DESIGNDIRECTORY Great Britain

A daring appearance
Mary QUANT brings
fashion up to the minute.

Collection 1967

Penny Sparke

DESIGN DIRECTORY
Great Britain

PAVILION

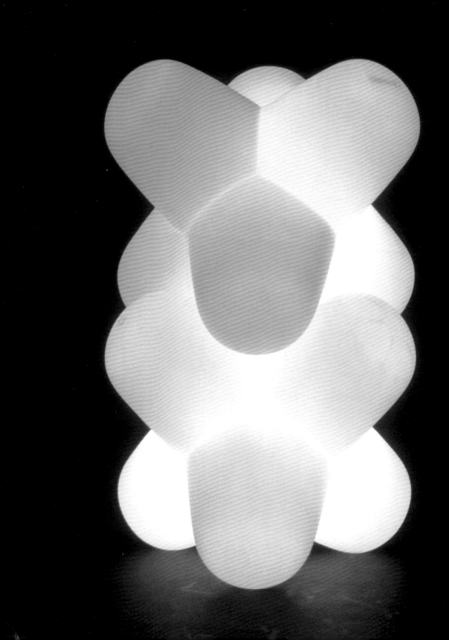

Systematically magical.
Tom DIXON combines lighting and seating
into one pop-object.

Jacks light/chairs for EUROLOUNGE, 1996

About this Directory

The first nation to become industrialized was also the first to feel the excesses of capitalism. Arts and Crafts was a reaction to this. As a reform movement, it leveled the road for modern design while spreading a notion of "Englishness" which has lost none of its fascination to the present day. The clash between grand traditions and creative revolt is the key to understanding the history of British design. The subversive transvaluation of all values began in the 1960's: London was swinging and at once Carnaby Street began to set the stylistic tone. Shock therapy followed in the form of Punk. Since then nothing has ever been the same, and everything seems within the realm of possibility. Great Britain has developed into a workshop for innovation, producing one star designer after the other regardless of the field, whether fashion, furniture design or graphic arts. This volume presents extensive portraits of both classics and newcomers under one cover for the first time. By employing an uncomplicated encyclopedic structure and by presenting numerous examples to illustrate the world of visual form, the book will render one of the most vital and extreme design scenes more accessible. The content focuses on product, furniture and automotive design, although areas such as interior design, fashion and graphic arts also receive their due. Additionally, styles and schools of design are explained and—for the first time in a handbook such as this—design companies are also discussed in depth, including not only renowned traditional houses but also the small innovative enterprises which have contributed to Britain's recent design boom. A detailed, explanatory index complements the book. Names and concepts in bold face refer the reader to the index.

Bernd Polster, HOWARD Book Production

The authors

Paola Antonelli is curator of the Department of Architecture and Design at the Museum of Modern Art. She has made numerous contributions to journals such as Abitare, Domus, and Nest. "Mutant Materials in Contemporary Design" numbers among her exhibitions for MOMA. She lives in New York.

Andrew Russell is Chief Executive of the Design Council in London, Britain's most prestigious design institution. In this function he is also responsible for the Millennium Products project, which presents Great Britain as a leading design nation.

Penny Sparke is one of the best known British design authors. Formerly a professor at the renowned Royal College of Art, she now teaches at Kingston University. Among her many publications are *Design in Context, The Plastic Age*, and *A Century of Design*.

A skillful short cut.
Alec ISSIGONIS.

Morris Mini, sub-compact car, 1959

Bookmark.
Ron ARAD puts an end to
the order of shelves.

Bookworm bookcase for Kartell, 1992

Despite the rather un-British slogan "Cool Britannia" devised by Tony Blair's spin-doctors to promote the resurgence of the country's influence in the visual arts worldwide, one cannot help but appreciate recent manifestations of yet another British renaissance. There has been the **Millennium Dome** at Greenwich, the growing success of the "100% Design" annual exhibition in London, the waves made by the "Sensation" exhibition in the United States and Australia, and the international success of unusual design companies such as **Tomato**. The latest update is the new Tate Modern gallery on the south bank of the Thames and the unveiling of Daniel Libeskind's vertiginous design for the **Victoria and Albert Museum**. Add all this to the exhibitions shown during the "Glasgow '99" architecture and design celebration, and Great Britain is, and deserves to be, at the center of the attention of the design world.

In matters of style, Britain is the place where avant-garde can become mainstream without losing its edge, and where the many attempts to shock rapidly become aesthetic paradigms inside and outside of the country. Such contrasts as high and low, Tory and Labour, old and new, European and "exotic," tasteless and refined can coexist and thrive in an unparalleled cultural synthesis that reveals the political power of the visual arts. The list could continue for pages and include such phenomena as the 1950s Independent Group, the visionary architects of the 1960s, and the 1970s **Punk** movement, all examples of art-political revolution. Across the centuries, because of its social and political structure, Great Britain has transformed its bipolar tensions in creative inspiration and class conflict into new, strange kinds of beauty.

Such creative tension rests on a solid tradition of structural engineering and economic rationality. The concept of mass-production was born in England when in the eighteenth century Josiah **Wedgwood** separated his ceramic wares production into two different locations, one factory for low-end, big-number series, and the other for more precious, "one-off" series. Britain is also the country where mechanization first took off, and where its limits and potentials were first debated. At the time, in the second half of the nineteenth century, the earthquake of the Industrial Revolution had momentarily separated the "good design" process from the manufacturing process. The **Arts and Crafts** Movement brought up the issue of ethics in the manufacture of design, and its protagonists, **William Morris** in particular, presented an ideal and somewhat bigoted view of the future. On one side of the pendulum, the righteous side, sat the craftsman, independent maker of ideas and enlightened master of beauty and honesty. On the other side was the industrial manufacturer, creator of the evil and the ugly, and manipulator of materials against their own nature. Yet the best design, Britain soon taught us, is created somewhere in between the two.

Britain is also a country in which structural engineering is considered a branch of aesthetics. *The Structural Engineer*, the official journal of the British Institution of Structural Engineers, carries prominently displayed on its contents page this definition of its subject: "Structural engineering is the science and art of designing and making, with economy and elegance, buildings, bridges, frameworks, and other similar structures so that they can safely resist the forces to which they may be subjected." Such a declaration partly explains our response to the many innovative buildings sprinkled around the world by **Norman Foster**, Richard Rogers, James Stirling, **Roy Fleetwood**, and many other revolutionary architects, in collaboration with such engineers as the late Andrew Rice of Ove Arup, who was venerated and celebrated as a master of architecture in his own right.

This view of engineering also reveals a very British tendency to acknowledge the structural forces behind phenomena, which has helped the British government recognize the importance of design. "Much of the evidence shows that design continues to be seen as an increasingly important factor in determining the UK's competitiveness and our quality of life," declares Andrew Summers, chief executive of the **Design Council**, in its publication *Design in Britain 2000*, delineating the state of design and its future perspective. The Design Council was one of the first government-based institutions founded in order to promote design inside and outside Britain. Despite its many ups and downs, it has contributed, and it does even more so under the New Labour regime, to build the strong image British design enjoys worldwide.

Today, some of the most successful designers in the world, such as **Jasper Morrison**, **Tom Dixon**, **Marc Newson**, **Ross Lovegrove** and **Ron Arad**, either live in or have moved to London. New small companies such as **Inflate** and rejuvenated giants such as **Habitat**, whose program is directed by Dixon, are attracting design talent from all over the world. The **Royal College of Art**, whose design program is chaired by Arad, continues to draw lecturers of international renown, and all the while it produces the most sought-after alumni. Somehow, we can believe that this is not a fad. Trends and fashions come and go, but Great Britain's culture survives to provide the world with irony, innovation, and new suggestions.

Paola Antonelli
Museum of Modern Art, New York

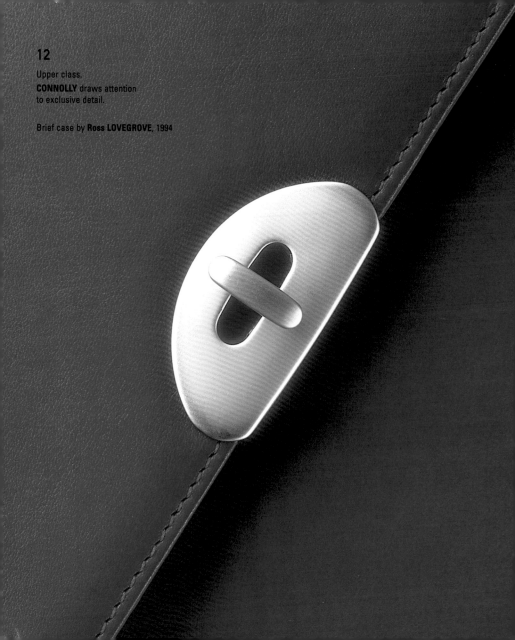

12

Upper class.
CONNOLLY draws attention
to exclusive detail.

Brief case by **Ross LOVEGROVE**, 1994

Lord of the sticks.
Charles Rennie MACKINTOSH declares structure as ornament.

Willow Chair, 1904 (reissued by Cassina)

NEVER MIND
THE BOLLOCKS
HERE'S THE
SeX PiSTOLS

Anti-design.
Jamie REID typesets
the alphabet of
the subculture.

Album cover for
Virgin Records, 1977

Street chic.
Vivienne WESTWOOD puts the subculture
on the runway.

Collection 1999

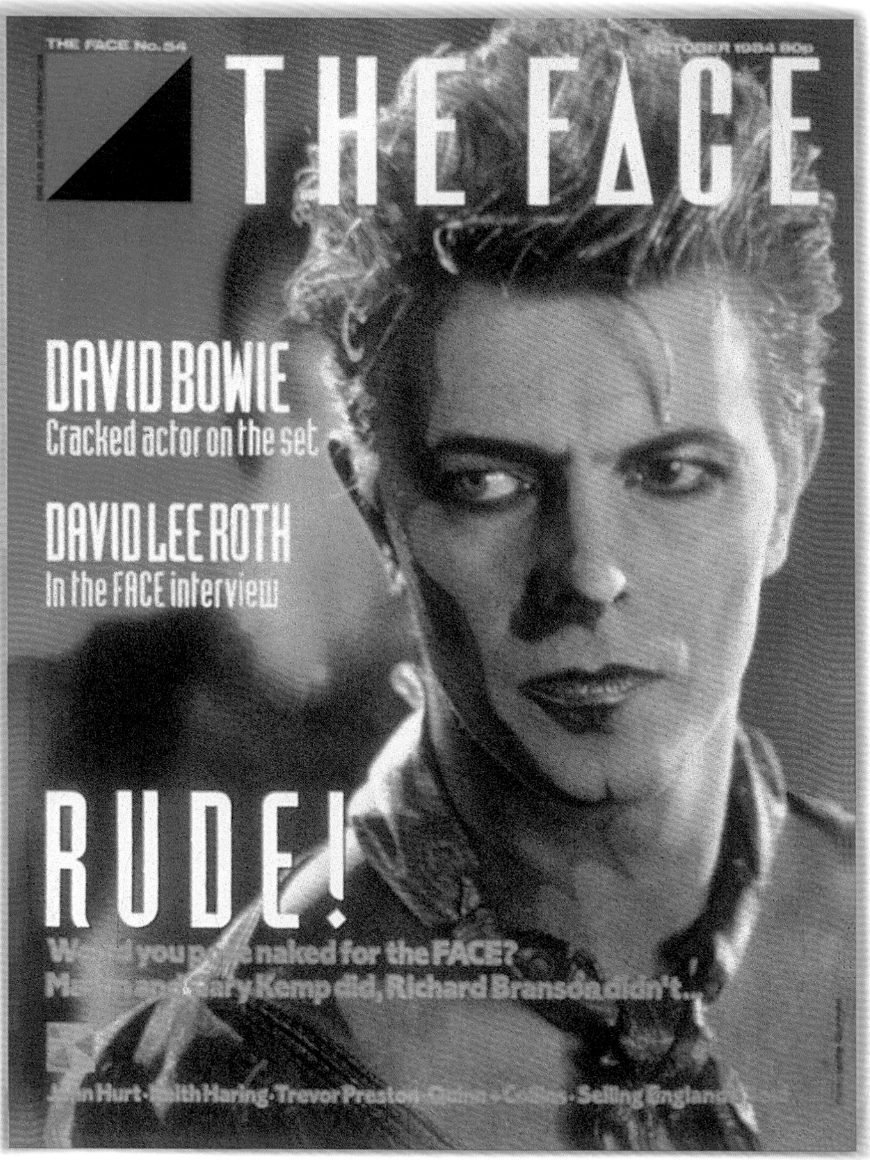

THE FACE No. 54

OCTOBER 1984 80p

THE FACE

DAVID BOWIE
Cracked actor on the set

DAVID LEE ROTH
In the FACE interview

RUDE!

Would you pose naked for the FACE?
Martin and Gary Kemp did, Richard Branson didn't...

John Hurt · Keith Haring · Trevor Preston · Quinn + Collins · Selling England

Postmodern typographer.
Neville BRODY forms the graphic
look of the 1980's.

The Face, magazine cover, 1984

Cutlery typology.
David MELLOR's
variations on
an everyday theme.

City cutlery, 1998

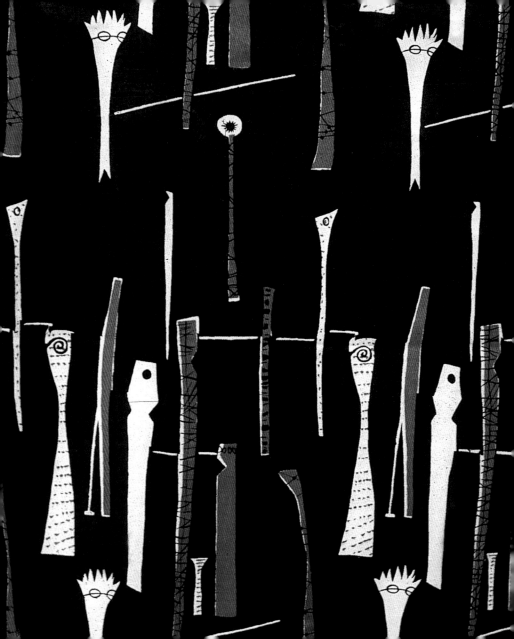

A canon of forms.
Lucienne DAY designs
back drops for the 1950s.

Spectators textile, 1954

Free development.
Gerald SUMMERS shapes a chair out of one
bent surface.

Chair by Gerald Summers, 1934

Return to the future.
Marc NEWSON draws on
streamline dreams.

Lockheed chaise longue, 1989

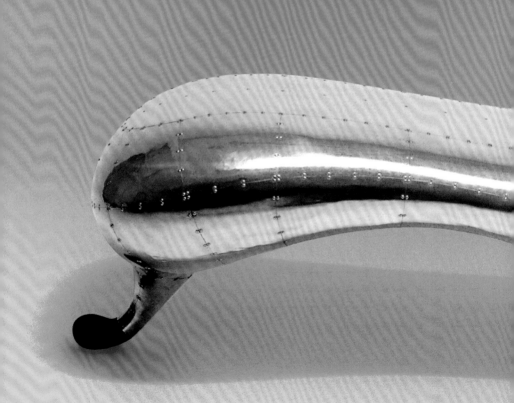

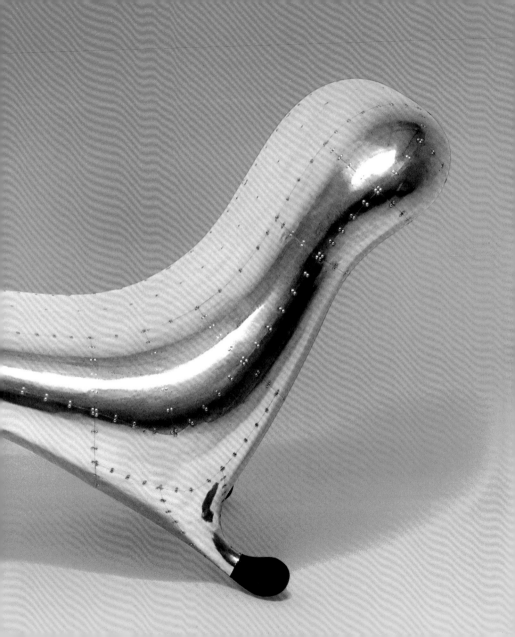

Reduced romanticism.
William MORRIS serves as
a model for simplification.

Brother Rabbit textile, 1892

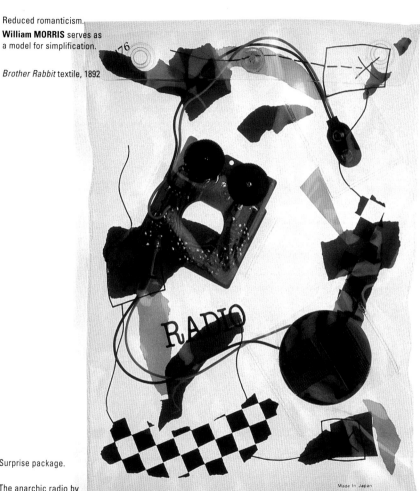

Surprise package.

The anarchic radio by
Daniel WEIL displays
its interior.

Bag Radio, 1981

Family gear.
Kenneth GRANGE designs for
everyday English life.

Brownie 44 B camera for Kodak, 1964

Fullness on principle.
INFLATE pumps fresh air into British
furniture design.

Lounge Chair by **Nick CROSBIE**, 1998

Moderate minimalism.
CONTEMPORARY STYLE makes modernism
for the masses.

Antelope Chair by **Ernest RACE**, 1951

Skillfully playing the angles.
Hinges and a steel spring allow the
Anglepoise to assume any position.

L 20 Anglepoise desk lamp by
George CARWARDINE, 1932
(reissued by Tecta)

Poetic purism.
Jasper MORRISON gives meaning to sitting.

Thinking Man's Chair for Cappellini, 1988

A playful machine.
James DYSON revolutionizes
a humdrum chore.

DC 02 vacuum cleaner, 1995

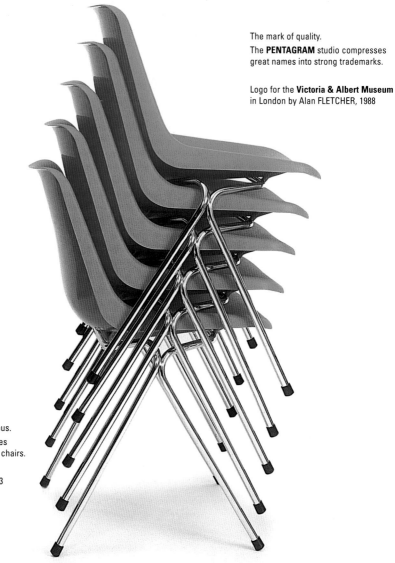

The mark of quality.
The **PENTAGRAM** studio compresses great names into strong trademarks.

Logo for the **Victoria & Albert Museum** in London by Alan FLETCHER, 1988

Useful and ubiquitous.
Robin DAY populates public spaces with chairs.

Polyprop chair, 1963

The art of proportions.
An eccentric design makes
JAGUAR a legend.

Type E Coupé by Malcolm SAYER, 1961

Playful symmetry.
Christopher DRESSER was
a pioneer of the Industrial Style.

Tea kettle, 1880 (re-issued by Alessi, 1991)

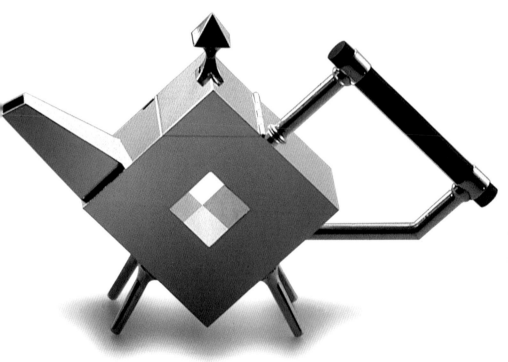

Pop comrade.
Peter MURDOCH folds cardboard furniture
for progressive children's rooms.

The Modern Chair, children's chair, 1963

A unique place to sit.
In the 1960's **POP DESIGN** specializes in breaking the rules.

Chair in 6 variations by **Allen JONES**, 1969

Brittle charm.
Michael MARRIOTT creates a design
collage by mounting everyday articles.

Drop vase, 1997

① *Debaser*

② *Tame*

③ *Wave of Mutilation*

④ *I Bleed*

Doolittle

PIXIES

Digital constructivism.
Montages by **Vaughan OLIVER** open up new
aesthetic terrain.

Album cover for the
Pixies: *Doolittle* for
4AD Records, 1989

Lollipop look.
Colorful housewares exude charisma.

Basic thermos flask by **Julian BROWN** and
Ross LOVEGROVE for Alfi Zitzmann, 1991

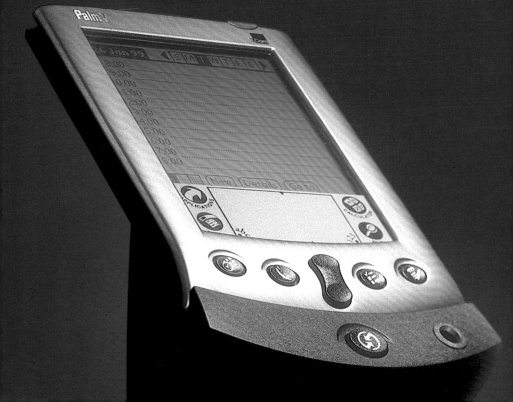

Well organized.
The hand held computer by
Bill MOGGRIDGE puts life in
perspective.

Palm V palmtop computer
for 3Com, 1998

Radiovision.
Wells COATES pours Bakelite into
new molds.

AD 65 radio for E. K. Cole, 1934

Foreign objects.
Nigel COATES dissolves shape.

Bulb vase series for Simon Moore, 1995

Glass cutter.
The avant-gardist **Danny LANE** invents a
new furniture type.

Stacking Chair, 1986

British cool.
Rodney KINSMAN produces furniture in the
high-tech style.

Seville (sic) modular bench system by
Rodney KINSMAN/OMK for the World's Fair
in Seville, 1992

Clear guidelines.
Edward JOHNSTON's signage for the
Underground retains its exemplary
character even today.

Johnston Sans Serif typeface
and logo for **LONDON TRANSPORT**, 1916

ABCDEFGHIJKLMN
OPQRSTUVWXYZ
abcdefghijklmnopq
rstuvwxyz 123456
7890 (&£.,:;'!?-*'"")

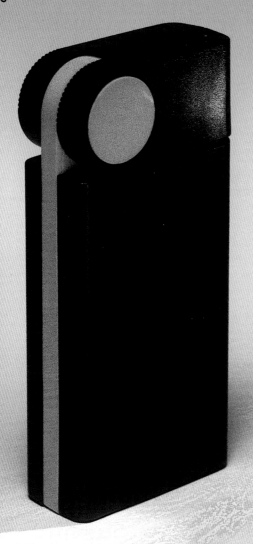

A giver of light.

Functionality pervades even minute detail i.
creations by the studio **BIB** (sic).

Durabeam flashlight by **Nick BUTLER** for
Duracell, 1967

Porcelain aristocracy.
WEDGWOOD sets classical standards.

Doric service, 1936

48

Romantic extremist.
John MAKEPEACE creates legends in
English furniture design.

Ripple chest of drawers, 1999

Page 49
Aston Martin DBR1, 1959

Decades

British Design History
from 1851 to the Present

1851-1939

Industry and Romantic Revolt
The First Designers

There is no single image of British design. Some people associate British design with "classic" traditional objects such as **Jaguar** cars, **Burberry** mackintoshes and **William Morris** textiles. Others will think of objects influenced by the more contemporary concept of **Street Culture**—the **Punk**-influenced clothes designed by **Vivienne Westwood**, or the striking graphics on record covers created by Malcolm Garrett and others.

Both impressions of Britain are equally valid, depending on one's viewpoint. The two extremes represent the diversity present within British society itself. There is a dramatic difference between the safe conservatism of upper-class taste, and the creative sense of risk and adventure grasped by its urban youth in the heady days of the 1960s. They are both manifestations of a society and a culture that have held firmly on to the past in the face of dramatic and turbulent change. Tradition and innovation exist side by side in British design, creating an eclectic diversity that makes a single image impossible.

This does not mean that, compared with Italy, Scandinavia, and the United States, Britain does not lack an important design culture. On the contrary, it means that British design, although more difficult to describe, is among the richest the world has to offer. It has influenced contemporary international design culture in a multitude of different ways.

The British design educational system, established in the mid-nineteenth century, provided a model that

"Except the goal to produce more beautiful things, the greatest motivation in my life was hatred for modern civilization."

William Morris

Room in Kelmscott Manor by **William MORRIS** and **Philipp WEBB**, 1860 has continued to be copied abroad. Equally influential has been the idea of social and moral reform through design—the belief that design can change people's lives for the better. The pioneering work of designers such as William Morris attempted to re-inject the values of craftsmanship into a world increasingly dominated by industrial manufacture. Their ideals have inspired many design initiatives both in Europe and the United States.

Nineteenth-century roots

The origins of modern British design are deeply embedded in the mid-nineteenth century. Conscious efforts were made at that time to raise the level of taste of the consuming public. The decline in taste was the result of the massive program of industrialization that had been taking place in Britain for over a century. The Industrial Revolution was a British phenomenon, after which the other European powers and the United States went through the same transformation.

At first the idea of designing a mass-produced object simply meant making it conform to the fashionable style of the day. Josiah **Wedgwood**'s neo-classical ceramics and Robert Boulton's metal goods reflected the same view of style as Thomas Chippendale's hand-made furniture of a century before. No longer the preserve of a social élite, these fashionable goods made it possible for the new generation of consumers to enter into the arena of taste. Artists were brought into the factories, and much copying went on to bring stylishness to the massmarket. Meanwhile, artisans in the different industries worked out ways to manufacture the goods that the artists had envisaged. Little by little, this divided labor system created a role for a new professional—the designer for industry, whose task it was to create new products and also to decide how they could be made. His role varied from industry to industry, but by the early years of the twentieth century the designer had become fully responsible for the appearance of the plethora of new goods which flooded the marketplace.

The Design Reform Movement of the mid-nineteenth century emerged in direct response to this sense of excess. Prince Albert himself, civil servants such as **Henry Cole** (who founded the **Victoria and Albert Museum**), art critics such as John Ruskin, and others banded together to rally against what they saw as the ubiquitous "bad taste" that surrounded them. They sought, instead, to instill in the general public the need for visual restraint. Designers such as Owen Jones and **Christopher Dresser** provided rules for ornament and "good design."

Two important cultural movements—Aestheticism and the **Arts and Crafts** Movement—added fuel to the campaign. Each promoted a different way of injecting new values into design, to help counter the disastrous effects of following the dictates of the machine. Among the individuals who played a role, William Morris stood

"When we acquire comprehensive knowledge of the material, we are liberated from the limitations of style or epoch."

C.F.A. Voysey

1888 first exhibit of **Arts and Crafts**; **C.R. Ashbee** founds Guild of Handicraft in Chipping Camden, Cotswolds

1890 the first electric subway runs in London

1891 London is the biggest city in the world with four million inhabitants

1893 the magazine *The Studio* is published

1894 Tower Bridge opens

1895 National Trust founded

1896 Chair with high back created by Charles Rennie Mackintosh

1898 Plain Oak Furniture catalog by **Heal's** in Arts and Crafts style

1900 Charles Rennie Mackintosh participates in the exhibit of the Wiener Secession

Page 55

top left: *Portland* vase by Josiah Wedgwood, 1789

top right: *Ingram Chair* by Charles Rennie Mackintosh, 1900

left bottom: soup tureen by Christopher Dresser, 1880

right bottom: textile *Union Of Hearts* by CFA Voysey, 1898

out as a beacon. Aestheticism, a powerful force in British architecture and design through the 1870s and 1880s, helped instill the concept of art into the mass British consciousness. Above all, it taught people how to make their own environments beautiful. Designers such as **E.W. Godwin** and J. Bruce Talbert created furniture items and interiors influenced by the simple lines of Japanese art. The Arts and Crafts Movement had a more overtly philosophical raison d'être. It focused on the desire to bring back the purity and integrity of the medieval craftsman into an age dominated by machinery. Morris led the way with his revolutionary furniture, textiles, wallpaper and other decorative objects, all of which rejected the heavy ornamentation of the early Victorian era. He replaced it with lighter, simpler, more two-dimensional patterns inspired by nature. **C.R. Ashbee** and **C.F.A. Voysey** also worked in a neo-medieval manner to evolve simple patterns for interior furnishings.

The influence of the Arts and Crafts philosophy and style was evident in British middle-class consumption throughout the late nineteenth century and early twentieth century. Its real impact, however, was felt in countries outside Britain which were trying to develop a concept of modern design suitable for the age of the machine.

One notable exception was the work of the Glaswegian architect and designer, **Charles Rennie Mackintosh**. He took British design to new heights and

1901 engineer Guglielmo
Marconi sends first radio
signal from Cornwall
across the Atlantic Ocean

1906 **Rover** and **Morgan**
founded

1907 introduction of the uniform
"Underground" logo

1908 first Ideal Home Exhibition
in London

1909 Glasgow School of Art
completed based on
design by Charles Rennie
Mackintosh

1910 flower-patterned fabric
becomes known as *Liberty
Print*

1914 **Aston Martin** founded;
German air raids on
London during World War I

1915 exhibition *Typifying
Successful Design in
London*; Design and
Industries Association
founded (today Design
Council)

Page 57

top left: poster for department store
Heal's, 1935

top right: table lamp by G. Russel,
1924

bottom left: bottle holder by Egon
Riss and J. Pritchard, 1939

bottom right: bowl by
Keith MURRAY for Wedgwood, 1933

made it a significant influence in Europe. His furniture
designs and interiors were exercises in abstract form,
combining geometry and nature in radically new
compositions. Once again, Europe was quick to respond
to this pioneering work and Viennese designers, in
particular, realized its significance. Britain's influence
was disseminated internationally through *The Studio*
magazine, which featured the work of the Arts and
Crafts designers and Mackintosh.

At the end of the nineteenth century, continental
Europe became increasingly gripped by the fever of Art
Nouveau. In Britain, however, only the London retail store
Liberty's responded to this new style. The vast majority of
Britain's designers adopted a more cautious approach.

Between the two world wars

Although Britain did not demonstrate the same intense
urge to move into the age of modernity as Germany,
Scandinavia and the United States, a few exceptional
individuals could see the writing on the wall. They
included **Ambrose Heal**, whose Tottenham Court Road
shop Heal's sold simple Arts and Crafts furnishings.

The British design educational system also received
much attention and energy. The work of C.R. Lethaby at
the Central School of Arts and Crafts was especially
pioneering. Lethaby was, with Heal, a founding member
of the influential Design and Industries Association,
formed in 1915 along the lines of the German Werkbund
established eight years earlier.

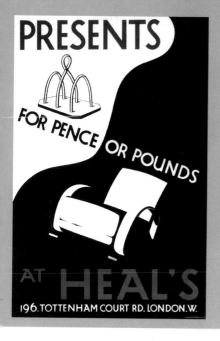

PRESENTS

FOR PENCE OR POUNDS

AT HEAL'S

196. TOTTENHAM COURT RD. LONDON. W.

As far as British design was concerned, the years between the two world wars were characterized by the same contrast between conservatism and progressiveness that had existed in the nineteenth century. The British Empire was still its main market, and there was little incentive to renew the design of goods that continued to be well received in the colonies.

New goods emanating from the new industries—transport, electrical appliances, radios, etc.—were also slow to adopt a "machine age" style, compared with developments in Germany and the United States. A notable exception was the **Ekco** company, which in the 1930s commissioned modern architects **Wells Coates** and **Serge Chermayeff** to design radio sets in Bakelite. The HMV company showed equal radicalism by collaborating with the designer Christian Barman on a number of highly innovatory designs, including an electric fire and an electric iron.

Although it never had the same wide influence as its German, French, Italian, and Scandinavian equivalents, modernism made a small inroad into English architecture and design in the 1930s. As elsewhere, architects led the way. Their ideas fed into their designs for interiors, furniture, and eventually into products. A few forward-looking manufacturers rose to the challenge. There was the tubular-steel furniture producer PEL (Practical Equipment Limited), and **Gerald Summers**'s "Makers of Simple Furniture", which worked with bent laminated plywood. Jack Pritchard's

Isokon company also produced furniture pieces in bent plywood, designed by the famous German émigré, **Marcel Breuer**, who was in Britain for a short period in the 1930s on his way to the United States.

Interior decoration also responded to the modernist call, at least to some extent. Syrie Maugham and the American Nancy Lancaster brought white into the domestic interior, and attempted to eliminate Victorian clutter.

The influence of Scandinavia was strong in Britain during these years, especially in the traditional decorative arts. Ceramic and glass manufacturers such as Wedgwood and Royal Brierley brought in artists and designers to give their products a new look. Eric Ravilious and Paul Nash produced stunning surface designs, and **Keith Murray** created radically simple, geometric forms. The theme of "art and industry" became highly visible, and it was clear that this was Britain's contribution to design modernism.

Graphic design also made enormous strides forward, with major clients such as Shell and **London Transport** playing an important role as patrons.

But for all the efforts made to bring British design into the twentieth century, the taste of the British public remained overwhelmingly conservative. It was not until after the Second World War that Britain really woke up to the idea that the objects that surround us can be made to reflect the values of the age in which we live.

"We cannot expect that everyone becomes a professional designer. That is neither possible nor desirable. Not everyone is a banker, but everybody can learn how to read a balance sheet."

Gordon Russell

1940-1959

War, 'Aesthetics', and Modern Style
"Good Design" as a Vision

One of the most interesting breakthroughs in British modern design came during the Second World War, when the government's Utility Scheme was introduced. The brief was to manufacture a standardized range of furnishing and fashion items for young married couples setting up home, at a time when most production facilities were concentrating on the war effort.

"I believe that the quality of design furthers humanity."

Robin Day

Gordon Russell, a Cotswolds-based furniture designer and manufacturer, was put in charge of the scheme. He commissioned a range of furniture pieces which combined **Arts and Crafts** tradition with a simplicity that was unequivocally modern.

The constraints of war showed that British design could straddle tradition and innovation, and that simple, functional furniture could be mass-produced. The experiment was enormously successful, and many people continued to live with Utility furniture long after.

It showed the potential within Arts and Crafts thinking—recognized many years earlier in Germany—to sow the seeds of a modern design movement for the twentieth century. Britain had finally evolved a new furniture aesthetic inspired by ideas and forms rooted in its own recent past. All that was needed was its application to the rest of manufacturing.

From war to peace

Ever since the mid-nineteenth century, Britain had been playing with the idea of embracing the concept of modern design. Because of its early industrialization

Page 60
Interior by **Robin Day** for the exhibit *Festival of Britain* (Pavilion Home and Garden), 1951

program, it had lost the craft base to its manufacture, and with it its national identity. This loss was too great to allow the country to commit itself fully to modernity.

Instead Britain concentrated on inventing a tradition for itself. The Arts and Crafts Movement was followed by the perpetuation of symbols—existing or newly created—of rural, aristocratic culture, for example, the Burberry mackintosh. By the 1920s, a range of icons of Britishness had come increasingly to represent British culture, at least in the eyes of foreign visitors. Cashmere twin sets and tartan scarves were soon joined by new products, such as the **Jaguar** car and later the Land Rover. Practicality and traditional thinking were combined in these products in such a way that it became increasingly hard for Britain to reject her past and embrace a modern, mass-produced, material culture. Until the post-war years, most of the British public favored the safety of the past and continued their search for their roots.

The pre-industrial eighteenth century was believed to be the age in which "taste" had ruled, unchallenged by the philistinism of the machine. When modernity finally entered British mass culture in the 1930s, it came through Hollywood films. These brought a new glamour and excitement, and were a form of escapism.

But it was not until after **1945** that people really began to purchase modern goods for their homes.

In the unsettled years after the end of the Second World War, the British public needed to project itself

---

1940 German bombers attack English cities and factories

1942 Committee on Utility Furniture founded

1943 Anti-Nazi poster by FHK Henrion

1944 British **Council of Industrial Design** founded

1945 **Ernest Race** Ltd. and **Jaguar** Cars Ltd. founded; Radio A22 by **Wells Coates**; End of the Second World War

1946 *Britain Can Make It* in London exhibition; rationing of clothes, gas and food; coldest winter since fifty years

1947 **Gordon Russel**, director of the **Council of Industrial Design**; **Christian Barman** leads the public relations division of the British Transport Commission; portable radio *Princess Handbag* by Wells Coates; flooding in the south of England

into a new future. The appearance of the goods around them played an important role. Nowhere was this more in evidence than the "Britain Can Make It" exhibition at London's **Victoria and Albert Museum** in 1946. It was conceived by the newly formed **Council of Industrial Design**, whose brief was to improve the standards of design in British goods in the face of foreign competition from the United States, Scandinavia, and elsewhere. Gordon Russell was the Council's first director. The Labour Party had just come to power in 1946, and the British public were starved of goods and hungry for novelty.

"Furniture with good, solid construction in a simple, but acceptable design that is offered for decent prices."

Committee on
Utility Furniture

The exhibition opened amidst enormous enthusiasm and queues of people waited patiently to see what the new post-war world had in store for them. Unfortunately most of the goods on display were either not yet in production or were destined only for export.

The contents of "Britain Can Make It" spanned the whole range of British manufactured products, including furniture, ceramics, glass, and textiles. It was strongly didactic, explaining who each industrial designer was and what he did. Many products were shown in interior settings destined for different social groups.

Among the stars of the show were **Ernest Race**'s little BA chair with its tapered aluminium legs and strikingly modern appearance. New materials were in evidence such as small plastic products in Runcolite, designed by Gaby Schreiber, and plywood furniture. The Ercol

1948 radio in walnut wood by **RD Russell**; introduction of the Land Rover as competition to Jeep; **Morris** Minor small car by **Alec Issigonis**; Commonwealth tableware by **Keith Murray** for **Wedgwood; Lucienne Day** and **Robin Day** found joint studio; "New Towns" planned; Immigration from the Commonwealth begins

1949 The British Iron and Steel Federation introduces the *Kitchen of Tomorrow*

1951 *Springbok Chair* and *Antelope Chair* by Ernest Race; *Festival of Britain* in London; *Calyx* textile by Lucienne Day; *Victorian and Edwardian Decorative Arts* exhibition in the **Victoria & Albert Museum**, London

Page 65

top: bus routemaster by Douglas Scott for London Transport, 1953

bottom left: Calyx textile by Lucienne Day, 1952

bottom right: garden chairs by AJ Milne, Festival of Britain, 1951

furniture company re-styled the classic Windsor chair to show how tradition could also be in step with modernity.

The imagination of the British public was captured by the idea of goods designed for the future. They were delighted by a streamlined bicycle and an air-conditioned bed. They saw the way forward towards a better quality of life, and the industrial designer was the magician who could make it possible.

The posters on display at "Britain Can Make It" demonstrated one of the strengths of British design in the 1940s. During the war, the Ministry of Information had commissioned men such as Abram Games and the French immigrant **F.H.K. Henrion** to design propagandist posters. Their striking designs provided the foundation for a post-war British poster movement that was without equal elsewhere.

The Contemporary Style

The 1950s were characterized, as elsewhere in the Western industrialized world, by an unprecedented expansion in mass consumption. There was a rise in the general level of expendable income, and in the increasing availability of consumer goods. The 1950s also marked Britain's mass entry into modernity. For the first time, the majority of the British public wanted their homes, and their surroundings in general, to look as if they belonged to the modern age.

A growing internationalism also came to the fore. The increasing impact of American mass culture

needed new goods with which to express itself. The concept of the "teenager" meant life-style accompaniments such as clothes, juke-boxes, and transistor radios. In the domestic decorative arts, the abstract sculptural forms of contemporary Italian products and softer, more natural Scandinavian products made a significant impact. A teak dining suite was coveted by many aspiring British housewives.

This general desire to modernize domestic environments was encouraged by manufacturers and design reformers alike. Nowhere was this more apparent than at the 1951 **Festival of Britain**, a vast exhibition held on the south bank of the River Thames in London. Intended to commemorate the centenary of the 1851 Great Exhibition in Hyde Park, it also celebrated post-war Britain and its future. The Council of Industrial Design again played a crucial role.

The Festival included stunning new buildings such as the Dome of Discovery, designed by Ralph Tubbs, and the dramatic Skylon, designed by Powell & Moya. The most ubiquitous design items were once again the simple, sculptural forms of Ernest Race's small steel rod chairs, used as outdoor seating throughout the site. Jack Howe's litter bins showed that even the most mundane objects could be given a contemporary appearance.

The Council of Industrial Design invited all the leading members of the new, post-war generation of British designers to contribute. **Robin Day** and **Lucienne Day** provided strikingly modern-looking furniture and light decorative textiles, which quickly became hallmarks of the contemporary interior. The "Homes and Gardens" pavilion, in particular, was packed with displays to inspire the British public.

One of the most interesting, and lasting, aspects of the exhibition was the work of the Festival Pattern Group, which looked for a new source of decorative imagery in chemical structures viewed through a microscope. These patterns were visible everywhere at the Festival, adorning the surfaces of textiles, wallpaper, ceramics and glass.

By the mid-1950s, this new kind of decoration had significantly infiltrated the mass environment. The accompanying belief in a future made possible by science was reflected in the expansion of technological goods.

The American concept of the "gadget" became increasingly appealing. Housewives succumbed to the lure of giant, colorful refrigerators, and food-mixers and coffee-makers were given pride of place on the formica surfaces of their new fitted kitchens. Women became key consumers, but husbands still controlled major purchases such as the family car. **Alec Issigonis**'s delightful little "Morris Minor" was a classic car of this period. "Do-it-yourself", another American import, became a popular pursuit in the "modern" home.

This was also the era of new materials. Plastics, in the hands of designers such as **Gaby Schreiber**, **Martyn**

"Some of the best pieces in English Art are rather conservative, but display dignity and balance, that are only possible in one country where traditions were never disrupted by a revolution."

Nikolaus Pevsner

1957 plastic furniture at the *Ideal Home Exhibition*; Anti-nuclear movement (CND) forms up in England

1958 P5 Limousine introduced by **Rover**

1959 Morris Mini compact car introduced by **Alec Issigonis**

1959 4A photo camera by **Kenneth Grange** for Kodak; *The Face of the Firm* exhibition in London; first air-cushioned boat by Hoovercraft; **John Stephen** opens first fashion store at **Carnaby Street**; hoola-hoop causes leisure time frenzy

Page 69

top: *Cambridge* table radio by Robin Day, 1964

bottom left: bedroom closet for *House of the Future, Ideal Home Exhibition*, 1956

bottom left: *Telechair* by Robin Day, 1952

Rowlands, and David Harman-Powell, took on new and exciting forms. Indeed, this was the decade of the industrial designer, the American concept of such an individual having been imported in the late 1940s. Independent designers and design teams—the **Design Research Unit**, Douglas Scott, Jack Howe, Allied Industrial Designers, and others—began to demonstrate that design could become part of British culture in general.

The art educational establishments re-organized their courses to meet the needs of the new design profession. By the mid-1940s, they were turning out designers such as **David Mellor**, Robert Welch, and **Robert Heritage**, who enthusiastically took up the challenge. The Council for Industrial Design encouraged them by introducing an annual awards scheme. Several manufacturing companies—prominent among them Race, **Hille**, **Ercol**, and Concord Lighting—also responded positively. By the end of the decade it was possible to talk about a modern design movement existing in Britain.

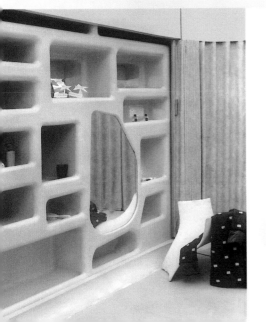

1960 - 1979

Commercial Design and the Pop Revolution

The changes within British society and culture that had begun in the 1950s accelerated in the 1960s. Britain ceased to follow other countries and began to lead the way. This was especially evident in the emergence of popular culture, and its accompanying shifts in values. A large youth market emerged in Britain ready to challenge its parents' generation.

This was manifested first in music and clothes, followed closely by other life-style areas. By the mid-1960s, the "pop revolution", as it came to be called, had brought about a major shift in thinking which also affected design. British goods began to make an impact in the international marketplace.

This was particularly obvious in the area of fashion. Designers such as **Mary Quant** and, a little later, **Barbara Hulanicki Biba** with her shop Biba, began to cater for the first time to young consumers. The mini-skirt and motifs derived from pop and Op Art demonstrated that Britain had moved enthusiastically into the second half of the twentieth century.

Inspiration for the new patterns and designs came from everywhere—space travel, contemporary art, and at street level, where youth-oriented style was having a dramatic effect. Union Jack motifs on plastic shopping bags, mugs, record covers, and T-shirts presented a single dramatic statement that was, above all else, new.

Primary colors were widely used, and mechanical forms symbolized the technology-dominated age. **Peter**

"We do not know Brigitte Bardot. We only know her (from) pictures in the newspaper."

Gerald Laing

Page 70
Street Scene, London, 1968

Murdoch, fresh from London's Royal College of Art, embraced the new, ephemeral aesthetic with his flat-pack "paper" chairs. Paul Clark put bull's-eye target images on to mugs, tiles, and clocks. Shop interiors in London's **Carnaby Street** and King's Road—the centers of the pop consumer culture—were transformed into environments for the young only.

Pop was essentially frivolous, and ephemeral, but its underlying message was more serious. It constituted a real threat to the "good design" values of the previous generation of designers who had shown their work at the "Britain Can Make It" exhibition.

At the end of the 1960s, the Council of Industrial Design (now re-named the **Design Council**) admitted it could no longer impose its values on a public which was clearly rejecting it in favor of what appeared to be an outbreak of "bad taste."

The crisis that ensued reached to the very roots of British society. For the first time, design and life-style were linked in the eyes of the British consuming public.

Meanwhile, a number of significant breakthroughs were made in this turbulent decade. **Alec Issigonis**'s "Mini" revolutionized the concept of urban transport. In the field of product design, **Kenneth Grange** produced several important kitchen appliances for the Kenwood company, notably his elegant "Chef" food-mixer.

Graphic design also moved ahead in this exciting decade. Michael Wolff's inspired corporate identity schemes for Bovis and Hadfield's paint company showed that such projects could also be young in spirit. The **Moulton** bicycle was yet another example of how radical British thinking could be.

Furniture design was significantly influenced by the pop revolution. **Roger Dean**'s fur-covered, blow-up chair for **Hille** was one obvious example.

Young design groups such as **OMK** were formed, producing stunning neo-modern designs in black leather and chromed steel. **Terence Conran**'s Habitat store made contemporary Italian and Scandinavian furniture available to a style-conscious London market, alongside French provincial pottery and ethnic rugs.

The 1960s showed that British design could be original, exciting and modern. Even more important, there was a desire for such goods among the British buying public. It was a turning-point that was to have significant repercussions.

The 1970s: consolidation and renewal

In some ways, given the excitement and energy of the 1960s, the following decade seemed a little lacklustre. It proved, however, to be an important period of consolidation and growth, which enabled the energetic 1960s to become the stylish 1980s.

The late 1960s had seen a growing interest in past styles. Interior design and poster design both looked back to **Arts and Crafts** and Art Nouveau decorative inspiration.

In the 1970s this retrospection expressed itself in different ways as the excitement stimulated by faith in

"The equilibrium between the intention to do a good job and to be financially successful is delicate."

Pentagram

1965 Plus 4 sports car by **Morgan**; Studio **Wolff Olins** founded; first black carnival in London district Notting Hill; Good Form exhibition about German design in London

1966 first ladies' collection by **Laura Ashley**; Studios **OMK** and **Queensbury Hunt** founded; "Swinging London" is the center of the pop revolution; Twiggy becomes *Woman of the Year*; Aubrey Beardsley Exhibition at the **Victoria & Albert Museum**; England becomes world champion in soccer

1967 logo for **Harrod's** by Minale Tattersfield; Studio **BIB** Design Consultants founded; "concept album" *Sgt. Pepper's Lonely Hearts Club Band* by The Beatles is released with a cover by Peter Blake

top left: *Cantilever* table lamp by Gerald Abramovitz for Best & Lloyd, 1966

top right: Mary Quant with models

bottom left: cover Pink Floyd *A Saucerful of Secrets* by Hipgnosis, 1968

bottom right: inflatable armchair (anonymous), 1968

technology gave way to a growing disillusionment. The oil crisis of 1973 played a key role in this cultural shift, putting an end, among other things, to cheap plastics. The hippie youth movement of the late 1960s had also favored the past in its choice of imagery and materials.

In 1973, American Victor Papanek's book *Design for the Real World* had a large international impact. It made British designers and consumers alike re-think their unbridled rush into the future.

The climate of the 1970s favored stylistic revivalism. Art Nouveau quickly gave way to Art Deco in the rapid turn-over of popular imagery—the grand 1930s interior of Biba's latest store in London's Kensington High Street was much talked about. Glamour and nostalgia combined to create a new design ethos that was a long way away from space travel and futuristic technologies.

Retrospection was also evident in the Crafts Revival movement. Founded in 1972, the Crafts Advisory Council organized a major exhibition of British crafts at London's **Victoria and Albert Museum** the following year.

The movement looked backwards and forwards at the same time—one side revered the pioneering work of **William Morris** and his nineteenth-century Arts and Crafts contemporaries, while another side saw a role for the modern craft object. Jewelry designers such as Wendy Ramshaw and David Watkins experimented with new ideas and innovative forms. The **Crafts Revival** also acted as a spur to creativity in the design of progressive

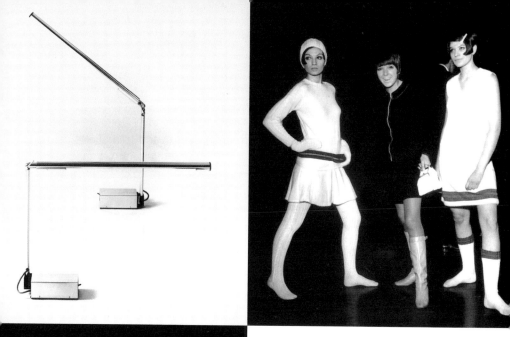

artefacts. Its influence was increased by the formation of the Crafts Council—created to balance the work of the Design Council—with its emphasis on the production of "one-off," rather than mass-produced, objects.

Soon individual designers linked with the Crafts Council began to blur the distinctions between the concepts of art, craft, and design. Furniture designers Eric de Graff and Floris van den Broecke, jewelry designers Caroline Broadhead and Susanna Heron, glass designer Simon Moore, and ceramic designers Alison Britten and Janice Tchalenko demonstrated the innovation that could be created by this ambiguity.

At the same time, a more commercial aspect of British design was being renewed by the formation of a large number of design teams, or consultancies. Their work mostly spanned the areas of graphic design and product design. Compared to the United States, Italy and Germany, the British design profession had been still somewhat underdeveloped until this point.

In these other countries, industry was used to calling upon the services of designers to help them with the appearance of their products, and with their own corporate identities. In the United States the design profession was a spin-off from the advertising industry, in Italy architects had taken the lead, while in Germany design was closely linked to engineering.

The British equivalent leant strongly upon the graphic and exhibition design tradition that had been established during and after the Second World War. The

1940s and 1950s had seen the formation and growth of the **Design Research Unit**, and of a group called **Allied Industrial Designers**, in response to the changing needs of British industry. It was not until the 1970s, however, that there was a significant expansion of this idea. British design consultancy took on an international dimension and became part of Britain's economic performance.

"Sex is fashion."
Vivienne Westwood

Design consultancy pioneers included **Pentagram**, **Kenwood**, and British Rail, as well as others outside Britain. Although rooted in graphic design, the British consultancies soon developed close liaisons with the retail sector. Conran Associates, formed in 1972, grew in response to the need to keep Terence Conran's successful Habitat stores stocked with goods, but it also developed links with other clients.

Many other design groups—among them **BIB** Associates, and **Fitch** and Company—set up in business, keen to get involved in the burgeoning design culture that was beginning to play a significant role in the British economy.

Another cultural phenomenon of the 1970s had enormous creative spin-offs, especially in the area of design. This was the youth movement dubbed "Punk." Its radical music and fashion-based subculture needed record covers, graphic signs and clothes with which to express itself. The "anti-taste" gestures associated with Punk had their roots in 1960s pop culture, but took new forms.

The "post-holocaust" work of **Ron Arad** and others in the1980s owes much to the legacy of Punk and its raw sensibility. The work of graphic designers such as Malcolm Garrett was directly dependent upon it, as were the fashion designs of Vivienne Westwood. Their "anti-establishment" attitude grew out of the atmosphere of irreverence that characterized the Punk revolution.

1975 100 Years of Liberty exhibition at the Victoria & Albert Museum, London

1976 **Punk** spreads in London Underground; record cover by **Peter Saville** for Factory Records; first collection by **Paul Smith**

1977 **Jane Dillon** works for Habitat; **John Makepeace** founds College for Furniture Design; Silver Jubilee by Queen Elizabeth II

1978 **James Dyson** develops vacuum cleaner without sack; Studios **Frazer Designers** and **Imagination** founded

1979 the movie *The Great Rock 'n' Roll Swindle* by Jamie Reid; **Timey-Fowler** studio founded; Margaret Thatcher becomes the first female prime minister (retires 1991), and enforces radical economic reforms; new class called "Yuppies" emerges

Page 79

upper left: *PH6* chair by Peter Hoyte

upper right: lettering by Roger Dean for the group Yes, 1973

lower left: house façade, London, 1968

lower right: pocket calculator for Sinclair, 1979

1980-2000

Pop-Baroque and Neo-Purism
The Invention of the "Creative Industry"

Early in the 1980s, design critic Peter York gave a lecture entitled "Punk and Pageant" in which he described the co-existence of both anti-establishment and traditional trends in British culture. One was subversive and radical, while the other was reactionary and aspired to be aristocratic—it was epitomized by the pearls and headscarves of the "Sloane Rangers," as York dubbed them.

Conservative thinking was widespread in early 1980s Britain. Margaret Thatcher had been elected Prime Minister in 1979 and she created a wealthy decade (for some), characterized by individualism and conspicuous consumption. Within this climate a new concept of design, linked overtly with conspicuous wealth and the concept of "life-style," flourished.

It brought with it a new approach to the modern designed consumer artefact and a new cult status for the "designer." Many design consultancies were set up and expanded quickly, the retail sector became increasingly dependent on design.

A handful of designers—**Terence Conran** among them—became household names. An infrastructure of museums and other institutions came into being to disseminate the new message, and the media—especially Sunday newspaper supplements—embraced the concept of design as never before. British product design, graphics and corporate identity were very successful, and British fashion became internationally famous.

"The changes remain the same. They make us human."

Tomato

Page 80
Interior by Marc Newson for the
Osman Restaurant, Cologne, 1997

1980 **Psion** founded

1981 "Collection Pirates" by **Vivienne Westwood; Ron Arad** founds One Off Ltd. (with Caroline Thorman); **Neville Brody** becomes art director of the magazine *The Face*; Crown Prince Charles weds Lady Diana

1982 *Oriental Cabinet* by **John Makepeace**

1983 *Bag Radio* by **Daniel Weil; Terence Conran** takes over Heal's

1984 CI for the oil company Q8 by **Wolff Olins**

1985 Studio **Branson Coates** founded; Gamma City exhibition of the group NATO

1986 Studio by **Julian Brown** and **Ross Lovegrove** in London founded; *Well-tempered Chair* by **Ron Arad**

1987 **Jasper Morrison** opens studio in London

Page 83

top left: *Cambalache* radio by Daniel Weil, 1982

top right: *Cabaret Voltaire* record cover; *James Brown* by Neville Brody for Virgin Records, 1984

bottom: *Nomos* table by Norman Foster for Tecno, 1987

The growth of the design consultancies was dramatic in this decade. Following on the heels of the 1970s pioneers, large design groups—**Addison**, **Seymour Powell**, **Michael Peters**, Roberts Weaver, **Wolff Olins** and others—took on projects that included design for retail, corporate identity schemes and products. These were widely publicized in the design press. The appearance of many towns and cities in Britain began to reflect their work.

The rise of the consultancies paralleled that of the design-conscious retail sector, which drew on their expertise. Conran's empire expanded to include the chains of British Home Stores and Mothercare. The series of Next stores also appeared, calling on the design skills of, among others, the **David Davies** group and **Din Associates** to create its modern interiors. Suddenly modern design was within the reach of almost everybody. British art schools continued to produce increasing numbers of young, eager designers ready to participate in the boom in their profession.

Other related innovations of these years included the stylish and much-acclaimed work of so-called "high-tech" architects and designers such as **Norman Foster**, Richard Rogers, and **Eva Jiricna**. Jiricna's store interiors for Joseph Ettedgui provided a model of urban chic that was widely emulated in British high streets.

The clothes and objects they featured epitomized the high end of the "design culture" that was invading British society and culture in this affluent decade.

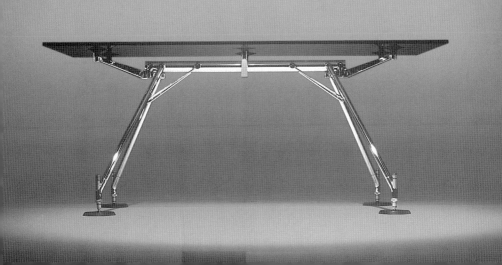

1987 Studio **Din Association** and furniture company **SCP** founded; **Tricia Guild**'s book *Designing with Flowers* is published; Nomos bureau system by **Norman Foster**; Studio **Why Not** founded; a post-modern shopping area is built in London's Docklands

1988 *Plywood chair* and *Thinking Man's chair* by Jasper Morrison; Mouse for Microsoft by **Bill Moggridge**; *Solomon Chair* by **Danny Lane**; Studios **TKO** Priestman Goode and v23 with **Vaughan Oliver** founded

1989 **Design Museum** in London opens

1990 Shelf Seven Series by **Michael Marriott;** Typo magazine *Fuse* is published

1991 *Blur* lettering by Neville Brody; furniture company **Aero** founded; Studio **Tomato** founded

1993 *DC01* vacuum cleaner by **James Dyson**; *Bookworm* shelf by **Ron Arad** for Kartell

A new generation of design magazines and support institutions emerged to spread the new gospel. **Blueprint** magazine, established in 1983, succeeded in bringing together the hitherto disparate worlds of architecture and design. The practice of exhibiting design objects in a museum setting also became widespread. The Boilerhouse, sponsored by Terence Conran, opened in 1981 in London's Victoria and Albert Museum, headed by Stephen Bayley.

It hosted a number of influential exhibitions before it moved to the Docklands to become the **Design Museum**. Design journalism expanded beyond the specialist press, finding its way into women's magazines and newspapers. Even BBC television attempted to disseminate the concept of design to a general audience through its Design Awards.

Some designers reached almost star status as a result of design's new-found popularity. Recent art school graduates such as **Daniel Weil**, **Ross Lovegrove** and **Julian Brown** received numerous commissions both at home and abroad. Britain's fashion designers, notably **Vivienne Westwood** and **John Galliano**, were widely celebrated for their innovative work.

There was a strong sense that British design had finally emerged, complete with an identity of its own and a self-confidence it had lacked hitherto, and that the rest of the world was ready to receive it.

Fin-de-siècle, twentieth-century style

The 1990s provided a very different context for design, however. A handful of superstars—**Ron Arad, Nigel Coates, Jasper Morrison** and, later, **Michael Marriott** and **Michael Young**—continued to flourish and make an international impact, but the optimism and extravagance of the 1980s took an about-turn. The economic boom years gave way to a recession, and the graph of consumption descended accordingly. A moral agenda and an anti-consumption ethic emerged, influencing a significant sector of British society as part of the wider concern with ecology and resources.

British design was quick to respond to the new ethical climate, however, and, in some ways, survived the sea change. The work of designers such as **Jasper Morrison** epitomized a rational approach towards the designed object. The simplicity and slight "retro" feel of his work felt comfortable in the new climate, in which practicality had come to the fore once again. The popularity of the Swedish store, Ikea, showed that the British public accepted good, commonsense design at a price it could afford.

A new interest in do-it-yourself in the home was promoted by the popularity of "make-over' TV programs such as *Changing Rooms*, which encouraged the public to express themselves by decorating their homes. The financial frugality of the 1990s did not mean an end to visual extravagance, and a new appreciation of color dominated popular consumption choices.

"It is a gigantic marketing plot that is designed to sell products by coating it with skin that spreads the scent of design. No one loathes the scent as much as the designer himself whose good intentions are cut into pieces and revarnished in black."

Jasper Morrison

1994 **FAT** and **JAM** studios founded

1995 **Azumi** studio founded; **Inflate** studio founded; Ikea takes over **Habitat**

1997 Series 5 hand computer by **Psion**; felt armchair by **Marc Newson**; re-design of the London Taxi by **Kenneth Grange**; Prime Minister Tony Blair regards the "Creative Industry" as an integral economic strength

1998 *Palm V* Hand computer by Bill Moggeridge; **Tom Dixon** becomes art director of Habitat

1999 Glasgow is the "City of Architecture and Design"

2000 Great Britain celebrates the turn of the century with a Millennium Dome in London and a selection of innovative Millennium Design Products

Creative salvage, pioneered in the work of Ron Arad, went from strength to strength. Arad received many commissions from manufacturing companies outside Britain, and showed how to be economical and expressive at the same time. The idea of recycling materials captured several other designers' imaginations also.

1990s British design showed a strong sense of escapism as well as practicality. The escapism was expressed in the interiors of the new restaurants and bars that began to fill the country's urban areas.

If the 1980s had been the decade of the designed retail outlet, the 1990s was that of the designer restaurant. Terence Conran again led the way with several restaurant projects such as the Bluebird in London's King's Road and others in Soho and the Docklands, which ranged from large and relatively cheap to small and exclusive. His ability to keep his finger on the pulse of public taste since the mid-1960s is unequalled.

Page 87

top left: table by David Mellor, 1997

top right: folding chair by Jasper Morrison for Vitra, 1999

bottom left: *La-Ola* thermos flask by Julian Brown, 1992

bottom right: *Typography Now 2* book shaped by Jonathan Barnbrook for Booth Clibborn Editions, 1994

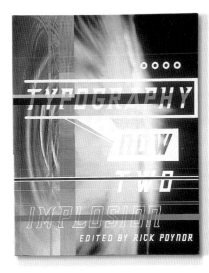

Designs for a New Millennium

The late 1990s saw the creation of two global icons that led to an international movement. Both were made in Britain. The first was the pop group, the Spice Girls, and the second, perhaps more remarkable, was Lara Croft, the gun-toting silicon heroine of the computer game, *Tomb Raider.*

"We were taking a risk," says Jeremy Smith, managing director of Eidos Interactive, the company behind *Tomb Raider.* "No video game had ever had a female lead and we had doubts that young men would be comfortable adopting a female character as a role model. But we have a company policy to let the creative teams run free and go with their flow. They were adamant it was going to be great."

Would-be design students the world over are beating a path to the doors of British design colleges. Some of the world's best-known fashion houses are led by Brits—**John Galliano** at Dior, **Alexander McQueen** at Givenchy (now at Gucci), and Stella McCartney at Chloe—and car design houses all over the world are dominated by ex-Royal College of Art students. Think of the most iconic, contemporary, worldwide designs, and you will be surprised how many originated in Britain. Cars such as the Ford Ka and Ford Focus, for example, were both developed by British design teams. The iMac, one of the most successful computers ever introduced by Apple, was designed by British-born and British-trained Jonathan Ive. Indeed, *Tomb Raider* is among more than 1,000 products and services recently created in Britain to be selected by the **Design Council** as Millennium Products for being the best, most pioneering, most creative, and most innovative.

Tomb Raider and Millennium Products are all about design and the peculiarly British way of solving design problems. "We are more intuitive, and Lara is the perfect example of how that instinct can pay off," says Jeremy Smith. "The guys working on the game were in touch with an emerging national mood and had no problem with the idea of a powerful female role model." The same intuition—not to mention dogged persistence—has created another powerful icon of contemporary British design in the Dyson vacuum cleaner. "If there was a better kind of cleaner, someone would have invented it," **James Dyson** was told, time and again, as he spent years trying to get his concept of a bagless cleaner accepted. "It was an idea born and nurtured in the cradle of frustration. I took the idea to most of my current competitors but they all rejected it. They were more concerned about arguing that their product was quite good enough, thank you. They weren't interested in a new approach." In the end, the combination of an unusually entrepreneurial bank manager and a Japanese firm that spotted a gap in the market led to perhaps the most famous British vacuum cleaner— certainly one of the best ever designed—in homes across the land.

Such innovative thinking can be seen in evidence throughout Millennium Products, many of which have rapidly become icons of the new millennium. **Tom Dixon**, for example, now head of design at the seminal home furnishing retailer **Habitat**, got the idea of his Jack light from looking at the industrial process of rotational moulding. He came up with the idea of designing a multi-functional lighting seat which stacks or creates sculptural towers of light. The result has been an extremely popular and sought-after piece of contemporary British furniture, often spotted in color supplements gracing ultra-chic modern homes worldwide, and one of Habitat's most popular lines. The idea of being not just the best but also the first is a key distinction of well-designed Millennium Products. Who but a British designer, for example, would have thought of creating a radiator coiled like a giant spring? "We wanted to come up with our own design for an innovative radiator. We wanted our product to differentiate ourselves in the UK market, and were also keen to have a product that we could export," says Peter Peirse-Duncombe, director of Bisque, the firm which makes Hot Springs. Bisque realized that a coil-shaped radiator might provide an alternative to the traditional tubular one, which is not as thermally efficient as it could be and often takes up valuable space. Moreover, its manufacturing involves welding and finishing. In contrast, Hot Springs is produced as a continuous length of tube and is installed vertically, taking up less space. Its larger surface area means a higher heat output. It is an innovation that is both functional and aesthetic.

Function and aesthetics have long been bywords for British design. The classic approach is to find an elegant, ergonomic solution to practical everyday problems. Take the AnywayUp cup. While the most determined of toddlers, who simply shake a vessel until they can sprinkle the liquid from out of the end of the spout, British housewife Mandy Haberman came up with a solution—a spout with a valve in it, or to be more precise a membrane with a slit. The slit stays closed until the spout is sucked by the toddler. Haberman was named "Female Inventor of the Year" and the AnywayUp sells in more than seventy countries worldwide. Once again, British doggedness coupled with ingenuity won through. Ingenuity does not necessarily come in domestic sizes, however. Thinking ingeniously on a grand scale has helped yet another clever British design overcome another British problem—traffic congestion. Heavy use and deterioration caused by the weather meant that two bridges and their slip-roads needed to be replaced on the main route into Plymouth that, being the main road into Cornwall, is one of the heaviest-used tourist routes in the country. The problem was how to embark on such a major, lengthy project while keeping the route open to allow a reasonably maintained flow of traffic. Unusually, two construction companies, Tony Gee & Partners and Hochtief UK, had exactly the same idea—to construct a new viaduct off-site and simply wheel it into place. Bob Spackman of Tony Gee explains:

"We were excited by the idea to slide the new roads into position, but worried if we would be able to persuade Hochtief to agree to the scheme before submitting our joint tender. When we discovered that Hochtief had come up with a similar concept, there was no stopping us. The atmosphere was fabulous—everything was 'can-do.' There were two bridges in place, together with connecting slip-roads. The bridges were decaying and crumbling, and had to be replaced as soon as possible. We built the two new bridges temporarily beside the existing ones so that traffic wasn't disrupted. When they were ready, Hochtief diverted the traffic on to the new viaducts in their temporary positions and then demolished the old ones. Finally, in two weekends, we slid the new ones into place, one each weekend."

This kind of lateral thinking in which British designers excel can produce quite extraordinary results . B&W, for example, have designed perhaps the most beautiful—certainly the most striking—loudspeakers ever to grace a hi-fi system, simply by copying nature. The *Nautilus* speaker, as the name suggests, borrows its shape from the spiral of a shell. "The curved sections of the spiral shell manage bass frequencies much better, and the horn-shaped pipes enhance treble sound. We think we have achieved 'transparency,' the perfect reproduction of sound as it was originally performed," says B&W marketing manager Clive Funnell. *Nautilus* began in the research and development section of B&W, and went through a series of prototypes. What resulted was a beautiful speaker set that was the culmination of all they had learned in more than half a century of experience.

Innovation tempered by experience is surely one of the key combinations behind any successful design. Take the Ford *Ka*. It took Ford's immense experience of the car market in Britain and abroad to identify a new niche for a small, highly radical car: the Ka. Winner of more than twenty awards and designed at Ford's Vehicle Centre at Dunton in Essex, the Ka was made for a whole new market. The need for a non-budget, stylish small car was supported by research, and the revolutionary *Ka* is now seen as the first small car to offer the features and performance of large cars. It is also efficient, running at 48 miles per gallon, and aims to be more recyclable, more compact, quieter, safer, and cleaner than its rivals. John Gardiner, corporate affairs manager for Ford UK, has no doubt that the secret of a success like the *Ka*'s lies in the design:

"Everyone on the product launch team played a major role in ensuring the *Ka* was a success, but special mention must go to the design team. They really believed in the design of the car, even when some of the initial market research was sceptical about the innovative shape of the car. The design team realized that by the time the car would come to market, its novel shape would be more in keeping with other growing design trends and thus would be acceptable and seen as innovative by the public."

Andrew Summers
Chief Executive, Design Council

Page 97
Well-tempered Chair
by **Ron Arad** for Vitra, 1986

Directory

From Aero to Young

AERO

Lamp and furniture manufacturer

Aero Wholesale Ltd.,
London

1991 founded by Paul Newman

1995 **Nazanin Kamali** works for
Aero (Creative director
in 1996)

1999 fifty new products for the
Millennium Collection

Products

1993 kitchen wall system in
high-grade steel

1995 Edison lamp by
Winfried Scheuer

1997 tilted, extending TV coffee
table

2000 *Valentina* coatrack

Page 95
top left: paper table lamp, 1995
right: closet system, 1996
bottom left: wall clock, 1993
all by Nazanin Kamali

TV table, 1997

It was the classical notion of marrying form and function that prompted Paul Newman in the early 1990's to found a new firm, which today—along with **Habitat** and **SCP**—upholds the concepts of modern furniture design in Great Britain. Creations like the *Flowerchair*, a metal piece by Rob Whyte, or Sebastian Bergne's bath accessories are based on a firm belief in the elegance of simplicity. While the idea was first applied during the Bauhaus period, British furniture design is producing perfect examples of it today. Paul Newman's side table of laminated beech is open on one side and, with its rectangular minimalism, can be placed in the tradition of Max Bill's Ulm Stool. The same functionalist spirit inspires Aero's tubular steel chair *Tuesday*. Since the mid-1990's—this newcomer has established itself as a mail order company in the interim—Creative Director **Nazanin Kamali** has contributed the majority of the company's understated furnishing designs. Offerings have expanded significantly meanwhile, and for example now include lamps and clocks. Currently, some designs are just a shade more permissive, such as the fluorescent wall clock by **Winfried Scheuer**, a German and Londoner-by-choice, which features the play of light and shadow as a visual extra.

Ron ARAD

Furniture Designer

The Israel-born Ron Arad is one of Britain's "superstar" designers, and it has been said that he is Britain's answer to Philippe Starck. There is some truth to this statement in that he, like Starck, is a highly individualistic designer whose ideas stem from a mental process that has more in common with that of the fine artist than of the jobbing designer for industry. Like Starck also, Arad's imagination expresses itself in the form of things—especially buildings, interiors, chairs, and everyday goods. His talent needs the world of goods to be actualized. By the early 1990s he had become internationally recognized for his work, which emphasized the role of the "ready-made," the found or salvaged object that could be transformed by the hand of the artist-designer. His work was highly evocative, suggesting a post-industrial world in which the urban landscape was characterized by materials in a state of decay. More recently, through collaborations with Italian and German manufacturers, his work has reached a new level of sophistication and finish, which differentiates it from the earlier designs.

It is only recently that Arad has applied this talent to mass-produced goods. The first part of his career was dedicated to designing and making "one-offs," a term he used in naming his own firm and retail outlet. His training was in architecture, which he studied at London's Architectural Association, and it was there that he came into contact with men such as Peter Cook. It is as an architect that he has allowed himself the freedom to work across a wide range of material goods, from furniture to products, with such ease. On completing his training, he established One-Off Ltd. in the early 1980s with Caroline Thorman in London's Covent Garden. It consisted of a design studio, workshops, and a showroom from which his designs were sold. From this base, he made his living at first by creating furniture and fittings out of metal tubes and cast-iron fittings for individual clients. These "KeeKlamp" structures could be transformed into beds, shelving systems, and other furnishings, and helped to establish the raw, industrial aesthetic

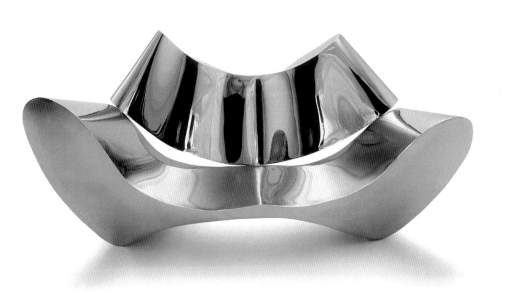

that characterized Arad's work at this time. The dominance of the "High-Tech" aesthetic of those years helped give credibility and visibility to his work, and he soon moved to a range of more individualistic designs that showed his developing philosophy. The *Rover* chair of the early 1980s is without doubt the piece that brought Arad into the public arena. In essence, he recycled old leather seats from Rover cars and fixed them on to tubular steel bases that he made himself. The chair quickly became an icon of the period.

Arad followed this with a succession of other designs that were all equally original. His *Aerial* light was another recycled object—this time a car antenna—brought to life by being used in a new way, and his *Transformer* seat, a granule-filled vinyl sack, broke new ground by being adaptable to the shape of each individual user. Although Arad made all his pieces by hand, they were not "craft" pieces but rather individualized examples of workshop-manufactured items in which technology was re-defined and made applicable to new uses and new contexts. Other pieces followed in which the use of tempered steel featured strongly, seminal among them being the *Well-Tempered Chair* and *Bookworm*, a bookcase made from one piece of steel that curved organically back upon itself.

At the end of the 1980s Arad created Ron Arad Associates, again with Caroline Thorman. It was an architectural and design practice, based in Chalk Farm in north London. At this point Arad's career as an architect took off, with an emphasis on interiors. Among the best known is his work for Belgo Central, a restaurant in London's Covent Garden, which was a conversion of three stories of a nineteenth-century warehouse. It was characterized by Arad's by now well-known organic forms, combined with a subtle use of lighting and an inventive use of materials. He worked on a number of interiors for private residences, but his architectural skills are perhaps best shown in his design for the foyer of the new Tel Aviv Opera House, completed in the mid-1990s, in which his firm worked on a number of retail outlets as well as exhibition spaces and showrooms.

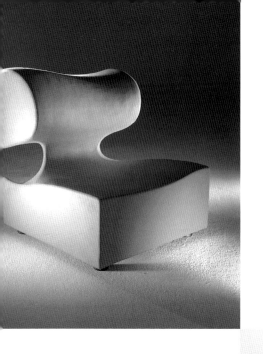

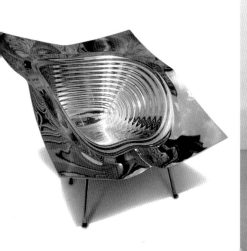

Alongside the expansion of architectural work undertaken by Arad Associates through the 1990s were numerous product designs, which were realized in significant numbers by a wide range of manufacturers. The Swiss manufacturer, Vitra, was the first to work with Arad in this way, moving from the steel *Well-Tempered Chair* to a molded plastic, low-cost, stacking chair. With the latter, Arad's reputation as a designer of workshop-based furniture came to an end and the era of "democratic" Arad furniture came into being. The experience was repeated with a number of Italian manufacturers—Moroso, Driade, Artemide, Kartell, and Alessi among them—and by the middle of the decade Arad had become one of the most-discussed designers of the day. Furniture, exhibiting a wide range of organic forms and executed in both metal and plastic, provided the backbone of his output but other objects also emerged from Arad's drawing board, including a brandy flask (for Martell), a CD storage system (for Alessi), a lighting system (for Artemide), and a toilet (for Allia).

The 1990s were prolific years for Arad. This highly individual designer also entered the British establishment by taking on the role of Professor of Furniture and Product Design at London's Royal College of Art.

1993 *Bookworm* shelf for Kartell

1994 *Schizzo* chair for Vitra; *Europa* steel sofa for Draenert

1995 *Sof-Sof* seat for Moroso

1997 CD shelf for Alessi; *After Spring/Before Summer* steel couch

1998 *Fantastic Plastic Elastic* armchair for Kartell

1998 *Reinventing the Wheel* shelf

Page 101
top left: *Fantastic Plastic Elastic* chair for Kartell, 1998
top right: *Rolling Volume* armchair, 1990
bottom: *Big Easy Reed* sofa for Moroso, 1989

Book table, 1993

left: textile by Liberty's and Co., 1891
right: commode by E. Gimson, 1908

Britain's most important nineteenth-century contribution to twentieth-century international design was the work of the members of the Arts and Crafts Movement, Britain's answer to Art Nouveau, who brought a new simplicity, a new quality, and a new sense of modernity to the backward-looking chaos of Victorian material culture.

Well-known designers such as **William Morris**, **C.R. Ashbee**, **C.F.A. Voysey**, Lewis F. Day, A.H. Mackmurdo, and Walter Crane created a body of architecture and interior artifacts, primarily furniture, wallpaper, textiles, and metalwork. Their work was characterized by a light, decorative aesthetic, which relied on vernacular models for its three-dimensional designs, and in its two-dimensional work on the world of nature for its stylized images of birds, trees, and plants.

The group followed the rule of "truth to materials" at all times. It was also deeply committed to design for everyone, expressed in Morris's famous words, "I don't want art for a few, any more than education for a few." Their work was a response to the growth of factory production, the impact of mechanization, and the increasing numbers of poor-quality goods in the marketplace. They sought to retain the principles of craftsmanship that had underpinned manufacturers in the medieval world. They set out on a path of design reform that was to last well into the following century, strongly influencing European modernism.

John Ruskin's writings lay at the core of Arts and Crafts thinking and hugely influenced William Morris, who translated Ruskin's ideas into material

form. His firm, Morris and Company, was responsible for the design and manufacture of a wide range of furniture items, textiles, wallpapers, and other decorative goods, all of which respected the principles of craftsmanship and the dictates of the materials and manufacturing processes involved. His simple, stylized patterns provided a model that others were to follow. Voysey's textiles, for example, with their stylized birds and flowers, rejected the illusory style of the High Victorian era and advocated instead a simplicity of form and pattern, and a respect for the materials and techniques used. Similarly, Voysey's architecture and furniture looked back to vernacular models, the furniture featuring bold metal hinges and heart-shaped cut-outs.

Each member of the Movement, in his own way, found a personal means of expressing his commitment to reforming design and the decorative arts by embracing craftsmanship, respecting materials and re-interpreting the message of the Middle Ages in the context of the late nineteenth century. Ashbee founded the Guild of Handicraft, which functioned along medieval lines, first in the East End of London and later in the country setting of the Cotswolds, while Voysey created several rural villas that combined vernacular details with a modern approach to architectural design.

The Arts and Crafts Movement was never a formally constituted group but its collective ideals were expressed in exhibitions and publications. The Arts and Crafts Exhibition Society was central in this context, as was *The Studio* magazine which disseminated the principles of the key practitioners.

1897 first chair with high arms by **C.R. Mackintosh**

1899 C.F.A. Voysey designs Moorcrag at Lake Windermere

1900 Arts and Crafts represented at the Eighth Exhibition of the Vienna Secession; C.R. Ashbee meets Frank Lloyd Wright in the United States

1901 manifesto *The Art and Craft of the Machine* by Frank Lloyd Wright

1902 *Art-Workers Quarterly* magazine (1904 *Arts and Craft magazine* — both until 1906)

1909 the book *Craftmanship and Competitive Industry* by C.R. Ashbee is published

left: *Birds & Berries* textile by C.F.A Voysey, 1897
right: *Adjustable Chair* by P. Webb for Morris Co., ca. 1900

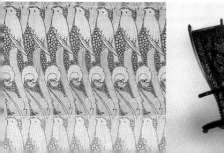

Laura ASHLEY

Fashion Designer

1925 born in Wales
1949 marries Bernard Ashley
1953 first work as designer;
     Audrey Hepburn wears
     one of her scarves in the
     movie Roman Holiday
1954 Ashley-Mountney Ltd.
     founded 1968, originally
     named Laura Ashley Ltd.
1977 Queen's Award for export
     series
1985 dies

Products
1966 first women's collection
1979 perfume and cosmetics
1999 Hydrangea furnishing
     collection

The name of Laura Ashley is synonymous with the British taste for nostalgic, decorative fashion textiles and interior furnishings. It is a "look" that has spread globally and which evokes an image of "Britishness" that is familiar to many. The small floral patterns of Laura Ashley fabrics and wallpapers represent the romantic mood of post-war British design.

This phenomenon was created by the self-taught designer, Laura Ashley, with her husband, Bernard. Their company was originally formed in the mid-1950s and a decade later a wide range of shops had been opened both in Britain and overseas to sell their designs. By the middle of the 1980s the number of shops had expanded to more than a hundred, while ten factories produced the goods to go into them. The range of goods grew wider and wider to encompass textiles, wallpapers, scarves, smocks, dresses, aprons, tiles, and perfumes. A complete Laura Ashley "life-style" was in place. It was one which from the 1970s onwards has captured the imagination of a large body of consumers, both in Britain and elsewhere.

Spring Collection, 1999

Page 105
Textile, Spring Collection, 1980

ASTON MARTIN

Auto Manufacturer

Aston Martin Lagonda Ltd,
Newport Pagnell

1914 founded by Lionel Martin
and Robert Bamford

1947 company takeover by the
industrialist David Brown
(DB)

1959 with the DBR1, Roy
Salvadori and Carroll
Shelby with the twenty-
four-hour race of Le Mans

1964 Sean Connery drives the
DB5 in James Bond movie
Goldfinger

1994 Ford completely takes over
Aston Martin

Products

1950 *DB2* sports car

1958 *DB4* sports car

1963 *DB5* luxury vehicle

1965 *DB6* sports car

1969 eight-cylinder *DBS V8*

1977 Lagonda limousine
(equipped with digital
instruments)

1980 two-seater *Bulldog*

1988 *Virage* sports car (follow-
up to the *DBS V8*)

1992 *DB7 Vantage* sports car

DB7 Vantage, 1992

Page 107
top: *DB 2/4 MK III*, 1954
bottom: *DB5*, 1963

Initially, automobile designer William Tows was only supposed to create an interior. But then in the late 1960's a sports car was developed under his supervision that represented the culmination of a classic series. The Aston Martin *DBS* was an angular, matter-of-fact and wider version of model run that began with the Italian-designed *DB4*. The Touring of Milan company specialized in light weight chassis, the so-called "superleggera," although the typical fish mouth grill which was originally designed by Englishman Frank Feeley remained. The *DB5*, which achieved high visibility as James Bond's roadster and was probably Aston Martin's most famous model, was another member of the legendary series. In the late 1970's the dream car maker from Feltham introduced the Aston Martin *Lagonda*, an extremely angular, wedge-shaped luxury automobile that now had not only an avant-garde look but also futuristic features such as touch-sensitive instruments. The first newly developed model to follow was the *Virage* in the early 1990's, with a high belt line, flush windows and proportions that are still recognizable in the *DB7 Vantage*. The top model of the year 2000 is a creation by young designer named Ian Callum.

1995 founded by Shin and
Tomoko Azumi in London

1997 Table=Chest in collection
adopted by **Victoria and
Albert Museum** in London

1999 Azumi solo exhibition at
the Lighthouse in Glasgow;
Future Furniture Award
from *Design Week* for
*Wire Frame Chair and
Stool*

2000 Tectonic exhibition at the
Crafts Council, London

Products

1995 *Overture* wardrobe, combi-
furniture *Table=Chest*

1996 salt shaker *Upright*

1997 clock/wardrobe
combination *Clock=Coat
Hanger=Shelf*; combi-
furniture *Armchair=Table*

1998 *Wire Frame Chair and
Stool*; salt and pepper
shaker *Snowman*

2000 *Penguin* Food Container

Page 109

top left: *Snowman* salt and pepper
shaker, 1998

top right: *Wire Frame Shelf*, 1998

bottom: *Wire Frame Chair and Stool*,
1998

Combi-furniture *Armchair=Table*, 1997

In the work of Shin and Tomoko Azumi, a London-based Japanese design
duo, concepts develop from the dialectic between simplicity and playfulness:
balance is key. The result is a characteristic syntax of visual forms which
distinguishes itself through lightness of material and construction. It is
occasionally reminiscent of the expressiveness of **Ron Arad**, while in other
cases it exhibits some of the unadorned persuasive power of the new purism
as represented by, say, **Jasper Morrison**.

Their S-shaped *Wire Frame Shelf*, for example, is a further step toward
dissolving the conventional order of shelves, while the functional, folding
Armchair-Table offers a rational approach to the perennial and often
underestimated question of how to save space. Recently, the Azumis have
begun to work for lifestyle brands like Authentics. Among other things, their
success points to the multicultural aspect of the recent British design boom,
with names like **El ultimo grito** and **Jam** serving as further examples.

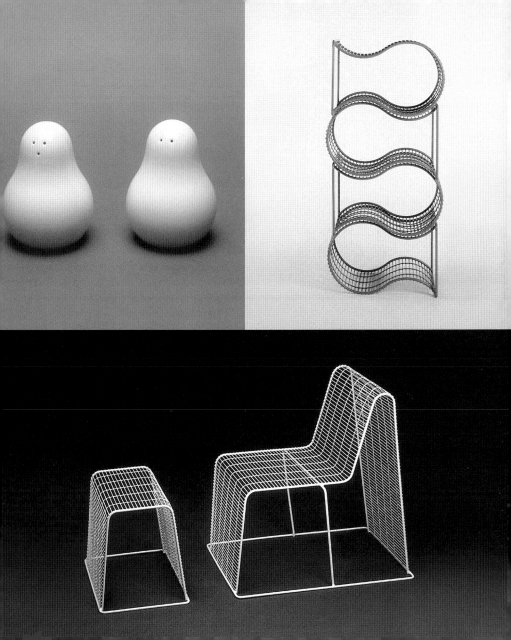

Fred BAIER

Furniture Designer

1949 born in Kingston-upon-Hull

1972 diploma from Birmingham College of Art; 1975 from the **Royal College of Art** in London

1976 teaches at the Wendell Castle School in New York; 1982 at the Royal College of Art

1986 participates in the traveling exhibition *British Design in Vienna*

1990 exhibition at the **Crafts Council**

Products

1979 *Star Wars* table

1982 *Smokers Bow*

1983 *Bay City Roller Cabinet*

1984 *Comfortable Chair*

1985 *Space Invader Cabinet*

1986 *Megatron*

1992 *Prism chair*

1993 *Half Cube+Cone-Cylinder=Table*

Page 111
top left: *Prism chair*, 1992
top right: *Torroid+Tetrahedron Table*, 1995
bottom: *Half Cube+Cone-Cylinder=Table*, 1993

Smokers Bow chair, 1982

One aspect of design in 1970s and 1980s Britain was marked by its close relationship with what was called "**The Crafts Revival**" of those years, which was characterized by a burst of energy in the area of "hand-making" in the fields of furniture, ceramics, glass, jewelry, etc. A number of creative individuals surfaced from the midst of this who favored an aesthetically progressive, rather than a backward-looking, approach. Fred Baier was one of these designers. Although they were hand-made, the furniture items he created were not "crafty" in any sense of the word. Instead they were brightly colored, highly decorated, eccentrically formed objects influenced by science fiction and popular culture. He said himself, "I wanted to bring decoration back into furniture and I wanted it to be structural, not just surface decoration." His designs had more in common with the Italian Memphis movement than with British **Arts and Crafts**. A music-stand from the mid-1980s, for instance, which combined aluminum and steel with sycamore wood, looked more like a futuristic robot than a piece of furniture.

Baier is a graduate of Birmingham Polytechnic and the **Royal College of Art**. He spent some time in the USA in the 1970s and taught in British art schools in the 1980s.

Ralph BALL

Furniture Designer

Page 113

top left: coffee table

top right: book table, 1998

bottom left: *Vienna* standing lamp, 1991

bottom right: *A Lighter Shade Up, A Lighter Shade Down* lamps, 1997

The design critic, Jonathan Glancey, has described Ralph Ball as "neither craftsman in the accepted sense, nor strictly designer," but rather "at once inventor, researcher, and maker with one eye on industrial production and the other on the handling of architectural space." Ball produces furniture and lighting designs, some of which are destined for volume-production and intended to inhabit spaces created by leading architects, while others are "one-offs" meant for galleries. Both sides of his work share the same interest in a reworking and questioning of modernism, and the relationship between ideas and forms. From the elegant *Aero* lamp of the late 1970s, a suspended wire, low-voltage lighting system, designed when Ball was still a student at London's **Royal College of Art**; his "high-tech" furniture designs of the early 1980s for **Norman Foster**'s *Renault* building in Swindon and for Foster's Hong Kong and Shanghai Bank; his *Summer Oak* furniture, a range of bedroom and dining-room furniture; his *Vienna* lights; and his recent gallery pieces, which take a more overtly ironic approach to modernism, his designs are recognizably his.

Ball trained as a furniture and lighting designer in the late 1960s and 1970s and has worked since for architects as an independent designer and, from the mid-1980s, in partnership with his wife, Maxine Naylor, also a furniture designer. He has spent some time in the United States and is a professor of industrial design at Washington University. Among Britain's contemporary designers, he is unusual in that he combines teaching (currently at the Royal College of Art) with personal works that result in exhibitions. His last two one-man shows, *Modern Movements* and *Introspective Furniture*, have both been well received. Ball has won several prestigious design prizes including, in the early 1990s, the Design and Industries Award.

Christian BARMAN

Product and Graphic Designer

1898 born

1933 works for **HMV** as product designer

1935 works for **London Transport** (until 1941)

1947 heads publicity division of the British Transport Commission (until 1963)

1948 elected *Royal Designer for Industry*; President of the Society of Industrial Artists

1963 receives *Order of the British Empire*

1980 dies

Products

1934 electric radiator

1936 electric iron for HMV

1935 routing system for London's traffic businesses

Christian Barman is a key figure among the handful of pioneer British industrial designers of the inter-war years. He was responsible for a number of highly influential products from this period that have since become icons of British modernism in design, among them an electric iron and a streamlined electric fan, both for the **HMV** company. They were among the few progressive British designs during these years that acknowledged developments in the United States and elsewhere.

Barman's influence was not simply as a product designer, however. Although his background was in architecture (he trained at Liverpool University), he started his career with **London Transport**—a very advanced organization then as far as design and visual identity were concerned—as head of visual public presentation. During his time there, which continued into the 1950s, he sat on a number of important panels that determined the design policies of large organizations involved with public transport of different kinds. He also played an important role as a writer, publishing several books on design and acting as editor of both the *Architect's Journal* and *Architectural Review* at different stages in his career. Although his name is less well known than many of his European and American counterparts, his significance in the British context as a promoter of modern design is not to be underestimated.

Page 115
top: Electric Iron for HMV, 1936
bottom: Southgate Station, 1935

Electric fan for HMV, 1934

Jonathan BARNBROOK

Graphic Designer

1966 born in Luton

1985 studies graphics at Central St. Martins College of Art and Design

1988 **Royal College of Art** in London (until 1990); graduated from the RCA and set up on his own

1997 founds Studio Virus

Products

1990 *Bastard* (DC) lettering

1991 *Exocet* lettering

1997 *Apocalypso* lettering; *Nylon* lettering; *Typography Now 2* book design

1998 concept book for the artist Damien Hirst for Booth Clibborn Editions

The group of radical graphic designers that grew out of **Punk**—**Peter Saville**, **Neville Brody**, and **Malcolm Garrett**—was the main source of inspiration for a new generation nearly a decade later, of which Jonathan Barnbrook is a key member. Trained at London's Central St. Martins School of Art and Design and Royal College of Art, Barnbrook has made a mark through an inventive approach to typography and graphic design, that acknowledges the links between graphics, pop culture, and music pioneered by Punk, as well as the subtle political and social power of graphic design. Unlike his inspirers, Barnbrook has been able to take advantage of new online technologies, and has increasingly oriented himself toward working on the screen and on advertisements produced by Tony Kaye films. His typefaces—among them *Prototype*, *Bastard*, *Mason*, *Exoset*, *Prozac*, *Patriot*, *Nylon*, and *Draylon* (the last two are based on lettering in medieval paintings)—are characterized by a deliberate sense of visual discord. In the late 1990s Barnbrook began to distribute his typefaces through his foundry, Virus and the print company FontWorks.

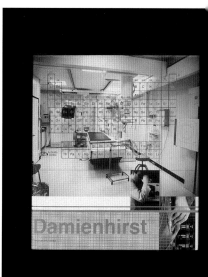

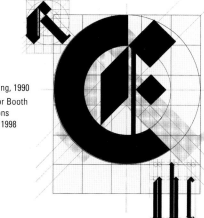

Bastard lettering, 1990
Damienhirst for Booth Clibborn Editions
Book-binding, 1998

Lamp Designer

The simple metal *Bestlite*, made from chrome and with a flexible metal shade, is a familiar lamp in contemporary British interiors that aspire to be "modern." Its design dates from the 1930s, a time when only a few British manufacturing companies responded to the ideas of modern design that were being generated in continental Europe. Best and Lloyd was one such company—and the lighting objects it produced in these years were the equal of anything being designed at Germany's Bauhaus. The firm was headed by Robert Dudley Best, who had studied industrial design in Germany. He took over what was a family lighting business and set about transforming the appearance of its products in line with the new aesthetic that he had seen in Europe. The *Bestlite*, available either as a standard lamp or as a desk or table model, has since become a classic of modern British design. Since the 1990s it has been back in production and continues to be a favorite with customers who want to create a highly functional-looking, minimal interior.

1892 born in Smethwick
1910 studies at the Arts and Crafts School in Düsseldorf
1915 member of the Design and Industries Association
1920 works in Paris
1925 managing director and product designer at Best & Lloyd
1984 died

Products
1930 Lamp *Bestlite*
1932 Standard Lamp *31766*
1991 Renditions of lamp *Bestlite* in different variations

Table Lamp *Bestlite*, 1930

BIB

Studio for Product Design

BIB Design Consultants,
London

1967 **Nick Butler** founds BIB
Design Consultants

1981 Nick Butler becomes
Royal Designer of Industry

Products

1969 medical tool for Ohmeda
(until 1983)

1986 television sets for
Ferguson

1990 *Tribune* telephone for
British Telecom; electronic
Rolodex *Agenda*

1992 *7000 SLR* camera for
Minolta

1998 desk System—UK

Page 119

top left: *Turbo Table* ironing board
for Oasis, 1998

top right: *7000 SLR* camera for
Minolta, 1992

bottom: *Tribune* telephone for
British Telecom, 1990

Durabeam for Duracell pocket lamp,
1989

BIB was founded by **Nick Butler** in the late 1960s. It remains one of Britain's strongest consultancies, with a reputation for a wide range of product designs that include pens for Dunhill, cameras for Minolta, earth-moving equipment for JCB, and radar equipment for Racal. It is best known, perhaps, for its neat little yellow-and-black flashlight, designed for Duracell, which reputedly helped Margaret Thatcher to safety when she was the victim of an IRA bomb attack at a Brighton hotel in the 1980s. The group's work has a sophisticated, international character to it and perpetuates the rigorous approach to product design that grew out of European modernism combined with American commercialism. Its only real claim to "Britishness" lies in its ability to bring these two approaches together successfully. The group's formula for good product design derives from "combining product aesthetics with function and sound engineering principles."

Butler trained at Leeds College of Art and the **Royal College of Art**. He came in contact with American thinking shortly after graduating, during a period spent in the United States on an IBM fellowship, where he worked under the leadership of Eliot Noyes. This was a formative experience which continues to influence his work. Other important BIB clients have included British Telecom and Ferguson. Several of BIB's designs have received prestigious awards.

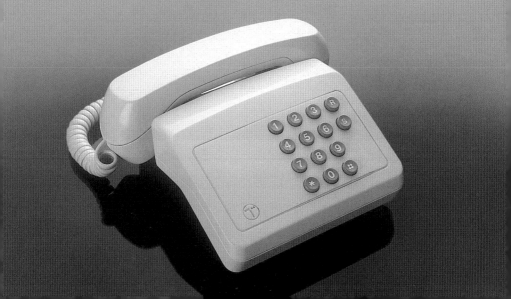

BIBA

Fashion House

BIBA of London, London
1964 Barbara Hulanicki opens fashion store in London
1965 BIBA-Logo by John McConnell
1966 fashion store in Kensington Church Street opens
1968 first catalog
1975 store closed
1995 relaunch by BIBA under Ellen Shek

Products
1968 *Pirate Set* with black-and-white trousers
1969 *Jumpsuit*
1970 BIBA-Cosmetics introduced; *Leopard's skin painting*
1997 BIBA-Cosmetics reintroduced

Logo for BIBA by John McConnell, 1968

Page 121
top: BIBA-Shop, London, 1974
lower left: Collection 1999
lower right: Collection 1999

The BIBA store was one of the most popular sources of fashion items for Britain's female youth in the second half of the 1960s. It provided its customers with clothing that had a nostalgic, glamorous, feeling. Their clothes helped to fuel the strong interest in escapist, fantasy dressing that characterized that era. During BIBA's lifetime it had a sequence of locations in and near London's fashionable Kensington High Street. It was a key component of "Swinging London." Set up by the fashion designer, Barbara Hulanicki, it sold highly feminine clothing to London's "dolly birds" in the second half of the decade and into the 1970s. Biba sold a whole "look" to its young customers, including hats and feather boas, creating an image that was based first on Victoriana but later on the "Art Deco" Hollywood look of the 1930s. Its last venue was on the site of the old Derry & Toms department store where the design of its interior was at its most extravagant, based on thirties cinema and the glamour of that era.

BRANSON COATES

Studio for Architecture, Furniture, and Product Design

Branson Coates
Architecture, London

1985 founded by Doug Branson
and Nigel Coates

1988 *Metropolis—New British
Architecture and the City*
exhibition, London

1995 *Objects of Desire*
exhibition, London

1997 Erotic Design for the
Design Museum exhibition,
London

The year 1999 saw the opening of a new National Centre for Popular Music (NCPM) in Sheffield. Built by the architectural partnership of Branson Coates, made up of Doug Branson and **Nigel Coates**, it is a impressive, highly sculptural, landmark building, characterized by four apparently floating drums clad in stainless steel and topped by four cowls that float in the wind. It is also a sign that, for the first time since its emergence in the 1960s, British youth culture has entered mainstream culture and is commemorated in a lasting monument. Coates describes the building as having "a swaying, jiving lilt. It celebrates Sheffield's industrial heritage and signals how buildings of the future don't need to ape the ones we already have. In the same way that pop music has no specific definition, the NCPM doesn't conform to any type."

The roots of this "typeless" architecture and interior design originated in the 1980s. A new, young, anti-heroic approach to architecture and interior design emerged in Britain, which, in the wake of pop and punk, allied itself to street culture, to urban decay and chaos, to salvaged materials, and, above all, to youth and fashion. In place of the heroic, simple, rational architecture that it rejected, it posited an approach to the environment that brought a number of disciplines—art, sculpture, curating, writing, film, and video—together in a new, subversive way. It touched taboo areas such as sexuality and acted as an irritant to mainstream values. Doug Branson and Nigel Coates were key advocates of this new movement. They based their philosophy on the ideas that "design should reflect the complex interaction of the city" and that it should be "knowing and reactive, encouraging involvement and inquiry." Their approach has resulted in an impressive body of work to date, which includes buildings in Japan and elsewhere, interiors, furniture, objects, and ephemeral displays.

Nigel Coates graduated from London's Architectural Association in the mid-1970s and returned to teach a very influential unit there until the late 1980s. In the early 1980s, with a group of friends and colleagues, he formed

Page 123

top: *Pillon* glass bowl series for Simon Moore, 1998

bottom left: *Legover* chair, 1997

bottom right: Powerhouse UK, Horseguards Parade, 1998

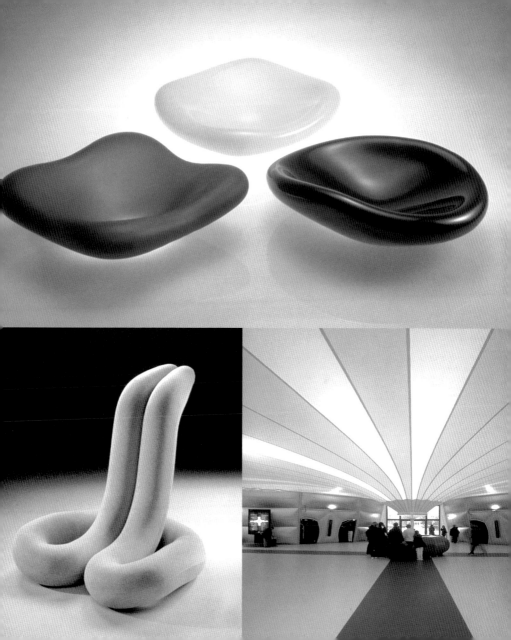

Products

1985 Metropole restaurant in Tokyo

1986 Cafe Bongo in Tokyo

1988 *Otaru* couch piping and *Tongue* armchair for **SCP** shop; for Katharine Hamnett in London

1989 shop for Jasper Conran in Tokyo; *Tongue* chair

1991 Jigsaw shop in London

1996 Bargo Bar in Glasgow

1997 Erotic Design exhibition for the Design Museum in London

1998 *Bulb* and *Pillon* glass vases and bowls for **Simon Moore**; *Oyster House* for the Ideal Home exhibition, London

1999 National Centre for Popular Music, Sheffield

Page 125

Top: *Daybed* couch for Lloyd Loom, 1999

bottom left: BargoBar,Glasgow, 1996

bottom right: *Genie* stool, 1988

NATO (Narrative Architecture Today), which hit the design headlines with its provocative, nihilistic work, the complexity and chaos of which echoed the anarchic condition of contemporary urban culture. Graffiti, found and recycled materials and objects, and a sense of "post-holocaust" decay and metropolitan malaise pervaded the work. At this stage the project was primarily limited to drawings and exhibition work. With the formation of Branson Coates in the mid-1980s, however, "real" projects began to come along. Within a few years, Nigel Coates had designed a number of interiors—among them the **Jasper Conran** shop in London, the **Katherine Hamnett** shop in Glasgow, the Caffe Bongo and the Metropole restaurant in Tokyo, and the Noah's Ark restaurant in Sapporo, also in Japan. Through his Japanese work Coates's reputation as an enfant terrible grew, as did a realization of the originality of his vision and imagination.

From the late 1980s onward, Branson Coates has gone from strength to strength, ceasing to work "at the edge" and becoming leading figures in the context of British avant-garde design. It has covered an unbelievably wide spectrum, creating buildings, interiors of all kinds, furniture pieces, and products. Some of the chairs have been created for specific sites such as the Noah's Ark restaurant or the Bargo bar in Glasgow, while others—the *Oxo* chair, the *Genie* stool, and the *Legover* chair among them—have become design icons in their own right. Shop interiors have been a mainstay throughout these years, providing a perfect outlet for their fashion-conscious approach toward the designed environment. While overtly commercial, Nigel Coates's designs are also personal, poetic statements.

The last few years have seen some important commissions, including the *Oyster House* for the Ideal Home Exhibition, the *British Pavilion* for Expo '98 in Seville, the Powerhouse::uk exhibit in London, and the Sheffield Museum. *The Body Zone*, a main attraction inside the Millennium Dome in Greenwich, is also by Branson Coates. In the mid-1990s Nigel Coates became Professor of Architecture and Interiors at the **Royal College of Art** in London, and he divides his time between this and his practice.

Neville BRODY

Graphic Designer

1957 born in London

1977 studies at London College of Printing (until 1980)

1981 works as art director for the new magazine *The Face* (until 1986); record cover for Fetish Records

1983 art director for publisher Conde Nast in Milan

1986 opens studio in London with Fwa Richards; bookcovers for Penguin Books

1988 solo exhibition at the **Victoria and Albert Museum**, London; the catalog *The Graphic Language of Neville Brody* is published (second edition, 1994)

1990 founds the Studio Research Arts; magazine *Fuse* is published

1998 *Meta Design* project in San Francisco

Page 127

top left: cover for magazine *New Socialist*, 1986

top right: record cover *23 Skidoo* for Fetish Records, 1982

bottom: cover and inside pages for magazine *The Face*, 1985

Neville Brody has played an important part in the story of progressive British graphic design since the 1980s. He has made his mark as one of the leading figures in the transformation of subcultural ideas into a mainstream context, and in combining these subversive ideas with those derived from the European modern tradition of the early twentieth century. The result was a new graphic aesthetic that was both raw and sophisticated at the same time. It was anarchic, yet respectful of the heroes of modernism such as the Russians Alexander Rodtschenko and El Lissitsky. Brody also admits his debt to Herbert Spencer's book *Pioneers of Modern Typography*.

Like many post-war British design innovations, Brody's work had its roots in music and its accompanying graphics, especially record covers. He explained, "We were trying to work against the kind of contrived and grandiose imagery that was significant on Ultravox sleeves, for example, seeking to engage an intuitive reaction that followed on from our own feelings about a sleeve's imagery."

This intuitive approach characterized all Brody's work, imbuing it with a strong fine-art content. It was also a reaction to the commercial nature of the business in which he was working. Brody began his career in music, working immediately after his graduation for Alec McDowell's Rocking Russian Company, and also for a short period with Stiff Records and Fetish Records.

When Terry Jones launched the magazines *i-D* (instant Design) and *The Face* at the beginning of the 1980s, he took on Brody as *The Face*'s art director. Brody created his own highly innovatory typeface and a new graphic imagery that was to influence other areas, especially advertising.

Frederique Huygen, in her book *British Design*, described how *The Face* contained pages of print, full of graphic symbols, used in juxtaposition with large photographs in a startling way. Brody explained, "I wanted to surprise people and maintain a rhythm that was based on a different set of elements. I felt that if you opened a page that stopped you in your tracks, then you

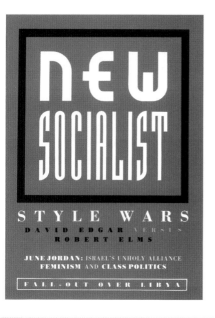

NEW
SOCIALIST

STYLE WARS

DAVID EDGAR VERSUS
ROBERT ELMS

JUNE JORDAN: ISRAEL'S UNHOLY ALLIANCE
FEMINISM AND **CLASS POLITICS**

FALL-OUT OVER LIBYA

Products

1981 layout for magazine *The Face*

1982 record cover for the band Cabaret Voltaire

1983 cover photos for the London magazine *City Limits*

1986 Six lettering

1987 art director of magazine *Arena* (until 1990)

from left to right:
Typeface *Six* lettering, 1986
Industria Inline lettering, 1990
Blur lettering, 1991

would want to read on." Catherine McDermott wrote, "type in *The Face* is used in an unconventional way: headlines turned upside down, serif and sans serif faces mixed, decorative devices thrown in and a range of detailing which includes dots, squares, triangles, and images from everyday life." Brody took this strategy with him in his work for other magazines such as *Arena, City Limits*, and *The New Socialist*.

He quickly moved beyond record covers and magazine layouts into the wider world of graphic design, including book design and posters. Art museums and galleries, among them the Museum of Modern Art in Oxford and the Photographers' Gallery in London, have also been transformed by him at particular moments. His work was celebrated by an exhibition at London's **Victoria and Albert Museum** in the early 1990s.

1991 *Blur*, *Gothi*, *Pop* lettering;
stamps for the Dutch Post;
routing system and design
for the Art and Exhibition
Hall in Bonn

1992 design for TV station ORF

1994 design for TV station
Premiere

Page 130/131

left: page for magazine *Interview*,
1989

right: brochure for Zumtobel, 1994

left: poster *F-State* for *Fuse 1*, 1991

right: software packaging for
Macromedia, 1997

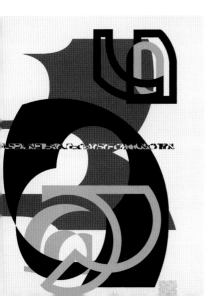

promise

shame

greed

destruct

disrspect

shame

damage

shame

disntgrate

Zumtobel AG

Annual Report 1994/1995

Julian BROWN

Product Designer

Laptop *La-Vie* for NEC, 1998

Page 133
top left: *Vercingetorix* alarm clock, 1993
top right: *Attila* can opener, 1997
bottom left: *Hannibal* tape dispenser, 1998 all for Rexite
bottom right: *Pump and Go* thermos, 1999

His studio cannot be identified with any one particular uniform style. Instead, Julian Brown employs a variable, theoretically grounded method which can be applied to a wide and sundry range of products, from office systems to cutlery, and from paper wares to garden furniture. The experience gained in one product area often overflows into another. Julian Brown, who founded his studio in the early 1990's not in London, but in Bath, has a consistent and highly individual approach. He was employed by **David Carter** for several years and worked in the mid-1980's at the renowned Porsche Design Studio in Austria. Here he designed the much-noted *Studio* eyeglasses, which have a leather nose piece which made them more comfortable to wear and was soon to become the brand's distinguishing feature. Among his best known products numbers the small colorful *Basic* thermos bottle he designed for the German manufacturer Zizmann. It was developed in the late 1980's when Brown partnered with **Ross Lovegrove**. This innovative and aesthetically pleasing object combines technology and design and is typical of Brown's work in that respect.

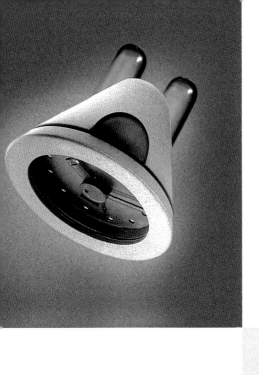

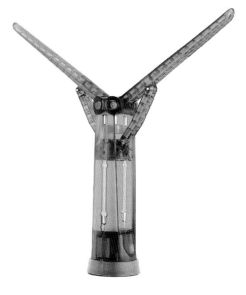

Products

His use of translucent plastic—for example in one of his more recent products, the *Hannibal* tape dispenser for the Italian Rexite company—illustrates his approach. When opened, the dispenser has the shape of an elephant. Julian Brown has repeatedly succeeded in synchronizing the main objectives of design by combining new materials, formal innovation and a strong visual aspect. Probably his most important trait is the dependable humor pervading his every design, whether it be a small article like a toothbrush, spoon or fountain pen, extensive electronic equipment(for NEC) or furniture, which he designs for such respected brands as Zanotta in Italy and Haworth in the U.S.A.

Intego thermos, 1999

Studio for Interior Architecture

Casson Mann-headed by Dinah Casson and Roger Mann-has carved a unique place for itself within contemporary British design in the areas of interiors, museum installations, temporary exhibitions and cultural events. While many of their designs are ephemeral, others have lasted and earned the team a reputation for rigorous and appropriate research and execution. Their designs of the mid-1980s for an ice-cream store, Grangelato, in Knightsbridge and for the interiors of the Headquarters of the Chartered Society of Designers in Bedford Square, showed how much they had learnt from the radical Italian experiments of that time. They have moved on from there. Their interiors for the Institute of Practitioners in Advertising of the mid-1990s, those for the offices of Hydra Associates in the later '90s, and their ongoing work for London's Science Museum and **Victoria and Albert Museum** show that they are led less by style than by a deep understanding of the way in which the old and the new can be combined-and of the complex relationships between spaces and users.

1984 founded by **Dinah Casson** and **Roger Mann**

Products
1986 CSD-Central, London
1995 garden design for the Science Museum, London
1997 exhibition design *Charlotte Perriand—Modernist Pioneer* in **Design Museum**, London
2000 fifteen galleries for the permanent exhibition New British Art and Design in **Victoria and Albert Museum**

below: reception room for British Council, Singapore, 1997

1895 born in Japan as a
Canadian citizen

1919 student of engineering in
London

1925 reports as a journalist from
the Exposition
Internationale des Arts
Decoratifs in Paris

1928 designs for Cresta Silks
store chain

1931 founds the firm **Isokon**
with **Jack Pritchard**

1944 elected Royal Designer for
Industry

1958 dies

Products

1931 furnishing for **BBC**
Broadcasting House,
London

1933 *Minimum Kitchen*
exhibited in the Dorland
Hall in London

1934 *AD 65* radio for E.K. Cole;
Lawn Road apartments
completed

1947 *Princess* Handbag radio
for E.K.Cole

Page 137
top left: *Typist's Desk*, around 1935
top right: *A22* radio for Ekco, 1945
bottom: *Radiotime* alarm clock for
E.K. Cole, 1947

Coates was born in Japan of Canadian parents. His mother had studied with the American architects Louis Sullivan and Frank Lloyd Wright. The Polyglot Coates first worked off and on as a journalist and a lumberjack, but then studied engineering and found employment with various architects, occasionally in Paris, before opening his own studio in London in the early 1930's.

Coates belonged to a small circle of progressive architects and designers who championed a Central European modernism. He became famous primarily through a series of apartment buildings, among them Lawn Road Flats in London's Hampstead, and Embassy Court in Brighton. As an interior designer he made a name for himself with his appointments for the **BBC**'s Broadcasting House. The history of design will remember him for the *AD65* Bakelite radio, which adopts the circular form of a loud speaker, gives the new appliance type an austere geometric form, and reveals the rationalistic perspective of an engineer. Coates treated the radio as the technical apparatus it was, not as a piece of furniture. It was the first time Britain had seen a modern product design in a household appliance, and it became one of the best known radios in the British Isles. Later Coates also designed portable radios such as the *Princess* model with its colorful plastic housing. During the 1930's he was additionally employed as a consultant by furniture manufacturer **Isokon**, which produced designs by Bauhaus-emigrant **Marcel Breuer** among others. Wells Coates' output was amazingly diverse, given the relatively short span of his career. He was also an enthusiastic sportsman and constructed an innovative catamaran for his own use. Toward the end of his career he left Great Britain and taught at various overseas universities including Harvard.

Britain leads the way internationally in what is broadly described as "communication design," a term that has come to refer to a multidisciplinary approach to design, which covers a broad field of activity, including graphic design, corporate identity schemes, advertising, pop videos, television commercials, the design of promotional material, and events of various kinds. It shows itself in a wide range of forms, from printed material to moving images and light shows. It has its essence in an abstract concept but manifests itself visually, although words and music also play an important role. It is essentially commercial and promotional, but its manifestations cut across the commercial/cultural divide in a unique way.

Communication design in Britain has its roots in at least two recent traditions. The first is the growth of "house styles" or visual identity schemes, created for the public and private corporations that emerged as a British strength in the 1950s in the hands of design groups such as the **Design Research Unit**. This phenomenon was a development of wartime propaganda schemes developed by the Ministry of Information and its protagonists all had some experience of that kind of work.

The second tradition is the British pop movement of the 1960s, which instilled in British cultural life the importance of the ephemeral and the transitory. It also provided a moment in which art-school–trained designers from different backgrounds worked closely together on a particular spectacle or event. The light shows, for example, that accompanied the pop

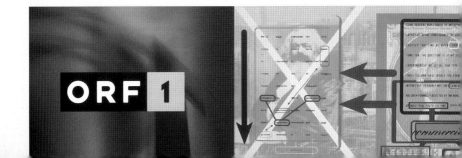

concerts of Pink Floyd are seminal in this context, as is the work of graphic artists such as Michael English and Nigel Waymouth, who saw any surface as one that could be covered with images. Pop provided the cultural, multidisciplinary face of British communication design.

With these two traditions colliding, a highly creative face of British design developed that is overtly commercial but also simultaneously cultural. Although it has its roots in the older, more traditional area of "graphic design," it now includes the moving image and, with the expansion of information technology and multimedia, has developed into a whole new area of creative endeavor in which young art-school graduates and a broader range of creative young people are making their mark.

As far as corporate identity is concerned, the work of the large design groups that emerged in the 1960s, 1970s, and 1980s—among them **Wolff Olins**, **Fitch** and Company, **Lloyd Northover**, and the **Michael Peters** group—established a standard that pointed the way forward. Many corporations were revamped visually in these years.

Advertising also developed into an increasingly sophisticated "communication design" area at this time. The line between it and corporate identity became hard to draw. The Benson and Hedges cigarette advertising campaigns, for example, showed how subtle British projects could be. As Frederique Huygen has explained in her book, *British Design*, "The dividing line between the two is vague: they merge into one another. Corporate

"The problem is not to create feeling but to have feeling."
Neville Brody

from left to right:
Visuals for the television channel ORF 1 and 2 by Neville Brody, 1992
Spread from the book *Typography Now 2* designed by Jonathan Barnbrook for Booth Clibborn Editions, 1994
Screen Design *The System* for the BBC by Why Not, 1996

identity and image overlap as regards content too." Groups such as Saatchi and Saatchi, Ogilvy and Mather, Bartle; Bogle; Hegarthy, and others have made a significant impact in the last few decades. In this context, design, marketing, and management have become mixed together. In the 1980s, especially, they worked together to great effect. The Saatchi firm, for instance, defined itself as the "foremost global know-how company" and worked in Britain, Europe, and the United States.

By the 1990s the pop video business had expanded considerably. Huygen explains again, "Here music, the visual arts, film, photography, graphic design and advertising are brought together, as are the avant-garde and the commercial." The pop video brought together all the areas in which Britain had developed strengths over the last few decades and represented a synthesis of talents. Creators such as Kevin Godley and Lol Creme, who had both been in the pop music business before they moved into videos, have produced some very innovative work as has the designer Alex McDowell who was quick to earn himself a reputation in this rapidly expanding field.

The area of the moving image, both videos and television commercials, picked up where graphic advertising and corporate identity had left off and created a new area in which Britain, with its strong art-school tradition, rapidly took the lead internationally. **Hipgnosis**, Roger Dean's design group, which had made its mark in the area of fantasy record covers, set up a small subsidiary to work on videos and commercials. The creative and financial potential of this new area was soon apparent to many. Film directors such as Julian Temple and Russell Mulcahey also found themselves being pulled into this exciting new direction.

One analyst of the phenomenon, however, claims that Britain's unprecedented success in this area is due to the fact that many of its protagonists have come not from a background in television commercials but from the creative free-for-all of the art schools. Although computers are increasingly used to generate this kind of work, it is still highly creative individuals who provide the visual ideas. Designers such as Martin Lambie-Nairn have played a crucial role in showing the creative standards that are possible in work for television.

The emphasis in British communication design upon the ephemeral rather than the durable led to dramatic new developments in the 1990s. The emphasis shifted from the static identity to the moving image and on to the "event," the ultimate throw-away concept. A number of multidisciplinary groups such as **Imagination** and **Tomato** were established, combining the skills of individuals from different backgrounds in such a way as to redefine the very meaning of communication design. Imagination focuses on events such as the launch of products, and on cultural events linked with the theater. Its approach also has its origins in pop culture, in this case in the concept of the "light show" spectacle that accompanied many pop concerts in the 1960s.

The emphasis in this kind of work is upon flexibility and open-endedness, and away from the single discipline or the simplistic concept. The end is almost always commercial in one way or another, but the means are highly creative and culturally significant. Young designers come from a wide range of backgrounds and constantly learn new skills. Ultimately the high level of achievement is due to them and their ability to change. As one graphic designer has commented, "Whatever else, young talent in the advertising world has managed to avoid contamination by ideas about design pureness or other weighty traditions."

"Create new loyalties, erase old ones, mark territories, strengthen ideas, and find new ways to do things."
Wally Olins

CONNOLLY

Leather goods manufacturer

Connolly Ltd. London

1878 founded as a shoemaking company by Samuel and Joseph Connolly

1904 contracted to upholster Rolls Royce

1995 luxury leather store opens in London

1999 majority of company stock sold to **Joseph Ettedgui**

Products

1963 *Portofino* driving shoes

1992 luggage (until 1996)

1994 *Rucksack City* by **Ross Lovegrove**

1998 Racing Numbers silver cufflinks, umbrella with leather handle, traveling folding cup with leather case; leather upholstering for Aston Martin

Page 143

top left: *Rucksack City* by Ross Lovegrove, 1994

top right: belt by In House, 1997

bottom: tool kit by Sebastian Conran, 1997

Briefcase by Ross Lovegrove, 1994

When the King of England ordered leather seats for his carriages from the shoemaker Connolly, it was almost a foregone conclusion that Rolls Royce would place a follow-up order sometime thereafter. Connolly stands for a century of tradition in leather goods and continues to manufacture upholstery for Rolls Royce and other luxury cars makers today. "Design" only entered the picture in the 1990's, when the family-owned company opened a shop for luxury goods. It was no coincidence that the first collection stemmed from **Ross Lovegrove**, a young multi-talented member of the British design scene. Lovegrove's Coachline leather handbag series is striking in its simple elegance and excellent workmanship, and it combines his concept of distinctive class with Connolly's aristocratic design concepts. In the meantime other no less noted designers such as **Sebastian Conran** and **Seymour Powell** have added to the company's offerings, which now comprises not only leather goods like shoes, belts and jackets but also eyeglasses and a tool kit. The main product line is now defined by Joseph and Isable **Ettedgui**, who also own the Connolly-Design branch, and whose creations are distributed in two exclusive shops. The new store was created by French star designer Andrée Putnam.

Terence CONRAN

Entrepeneur, Furniture and Product Designer

1931 born in London

1947 studies textile design at the Central School of Art and Design

1950 works at Rayon Centre in London

1952 produces own furniture

1956 founds Conran Design Group, a studio for Design and Design consulting (with John Stephenson)

1964 Habitat store opens in London

1971 Conran Associates founded

1974 **Design Council** prize for a series of plastic containers

1981 opening of **Boilerhouse** design gallery at **Victoria and Albert Museum**, London

1982 Mothercare store chain bought (1983 **Heal's**, 1986 British Home Stores)

Page 145

top left: round wicker chair, 1954

top right: wicker chair, 1999

bottom left: Conran Shop, London

bottom right: *Minima* silver pot and tableware, 1997

The figure of Terence Conran has dominated post-war design in Britain more than any other single individual. Without him, the popular **Habitat** stores dotted all over the country, the chic Conran Shop in London's Fulham Road, and the **Design Museum** in London's Docklands would not exist. His larger-than-life personality and love of the "good life" have played a key role in the formation of British taste for things modern, and have influenced many design institutions. Conran has influenced the course of modern British design not only as a designer but, more importantly, as an entrepreneur, retailer, design reformer, patron of modern design and, most recently, restaurateur. His unremitting commitment to "good taste" has dominated British design for more than three decades, showing that there is a modern face to British culture, which is acceptable to a large sector of the population. He has helped bring influences from countries such as Scandinavia, France, and Italy into Britain. He also developed an approach toward "good design" that could be made available to many people, and his stores cater to the middle classes as well as the elite. His discerning eye favors a design style which is modern, simple but, above all, human.

It was as a designer that Conran was first active in the 1950s. Furniture, ceramics and textiles all bore his signature and his output soon came to the notice of many who sought modern furnishings. Striking designs for Midwinter were among early examples showing that he could combine elegant simplicity with popular imagery. He also made an impact with a number of Italian-inspired furniture pieces. By the early 1960s Conran had become very disillusioned with British retailing and realized that the only way to improve things was to move into that area himself, and to make things available to people that hadn't been available before. To this end, he opened the first Habitat store in 1964, importing vast numbers of products for the domestic interior from Europe and creating a total "lifestyle" look that appealed to young, fashion-conscious consumers. The store was a huge

success and by the end of the decade he had opened branches in other British cities such as Manchester.

1989 **Design Museum** in London opens

1990 withdraws from trade

1992 buys Conran shop chain back

1990 *Bluebird* restaurant opens

Products

1954 wicker stool with metal legs

1955 Cafe Orrey in London designed

1958 stacking chairs made of laminated books

1974 the *House* book published

1993 tray for Quaglino's restaurant

1997 *Pont Occasional* table *Minima* silver pot and tableware and *Conran Watch*

1999 Great Eastern Hotel in London

Page 147
top left: Conran Watch, 1997
top right: shelf, 1999
bottom: table *Pont Occasional*, 1997

Through the success of Habitat, Conran earned a reputation for his meticulous eye and his ability to make things happen. He used this success to move back into design practice and formed Conran Associates, a design consultancy that focused on corporate identity and product design. A particularly successful example of a project undertaken by the group was the range of brightly colored plastic containers designed for Crayonne, a division of the Airfix Plastics Group. The combination of high quality, simplicity, and wide availability of these products lay at the heart of Conran's philosophy of "good design."

The 1970s saw both Habitat and Conran Associates go from strength to strength, and Conran increasingly became a spokesperson for modern design in Britain. His retailing interests and ambitions expanded, and he took over the chain of Mothercare stores, the prestigious **Heal's** shop in London's Tottenham Court Road and, later, British Home Stores, a large, popular, low-priced chain of clothing shops, applying his philosophy of "good design for everyone" to these new contexts. As his personal wealth grew, he sought to play a role in promoting "good design" in Britain, funding Britain's first exhibition space dedicated solely to designed artifacts—the **Boilerhouse** in London's **Victoria and Albert Museum**. The venture was a huge success and hosted a number of exhibitions, among them *Memphis from Milan, Issey Miyake, The Ford Sierra, Taste, National Identity*, and *Design*. At the end of the 1970s the Boilerhouse was replaced by the much more substantial Design Museum near London's Tower Bridge, which Conran also funded.

Conran left nearly all his retail interests (with the exception of the Conran Shop) behind him in the early 1990s and returned to an earlier love—restaurants. Since when he has opened a large number of eating places, large and democratic as well as smaller and exclusive. They include his Bluebird complex in London's King's Road, and various restaurants in its Docklands.

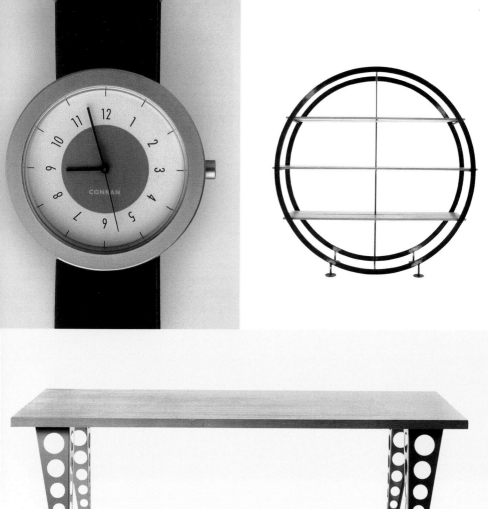

Post-war Britain witnessed the emergence of a new interior style. Characterized by organic forms in furniture, abstract patterns on wallpapers, textiles, ceramics, and metalware, it was a hybrid style, synthesizing new developments in the United States, Italy, and Scandinavia. The work of the American furniture designer, Charles Eames, and the Danish designer, Finn Juhl, was particularly influential. Britain's modern style quickly became popular, especially in the extensive post-war housing built for the newly affluent lower-middle-class and working-class population.

The "contemporary style" was first noticed by *Design* magazine, launched in 1949 as the mouthpiece of the recently formed **Council of Industrial Design** (later the Design Council). Where furniture was concerned, its protagonists were men such as **Ernest Race**, **Robin Day**, and **Clive Latimer**, who responded enthusiastically to the challenge of new materials such as aluminum, steel rod, and molded plywood, and worked for enthusiastic new manufacturers such as **Hille**. Before long, their designs were available in furniture outlets in provincial High Streets across the country and the Council began to worry about what it termed "repro-contemporary," which it considered to be a cheaper version of the "authentic" design aesthetic it had promoted.

Furniture played an important part but "contemporary style" was a total interior "look," in which textiles also played a key role. **Lucienne Day** designed some outstanding textiles, many of which were sold through the Heal's store in London's Tottenham Court Road. Ceramics and other

decorative items completed the effect, and many consumers began to move away from the more traditional designs produced by long-established manufacturers toward more up-to-date patterns and forms by manufacturers such as Midwinter, and designers such as **Terence Conran**.

"Contemporary" was the first truly popular modern British style. It penetrated deeply into British society in the wake of the **Festival of Britain**, a major event held in London in 1951. The Festival's displays of living spaces all embraced the new forms and patterns. Indeed, many of the patterns had been created by the Festival Pattern Group, formed to find new abstract patterns based on what could be seen when organisms were viewed through a microscope. A belief in science as the way forward was all-pervasive, and the organic motifs that resulted from these experiments rapidly found their way on to the surfaces of a wide range of goods.

By the late 1950s, however, the energy that inspired the "contemporary style" had evaporated and the generation of the immediate post-war years had been succeeded by one with a completely different set of priorities. This was the last time that the British public shared one view of the future as represented by one visual style. Once the pop generation emerged, British design became much more mixed. The contemporary style represents a moment of national unity and optimism that has not been seen again since.

"I believe that the quality of design strengthens the value of humanity."
Robin Day

from left to right:
Seats by Robin Day for S. Hille, 1960
A 262 radio by E Minud for Murphy, 1955
Dinner Occasional Chair by Ernest Race, 1946

One of the most familiar faces of British visual culture, as viewed from outside Britain, is linked to the nation's deep love of the countryside and the rural, aristocratic lifestyle that goes with it. A powerful image is evoked of a nation that spends its weekends in country houses engaging in the traditional sports of hunting, shooting, and fishing, accompanied by functional, hard-wearing clothing and items of equipment that are centuries old and smell of polished leather.

There is a high level of mythology and marketing "hype" attached to this image and it is, in reality, a vision of "Britishness" that has been constructed more recently than may appear obvious. It is rooted in what has been called the "invented traditions" of the nineteenth century and the early years of the twentieth century, and in the emergence of a range of goods that have been developed to act as the props in this staged fantasy. Although these artifacts are only props, many foreigners come to Britain in search of them and leave believing that they have bought into "Britishness." As a marketing exercise, its success is remarkable.

The country style exists on a number of different levels. First, there are the signs of a faded, aristocratic lifestyle, expressed in a "uniform" that is seen to operate outside fashion and to depend instead on concepts of quality, utility, and durability. Prominent are cashmere cardigans and jumpers by Pringle; tweed skirts and suits by Jaeger; hard-wearing, weatherproof jackets by Barbour; and sturdy boots and shoes hand-made by Lobb's.

This "look" is completed by such essential country items as green Wellington boots and a green sleeveless quilted jacket. No designer's name is attached to these items. They seem, instead, simply to have evolved from the requirements of utility and to have always been in existence. Their brand is their selling point, for example, the Burberry company and its mackintoshes. The names of **Pringle**, **Jaeger**, **Barbour**, and others act as guarantors of a certain "authenticity" and quality, which, it is believed, stem from a rural idyll now for the most part lost to us. It still lingers on, or so one is made to believe, in the British countryside, which remains unchanged and true to the past. In reality, all these companies have been formed within the last hundred years or less.

The British's love of the country shows itself in other ways. The continued admiration of foreigners, and indeed of many British consumers, for the Land Rover and, more recently, other four-wheel-drive cars (many not of British origin) is a symptom of the same desire to return to the land, although most can be seen trying in vain to park in narrow urban and suburban streets. The "country look" has invaded the town in recent decades and the popularity of these objects of transport is yet another sign of the strong sense of nostalgia that underpins contemporary British society, and is very visible to visitors from abroad.

The "country style," particularly in its urban manifestation, was given a huge boost in the 1970s when Britain was experiencing economic decline

"The right place for the handicraftsman is the countryside."
C.R. Ashbee

from left to right:
OSE basket by Highland Home Industries, 1950
Chair by C.F.A.Voysey, 1902
Wastebasket and bread basket by M. Kloss, 1948
Chair and kitchen cupboard by Ambrose Heal, 1908–1910

and was once again in search of its lost cultural roots. The textile designs of the Laura Ashley company brought this ideal to a mass market for the first time. Based on a popular, rather than an aristocratic, view of the countryside, its ubiquitous flowered cotton fabrics and wallpapers were based on cheap textiles supplied to the Victorian market. After the science-fiction atmosphere of the "artificial" 1960s, British mass taste swung back in search of the "natural." This was the era of the pine kitchen, when housewives discarded their formica-covered surfaces and replaced them with wood. The solid warmth and comfort of an Aga range-style cooker, a product of the 1920s, was introduced as another mythical component of traditional country living that had (and still has) a powerful symbolic message.

The British "country-house look" dominated middle-class urban and suburban interiors. Venetian blinds gave way to swagged curtains and decorating companies such as Colefax & Fowler became enormously popular, supplying traditional chintzes to huge numbers of customers. The "look" was widely exported and was especially appreciated in the United States. With this interest came a sudden expansion of mass-market magazines such as *Traditional Homes* and *Country Living*, which filled the shelves of urban supermarkets across the country.

As well as clothing, interior decor, cars, and cookers, the British "country look" has also been widely adopted by packagers wanting to give "added value" to the goods they are selling. Nowhere is this more obvious than in toiletries.

Soaps and bath oils manufactured by a number of companies use this strategy to give their merchandise extra appeal. Crabtree & Evelyn, for example, bases its apparent exclusivity on its sophisticated packaging, which evokes a lost past.

As urban life becomes more complex, the British "country look" is more successful. It stands outside the world of high design, yet it occupies vast numbers of packagers and designers. The up-market, craft end—Lobb's shoes, Burberry mackintoshes, etc.—continues to flourish with the help of foreign tourists, but of more significance to British culture in general is the entry of this idealized, "country look" lifestyle into the mass marketing and advertising of countless products that affect the lives of vast numbers of people. It is a "look" that shows no sign of going away and, with the growing interest in organic food and natural toiletries, is likely to be around for some time to come.

"Forget the bursting, terrible city. Rather dream of a horse wagon in the mountains."

William Morris

Lucienne and Robin DAY
Textile Designer and Furniture Designer

1915 Robin Day born in High Wycombe

1917 Lucienne Day born in Coulsdon

1942 Robin and Lucienne get married

1948 common studio in London; Robin Day wins a design prize at the Museum of Modern Art

Page 155

top: bench by Robin Day, around 1980

bottom left: *Trig* textile by Lucienne Day, around 1950

bottom right: *Sommerset* tablecloth by Lucienne Day for Thos, 1960

Polyprop chair by Robin Day, 1962

The Days are two of Britain's leading designers of the post-war years. Together they helped bring progressive ideas about modern design into the British interior—Robin through his innovative furniture, which used new materials such as bent plywood, steel rod and plastic in original ways, and Lucienne through her biomorphic-patterned textiles. Their influence marked an important turning point in the story of modern British design.

Robin Day's first breakthrough came when, with **Clive Latimer**, he designed a piece of storage furniture for a competition at New York's Museum of Modern Art, where they were awarded first prize. The Hille company offered to manufacture Day's designs and has continued to do so throughout his long career as a furniture designer. He is best known for his molded polypropylene chair, which has been manufactured in vast quantities since its introduction and has become a ubiquitous object in Britain's public spaces. His work was featured strongly at the Festival of Britain in 1951, and he also exhibited at the Milan Triennale exhibitions of the 1950s, along with

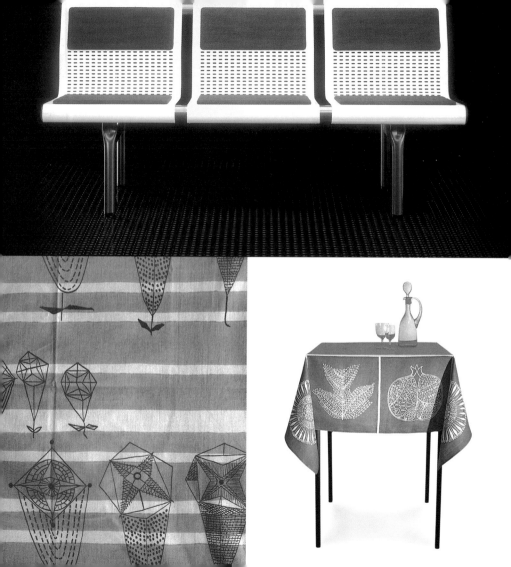

1963 Lucienne Day is on the board of the Royal College of Art (until 1968)

1974 **Robin Day** leads the London School of Furniture (until 1980)

Products

1951 *Calyx* fabric by Lucienne Day for the Festival of Britain

1955 *City* wallpaper by Lucienne Day for Rasch

1959 *4 Seasons Service* by Lucienne Day for Rosenthal

1962 *Polyprop* plastic chair by Robin Day for **Hille**

1970 *Sunrise* fabric for **Heal's** by Lucienne Day

1980 couch for the Barbican Centre in London by Robin Day

1983 *Sad Lady* fabric mosaic by Lucienne Day

Page 157
Textile by Lucienne Day

Sofa by Robin Day

Lucienne, winning a number of prizes. He has also worked as a product designer creating radios and television sets for the British firm, Pye.

Lucienne Day also came to the fore professionally in the 1950s. Her innovative textiles were sold through Heal's on London's Tottenham Court Road. One of her most notable designs, *Calyx*, was created for the Festival of Britain and earned her design awards in both the United States and Italy. The Day's designs are still much admired.

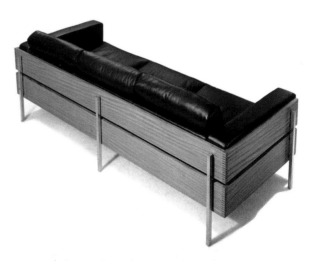

DESIGNERS GUILD
Textile Manufacturer

Recent decades have seen a dramatic growth in the public's interest in furnishing domestic interiors. A number of companies and stores—Habitat, the Conran Shop, Heal's, Osborne & Little, and others—have played a significant role in encouraging this trend, and in providing the necessary artifacts and furnishings. They have helped to form the dominant public taste, which is characterized by a modern "look" offset by nostalgia for the past, natural material and a "soft" image of domesticity. It is a particularly British style, which owes much to the country-house tradition but is not limited by the need to reproduce the past.

No single company has played a more important role in disseminating this style, as far as interior fabrics are concerned than Designers Guild, the retail outlet located on London's fashionable King's Road. Opened in the early 1970s, the firm owes its existence to its founder, Tricia Guild, who set out designing ranges of coordinated fabrics and wallpapers. Since then, it has grown into a highly profitable business and has expanded considerably. The

Textile *Quanjin* collection, 1999

range now includes furnishing fabrics, wallcoverings, upholstery, bed linen, towels, and table linen, sold in more than fifty countries. They are imbued with the quality of design that is the result of Tricia Guild's highly individual eye. She has a strong sense of color, often muted and combined with other colors in a unique way. Her inspiration comes from her love of nature, gardens, and flowers, and from her extensive travel during which she has seen a wide range of exotica. Over the years her palette has changed from pastels to much stronger colors, and her imagery from flowers to more abstract patterns and motifs derived from Europe, the East, and Africa. Recently, upholstered furniture has been added, and the London shop sells many other items—giftwrap, other paper products, and paints—which extend the company's "look" into new directions. Designers Guild has an in-house design group overseen by Tricia Guild and collaboration with "outside" artists and designers—among them Kaffe Fassett, Howard Hodgkin, Janice Tchalenko, and Michael Heindorff—have enriched the company's variety. Tricia Guild is a strong supporter of contemporary British crafts and sells a number of items made by young craftspeople.

Products
1975 *Village* collection
1984 *Natural Classics* collection
1992 *Harvest* wallpaper
1993 *Kusumam* collection
1998 *Candassa* collection
1999 *Passiflora* collection

Candassa collection, 1998

Jane DILLON

Furniture Designer

1943 born in Manchester

1965 studies interior architecture at Manchester Polytechnic

1968 studies at **Royal College of Art**; works at Knoll International UK and at Olivetti under Ettore Sottsass (until 1969)

1971 works at Terence Conran (until 1972)

1972 works at Disform, Spain

1977 works at **Habitat**

1978 consultant for **Wolff Olins**

Products

1968 *Synthesi 45* furniture series

1971 *Tallo Lights* lamps (with Charles Dillon)

1972 *Cometa* hanging lamp

1992 *Multipla* sitting area (with Peter Wheeler) for Kron

Page 161

top left: *Multipla* sitting area (with Peter Wheeler) for Kron, 1992

top right: *Movable Chair*, 1968

bottom left: *Tallo* light, 1971

bottom right: *Conference Table* for Cassina, 1987

Jobbes Chair, 1979

Jane Dillon's career is a concrete example of the often cited bordercrossing, international aspects of the current design scene. She studied art in the 1960's at the **Royal College of Art** and was employed in the early 1970's in the design department—then directed by Ettore Sottsass—of the legendary Italian office machine manufacturer Olivetti. Today, the clients of her studio in central London include such illustrious companies as Amat from Spain, Cassina from Italy, Herman Miller from The USA and Thonet from Germany. Furniture for both home and office from studio Dillon enjoys worldwide esteem because its design generally results from an intense analysis of new materials and technologies. Her speciality is seating. the ultimate test of skill in furniture design. A major success, for example, was her *Multipla* variable chair program of cold-formed foam, which she developed in the early 1990's with Peter Wheeler.

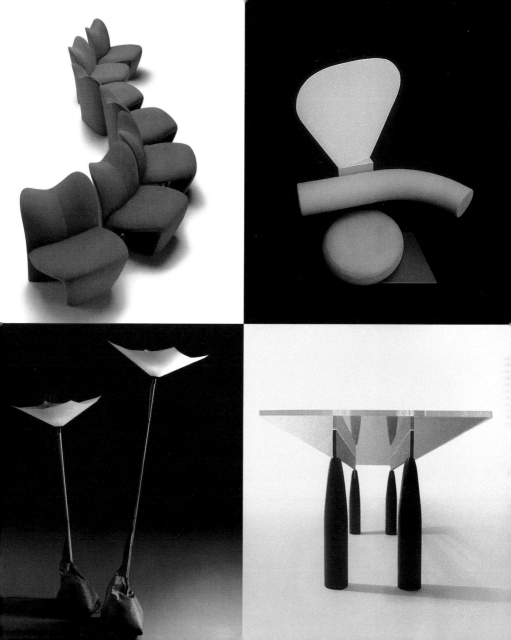

DIN ASSOCIATES

Studio for Interior Architecture

Din Associates, London

1986 founded by **Rasshied Din** and John Harvey

1989 *Design Effectiveness Award* for Dept. X

1990 the *Observer Magazine* selects Rasshied Din as *Young Business Person of the Year*, *D&AD* Silver Award for the Nicole Farhi Showroom

Projects

1987 store and buro for Next in London

1988 Department X in London's Oxford Street

1993 CI for W.H. Smith

1994 exhibition on **Habitat** at **Victoria and Albert Museum**; Dr. Martens Department Store, London

1995 two cafes for Habitat in London and Dublin; Shoeless Joe's restaurant

The design consultancy, Din Associates, made a name for itself in the second half of the 1980s at a time when the design of British retail spaces was receiving a great deal of attention. Its interiors for the Next stores led the way in the concept of "lifestyle shopping." Britain was foremost in this field, influencing other countries to a considerable extent and providing a new look for the contemporary retail environment at an international level. The innovations that occurred were the result of close collaboration between forward-looking retailers and design consultancies. Pioneering links with George Davies at Next and Stephen Marks at French Connection—two of Britain's fastest-expanding retail chains at that time—ensured that Din Associates quickly earned a reputation for innovative interior design in the retail context.

More recently the group has moved into new areas such as restaurants and cultural spaces, one of its most prestigious projects being the adaptation of a stable block at Althorp House to house a commemorative exhibition dedicated to the life of Diana, Princess of Wales. This involved not only creating an exhibition space but also converting the building to include a café and a small shop. Describing its approach to the project, Din Associates explained, "We decided our approach would be to 'slot' the new into the old and that both should have a harmony. We were careful not to overpower the existing character which led us to a minimal design philosophy, with junctions clearly defining new from old."

The consultancy, which currently employs more than twenty staff members, was founded by Rasshied Din in 1986. He graduated from Birmingham Polytechnic and undertook an apprenticeship with a number of London's leading design groups before setting out on his own. The link with Next provided a "lift-off" for the group. The first Next store on London's Kensington High Street was completed soon after the formation of the group, which went on to work on a jewelry store for the same company soon afterward. Other projects followed, including a large Next store on London's

Regent Street. This was the era of lifestyle retailing, and Din's approach fitted it perfectly. He aimed to penetrate the essence of the lifestyle message of a particular retailer and then to create an appropriate setting for it.

In the 1990s the consultancy spread its wings considerably, although the same approach underpinned all its projects. Din created offices for Next and French Connection; showrooms for Nicole Fahri, Ralph Lauren, Zygo, Escada, and Anne Storey; a wide range of restaurants, including the "X" café on London's Oxford Street, the Beak Street Restaurant in Soho, restaurants for several of the Habitat stores, and a large restaurant, Shoeless Joe's on King's Road; a number of exhibition spaces, and the set for London Television's *Weekend Live*. These are in addition to a wide variety of retail store interiors. Most recently the company has become involved with the areas of brand identity, labeling, and packaging, a logical extension of the lifestyle approach. The light, modern aesthetic favored by the group, albeit one that responds openly to the requirements of the client, is characteristically British. It has come to dominate the urban public commercial interior in Britain and is much in demand abroad.

1996 five divisions at the department store **Liberty's**, London; fashion store for Joop, Hamburg

1997 CI for Victim Support

1998 glass and porcelain division for the department store Selfridges, London, Diana Museum on the farm, Althorp, Restaurant Soup Opera in London

Fashion store for Joop, Hamburg, 1996

Tom DIXON

Furniture Designer

1959 born in Tunisia
1963 moves to Great Britain
1981 works for nightclubs
1983 first interior architect
1985 founds **Creative Salvage**
1985 furnishes the Boutique
       Rococo Chocolates in
       London
1991 SPACE studio opens
1994 SPACE Shop opens
1998 art director at **Habitat**

Products

1985 one-of-a-kind items, for
       instance, chandelier
1986 Organ-pipe screen made
       of steel

Page 165
Pylon chair for Cappellini, 1991

"Whatever mainstream designers are up to, Tom takes a pleasure in the opposite line. He has proven that designer craft is alive and well. He has also shown that it doesn't have to cost thousands of pounds apiece," wrote a *Vogue* journalist in the mid-1990s of this designer's work.

Unlike many of his contemporaries, Dixon did not come through the orthodox route of a post-graduate degree at London's **Royal College of Art**. Instead he started out as a sculptor, spending some time at Chelsea School of Art in London, and then discovered welding—an important technique for many of his scrap-metal designs—because he needed to fix his motorcycle.

This unusual background made him an unusual designer for whom salvaged materials were the main source of inspiration in his early career. He also, in the mid-1980s, promoted nightclubs and used welding scrap metal as a stage act at the Titanic club. It was this act, in fact, that resulted in an exhibition, followed by a number of furniture commissions, which set Dixon on the path he was eventually to pursue. In the years since then he has become one of Britain's most original and imaginative designers.

Dixon's work has been highly expressive from the outset, embracing rococo-like curves and sinuous forms in pursuit of a new form of hand-built furniture that is nearer to sculpture than anything else. The mid-1980s saw the formation of his own studio/workshop, **Creative Salvage**, which a few years later was replaced by SPACE. SPACE was later turned into a shop.

From his workshop, Dixon has worked on many fronts, creating stage sets, furniture, sculpture, architectural installations, chandeliers, and numerous other objects. The workshop has also provided an opportunity for other young designers to develop their ideas and Michael Young, among others benefited from it. The second half of the 1980s saw the emergence of what have since become "classic" Dixon designs. Best known of all, perhaps, is his "S" chair in rush and wicker on a steel frame, whose curves are evocative of earlier designers such as Carlo Mollino. The forms that

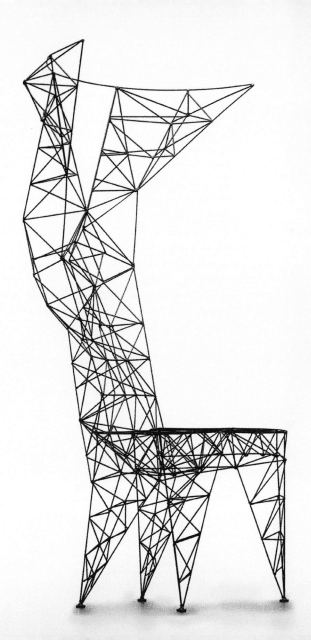

1987 table made of steel and glass; chairs made of metal pieces

1991 *"S"* chair and *Pylon* chair

1992 *Bird* armchair for Cappellini

1996 *Jack* lighting and sitting object; product series for Eurolounge (among others, lamp *Star Light*, *Tub Chair*, *Stump* stool, *Nob* barstool)

2000 *Octo* lamp for EUROLOUNGE

Page 167

top: *Bird* armchair for Cappellini, 1992

bottom left: *Maze* carpet for Asplundl, 1999

bottom right: *"S"* chair for Cappellini, 1991

Dixon evolved and the materials he used helped British design to move away from neomodernism and to become more overtly sculptural. In the mid-1980s also, with Andre Dubreuil, Dixon decorated the Rococo chocolate boutique on London's King's Road, a perfect opportunity to indulge in his preferred aesthetic. The 1990s saw his work beginning to reach a larger, more mainstream audience through the intervention of manufacturers such as Cappellini in Italy. His work became more sophisticated, more elegant, and internationally oriented. The second half of the decade saw the launch of a product range designed for EUROLOUNGE, and his appointment as head of design at **Habitat**, a real achievement for someone who discovered design just by chance.

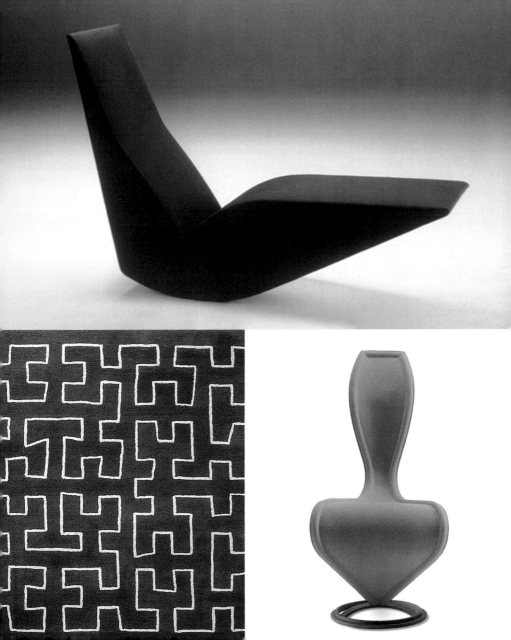

Christopher DRESSER
Product Designer

1834 born in Glasgow

1847 studies at the School of Design, London (until 1853)

1857 becomes professor of botany

1862 the book *The Art of Decorative Design* is published

1871 works for **Mintons** and **Wedgwood**

1876 United States and Japan trip

1880 founds Art Furnisher's Alliance

1889 studio in Barnes at London

1904 dies

Products

1864 sugar bowl with feet (1991 re-edition by Alessi)

1871 furniture made of iron for Coalbrookdale Ironworks

1875 tiles for Mintons

1880 square teapot (1991 re-edition by Alessi)

1884 carpet for Brinton; wallpaper for Jeffrey; fabrics for Warner

Page 169

top right: wall painting for a church, around 1900

top left: chamber lights Spun Brass, 1883

bottom right: Christopher Dresser Collection by Alessi, (re-edition 1991)

At the School of Design in London this born Scotsman was an exemplary student. His true interest was botany, however, and he taught this subject at several universities. As a sideline, Christopher Dresser cultivated his love of Japanese craftsmanship. In the '60's of the nineteenth century he established himself as a leading commercial product designer and authored several important books on the field. An intermezzo at the journal *Furniture Gazette*, where he made a hopeless attempt to promote a design reform in England, lasted only a year. His practical activities, on the other hand, were much more productive. This all-around talent designed carpets, glass and porcelain for leading British manufacturers. In the 1870's the very busy designer began working in silver, a medium in which he was to produce several of his most successful designs. Their clear geometric lines contrasted sharply with the historicism prevalent at the time and anticipated stylistic elements of modernism. This reflects not only Dresser's maxim of "honesty" toward his materials but also the rather systematic approach of the botanist.

Teakettle, *Triangular*, 1881

James DYSON
Entrepeneur and Product Designer

"I am a creator of products, a builder of things, and my name appears on them ... I imagine a time, years from today, when 'Dyson' replaces 'Hoover'." So writes James Dyson, inventor extraordinaire, in his recent autobiography. The object that he hopes will be one day be known by his name is his *Dual Cyclone* vacuum cleaner, which he invented and designed, and which has, after years of effort, finally taken off in the British marketplace in a major way, making him a rich man.

The product is technologically innovative (it doesn't need a bag), and its bright, clear colors—purple, pink, blue, red, yellow, etc.—have visually transformed household cleaning, taking it into the post-modern age. No other single household appliance has had such a dramatic effect on daily life in Britain, with the exception, perhaps, of overseas products in the early 1970s such as those created by the German company Braun or the Japanese companies Sony and Sharp. Dyson's cleaner brings with it a whole new attitude toward housework, one which crosses gender boundaries and makes it "fun."

The manufacturing and marketing implications of Dyson's success are enormous, showing that a company led by a single individual with a dream can compete with the huge, anonymous, multinational firms that have hitherto dominated the market for home appliances. Versions of the Dyson cleaner can today be seen in London's **Victoria and Albert Museum**, Science Museum, and **Design Museum**, marks of the incredible level of success and popularity that it has achieved.

James Dyson is a phenomenon, and a specifically British one at that. From a broad background in art and design (he studied furniture and interior design at London's **Royal College of Art** in the late 1960s, during which time he designed a number of theater interiors and created some public seating), he went on to create a set of objects that revised the function of several existing tools.

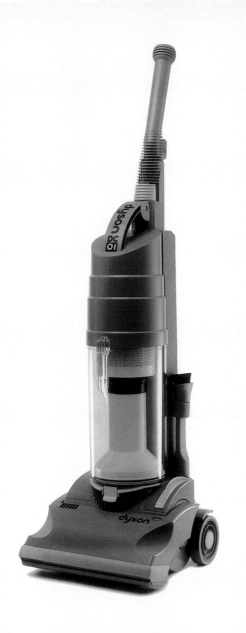

Products

1974 *Bailbarrow*

1986 *G-Force* vacuum cleaner

1993 *DC01* vacuum cleaner

1995 *DC02* vacuum cleaner

1996 *DC02 Absolute* and *DC02 De Stijl* vacuum cleaner in limited edition

1998 *DC03* and *DC04* vacuum cleaner

Page 173

top left: vacuum cleaner accessories DC05, 1998

right: vacuum cleaner DC04, 1998

bottom left: vacuum cleaner DC02 (prototype), 1993 (introduced 1995)

As a designer/engineer/inventor/entrepreneur, he stands in the British tradition of men such as Isambard Kingdom Brunel and has, as Brunel did in his day, helped to put Britain on the map in the 1990s. However, his success was relatively slow in coming. On graduating, he first dedicated himself to the development of the Sea Truck, which he designed for the inventor Jeremy Fry, and worked for the marine division of a company called Rotork, based in Bath. Before long he was given a directorship but left to work on his own in order to develop one of his first product designs, the *Ballbarrow*, a wheelbarrow with a ball at the front instead of a wheel so that it did not get stuck in mud or rough ground. It proved both a financial and a design success, winning the Building Design Innovation Award in the mid-1970s. Dyson went on to create a water-filled plastic garden roller and a boat launcher with ball wheels, but his greatest energies were dedicated to developing an idea he stumbled across at the end of the decade, a bagless vacuum cleaner.

From the early 1980s onward he worked hard at selling his idea but only Japan responded at first — in the mid–eighties producing a pink model named the *G-Force*, which, while expensive, became a cult object and sold well in the Japanese market. Back in Britain, the machine had been featured on the cover of *Design* magazine in the early 1980s, but it was to be some time before it became a reality in the marketplace. The intervening period was filled with lawsuits and a continued struggle on Dyson's part to get the manufacture of his design financed. Finally, in the early 1990s his dream was realized, and he opened his own research center and factory in Wiltshire. Since then it has expanded significantly and the story is one of remarkable growth, countless accolades, and financial success.

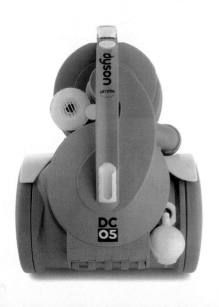

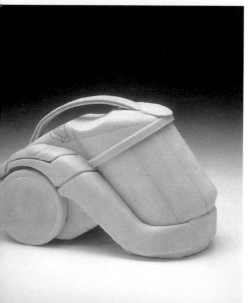

EL ULTIMO GRITO

Studio for Furniture Design

El Ultimo Grito, London

1997 founded by Roberto Feo, Rosario Hurtado, and Francisco Santos; wins 100% Design Award for the magazine *Blueprint* (again in 1998)

1999 solo exhibition at Institute of Contemporary Art, London

Products

1997 *Miss Ramirez Chair* and *Plug it* shelf

1998 *Brainstorming?* toilet paper holder and newspaper holder

1999 *Don't Run Away We Are Your Friends* lamp

Three young Spanish designers—Roberto Feo, Francisco Santos, and Rosario Hurtado—make up the exciting London-trained and London-based design group El Ultimo Grito ("the latest thing"). In the very short time during which it has been active, the company has made a strong impact with its simple, yet ingenious, furniture and interiors, which use materials and technology in innovative ways. The *Miss Ramirez* chair, for instance— winner of the *Blueprint* award at the 100% Design Show in 1997—is typical of the groups approach. It is made from cork and latex, creating both a striking form and comfortable sitting object. The *Mind the Gap* magazine rack and coffee table is another simple yet original solution, with a rubber element that simply "drops" through a gap in the table to make a space for magazine storage. Its title conveys the strong humorous element that pervades much of their work. As they explain, "We aim at creating a dialogue with the user, so the design is not giving just a one-way message, but it leaves itself open to exploration." Other designs in their *Minimal Maximum* collection have such evocative names as *Brainstorming?* and *Good Morning Moneypenny*. The group promises to contribute much to the London design scene.

Miss Ramirez chair, 1997

FAT

Studio for Interior Designer

Fashion Architecture Taste (FAT) Ltd. is very much a product of 1990s British culture in which the barriers between disciplines are continually being questioned and broken down. The precedents of **Pop** and **Punk** have played a significant role in this scenario, as FAT indicates in its description of its activities: "Drawing on sources as diverse as situationism and advertising, and as contradictory as Dada and Disneyland, the strategies employed by FAT derive explicitly from collaborations with practitioners of other creative disciplines and make use of visual languages which communicate complex and critical ideas to audiences beyond the usual architectural cognoscenti." With a base in architecture, the group focuses on experimentation, performance, and installations rather than buildings *per se*. Work to date includes built projects, among them the redesign of the bar for London's Institute of Contemporary Arts and a shop interior for Mambo; art projects, including an intervention at the Royal Academy Summer Show; and exhibitions such as *Disaster* at the Limehouse Arts Foundation in London.

Fashion Architecture Taste Ltd., London
1994 founded by Emma Davis, Sean Griffiths, Charles Holland, Sam Jacob

Products
1996 bus stops and flower graffiti in London
1997 billboard Installation
1998 transformation of a church into advertisement agency in Amsterdam

Burel Rooms Nightclub in Swindon, England, 1999

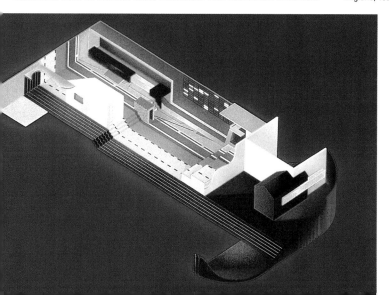

Roy FLEETWOOD
Product Designer

1946 born in London

1965 studies at the Architecture Academy in Liverpool (until 1970)

1973 works for Foster Associates (until 1986)

1988 *IF* design prize for lamp series *Gantry* (1989 and 1991 for *Axis* and *Emanon* lighting systems)

Products

1986 *Axis* and *Gantry* lighting systems for Erco

1990 *Wing* sofa for Vitra

1991 *Emanon* radiator for Erco

1992 M&E Center for the business YKK Architectural Products in Japan

1995 Museum of Literature, Tokyo

1996 *Geoscape* garden furniture series for YKK

Page 177

top: sofa *Wing* for Vitra, 1990

bottom left: Museum of Literature, Tokyo, 1995

bottom right: solar lamp for Geoscape, 1996

Bench for Geoscape, 1996

As a consultant, Roy Fleetwood is sought after by noted companies such as Corning or Vitra. In his Cambridge "Office for Design Strategy" he occupies himself with such basic questions as the relationship between light and shadow, solar energy, or the influence of the new media on interior design. Fleetwood's leitmotif is the question of "how the forces of industry can be harnessed to achieve peak performance in architecture and design." Formerly Managing Director for Project Design, Development and Strategy in the office of **Norman Foster**, he was involved with such prestigious projects as the Hongkong Bank, the Sainsbury Centre for Visual Arts and the Renault Centre. Since the late 1980's he has also been active as a product designer specializing in complex illumination systems, which have won numerous awards. His lighting track/lattice girder *Axis* is well-suited for extremely large spaces and is stunning with its laconic, technoid exterior. A pragmatic theoretician and an avid student of Japanese architecture, Fleetwood designed a comprehensive system of landscape furniture for a Japanese manufacturer; it consisted of benches, flower beds, and fences in addition to street lights and bollards.

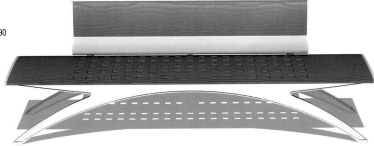

Norman FOSTER

Architect and Designer

The design for the new German Parliament, with which Norman Foster equipped the old Berlin Reichstag with a light-filled interior, a cupola with a viewing platform, and all manner of designer furniture, probably numbers among the most prestigious assignments in recent history. The man who creates tomorrow's monuments today, first studied in Manchester before collaborating with the American Buckminster Fuller, a specialist in futuristic although seldom realized visionary design. Since then Fuller's student has established offices in six major cities and employs several hundred people. He is considered the founder of **High-tech** architecture, and he has a preference for using modern materials to build dramatic structures which are open to the sky above. His product designs—the focus of a small "design group" within the Foster enterprise directed by John Small and Mike Holland—also conform with his technoid mind set. The office furniture series Nomos, configurations of aluminum, plastic and steel, offers solutions for flexible, aesthetically demanding white collar workers. The lighting system he developed for the Hongkong and Shanghai Bank became a part of the Erco program. His unadorned Alessi tray of aluminum with pear wood handles is already a classic.

Since his buildings, interiors and products are both equally uncompromising and "un-British," most of his clients come from abroad. Exceptions to the rule are the Sainsbury Centre for Visual Arts and Stansted Airport near London. An assignment from German furniture maker Thonet resulted from Foster's work on the Reichstag. For this renowned company the sought-after Briton designed a highly functional series of chairs, benches and tables, with a T-shaped aluminum profile developed especially for this purpose.

Page 179
top: doorknob for Fusital, 1995
bottom left: Airline bench system for Vitra, 1998
bottom right: tray for Alessi, 1988

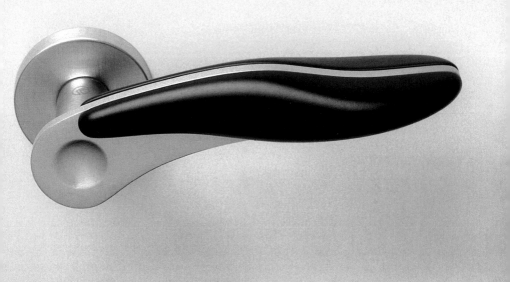

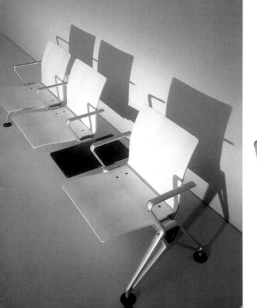

Stephen FRAZER

Product Designer

1948 born in London

1973 finishes design studies at the **Royal College of Art**

1978 Frazer Designers founded by Stephen and Pamela Frazer

1986 beginning of collaboration with NEC

1988 *IF* award for Psion Organizer

1992 *British Design Award* for **Psion** Series 3

Products

1991 *Palmtop Series 3* for Psion

1995 *HC600 Cellphone* product line for Alcatel

1996 *G800* telephone for NEC

1997 *Vision Cobra* microscope

1998 remote control for Sky and portable computer for Radix

Page 181

top left: *Rxl Rugged Portable* computer for Radix, 1994

top right: *Palmtop Computer* 3rd Edition for Psion, 1991

bottom left: remote control for Sky, 1998

bottom right: *Vision Cobra* microscope, 1997

"We all possess a natural gift for choosing the objects we want to have around us to meet our physical and emotional needs. At Frazer Designers we understand how these intuitive and logical processes of selection work." So wrote **Stephen Frazer** and Jonathan Knight in their company brochure. Frazer Designers is one of Britain's leading product design groups, responsible for a number of key designs, prominent among them their range of electronic personal organizers for the Psion company.

Frazer Designers was formed in the late 1970s by Pamela and Stephen Frazer, now the managing director, after studying at London's Royal College of Art and a few years as an independent industrial design consultant. The team's formation coincided with the expanding international profile of British product design. It was also the time when a number of British manufacturers in the area of high-technology goods emerged on the scene, in need of designers to provide them with product identities. Since the early 1980s, Frazer Designers has concentrated on creating the housings and electro-mechanical assembles for a wide range of computers, business machines, consumer electronics, instruments, domestic appliances, and toys, specializing in goods with plastic bodies.

The **Psion** *Series 3* was given a British design award and represents the way in which British product design and British electronics manufacturing can work together to provide truly innovative products, both technologically and visually. The unassuming effectiveness of this miniature object is a result of Frazer Designers' ability to provide a neat body shell for it, the fact that it is involved with the user interface system and its mechanical design. The company is rare in being able to cross these boundaries, and the result is an unusually unified product.

The group's highly successful designs include the strongly ergo-nomically oriented *BSkyB* remote control, the *Radix* handheld pc, and the *Vision* microscope.

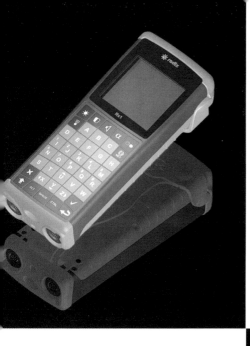

John GALLIANO

Fashion Designer

1960 born in Gibraltar

1981 studies fashion at the St. Martin's School of Art, London

1984 founds fashion house in London

1987 wins *Dress of the Year Award* from the Bath Costume Museum, and *Designer of the Year Award* from British Fashion Council

1995 chief designer for Givenchy in Paris

1996 first collection for Givenchy

1997 chief designer for Dior; *VH1 Fashion and Music Award*; *Oribe Award* for design; first Pret-a-Porter collection for Dior

Page 183
left: fall collection, 1989
right: fall collection, 1999

British fashion designers have made a significant international impact in recent years. John Galliano is among the most important of those whose designs have delighted the Paris catwalks since the 1980s. He has worked at the more sophisticated end of the industry, creating innovative items that extend the possibilities of the structure and cut of clothes themselves. His clothes are structurally complex and only really come to life when they are on a model. Galliano's imagination and his ability to take influences from a wide range of sources and transform them into something recognizably his, marks him out. Together with fashion designer **Vivienne Westwood**, he helped capture a moment in fashion history when it was possible to look back and sidewards for inspiration.

Galliano was born in Gibraltar but his years at London's St. Martin's School of Fashion made him into the designer he is today. Since the 1960s St. Martin's (now Central St. Martin's) has acquired a reputation for turning out the most daring and experimental of Britain's fashion designers—and Galliano clearly flourished in this hot-house climate of experimentation. His graduation show, with a collection named *Les Incroyables*, hit the headlines. Unlike most student shows, his had a real-world quality and maturity, which meant that the clothes were bought by the London shop, Browns, and entered directly into the fashion system. The clothes sold out very quickly and helped get Galliano the financial backing he needed to carry on working. Almost immediately, in the mid-1980s, he set up his own fashion house in London, when he was only twenty-four years old.

Galliano's originality lies in the way he has studied details from traditional clothing, subtly altering them to create simultaneously a historical feel and a strongly contemporary presence. His work is based on extensive research, undertaken in libraries and museums, adapted for his own creations.

Les Incroyables, for instance, was strongly influenced by eighteenth-century French dress, a period that had a wide appeal in Britain at that time,

Collections

1986 *Fallen Angels* spring
collection

1985 *The Ludic Game* fall
collection

1993 *Olivia the Filibuster* spring
collection

1994 *Princess Lucretia* spring
collection

1996 *Le Papillon et le Fleur* at
the Champs-Elysee
Theater spring collection

for example in films directed by Peter Greenaway. Galliano's collections of recent years have had such romantic and evocative names as *Afghanistan Repudiates Western Ideals*, *Fallen Angels*, *Forgotten Innocents*, and *Princess Lucretia*. As one writer has explained, "From the Highlands of Scotland to the Russian steppes, from thirties-style sleek evening gowns, to kilts, tulle ball gowns, farthingales, frock coats, hourglass silhouettes and 1940s gangster garb, he raids history for ideas." Galliano's sensibility is such that he is able to tap into this mood in a way that is easily emulated by High Street fashion.

Although Galliano is a strong inspiration for mass fashion, this does not prevent him being a "cutting edge" designer. Each collection brings new surprises. In one he created Napoleonic jackets in the shockingly new material, neoprene, while in another he drew upon the imagery of "drag" costume—satin knickers and feathered bras—to create an entirely new look. Galliano's main signature features, however, are his use of the bias-cut for dresses and sexy materials, such as velvet. In the mid-1990s he abandoned London and moved to Paris, where he became the head designer for Givenchy's couture and ready-to-wear collections. He left after only a year, however, to take over control of the house of Dior. Galliano remains in Paris but still has the reputation of being a British designer.

Page 185
top left: fall collection, 1999
right: fall collection, 1996
bottom left: fall collection, 1994

Eric GILL
Graphic artist and sculptor

1882 born in Brighton

1925 works for Golden Cockerell Press

1928 works at the **London Underground** headquarters

1931 Typography essay is published

1936 becomes Royal Designer for Industry

1940 dies

Products

1905 book covers for the Insel publishing house in Leipzig

1907 stone sculptures for the **BBC** house in London

1929 *Gill Sans Serif* lettering; Golden Cockerell Roman

1930 *Perpetua* lettering

1931 *Joanna* lettering

1938 stone inscriptions for the Volkerbund in Geneva

Joanna lettering, 1931

Page 187

top left: *Gill Sans Serif* lettering design for London and North Eastern Railway, 1929

top right: *Gill Sans Serif* lettering, 1929

bottom left: *Perpetua* lettering. 1930

bottom right: book cover, 1931

Although Eric Gill began as an autodidact and acquired his initial knowledge of typography in evening courses, he quickly attained professional standing as the assistant to Edward Johnston. Even before World War I he was already working for well-known companies such as the German Cranach-Presse, and later for Golden Cockerell Press and Monotype. But the name he later made for himself was not limited to that of an excellent illustrator and type designer. This trained stone-cutter also had a successful career as a sculptor. The first successful typeface he designed was *Perpetua*, an austere but elegant serif alphabet. It was first used in 1929 by Cambridge University Press and subsequently became extremely popular. Later, it was joined by *Felicity*, a sister in cursive, and was followed by fonts like *Gill Sans* and *Jubilee*. Gill, who himself authored important texts on typography and waged a life-long struggle against "typographical snobbism," later founded his own hand-operated press for bibliophile printing.

ABCDE
Abcdef

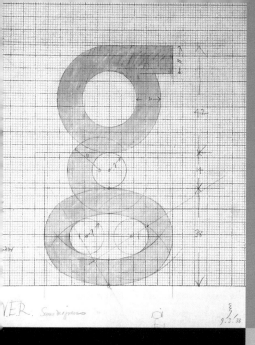

ABCDEFGHILKLMN
OPQRSTUVWXYZ
abcdefghijklmnopqrst
uvwxyz1234567890

V.E.R. Sans sérifs

S

ABCDEFGHIJ
abcdefghijklmno

Eric Gill and
Denis Teg

UNHOLY
TRINITY

Text by Eric Gill • Pictures by Denis
Tegetmeier • Published by Dents for

Kenneth GRANGE

Product Designer

London Taxi, 1997

Page 189

top right: *Instamatic 133* camera,
1970

top left: *Protector* razor, 1992

bottom: *804* sewing machine, 1972

Page 190–191

Kenwood Chef kitchen mixer,
left: 1986 right: 1961

From the early 1970s until recently when he retired, Kenneth Grange was a member of the **Pentagram** design consultancy, responsible for the product design side of the group's activities. He is best known, perhaps, for his work on kitchen appliances for **Kenwood** and his design for British Rail's high-speed train. However, he has undertaken a vast range of other projects over the last quarter of a century such as designs for B&W Loudspeakers, Kodak, Parker Pens, Ronson,and, in recent years, a range of Japanese companies including Shiseido and INAX. He is among the most prolific of Britain's product designers and has maintained a reputation for creating simple, functional goods with a minimum of ornamentation. His approach is that of a "problem-solver" and he combines this with a sensitivity to form and color.

Writing of his relationship with the consumer, he explains, "None of our heartaches and debates, our anxieties and revisions are ever known to the consumer, but when our product is excellent, the care and effort is felt and their valuation of the product is manifest in what is paid and with what care it is treated through its life."

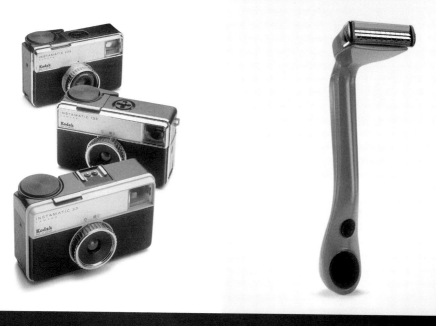

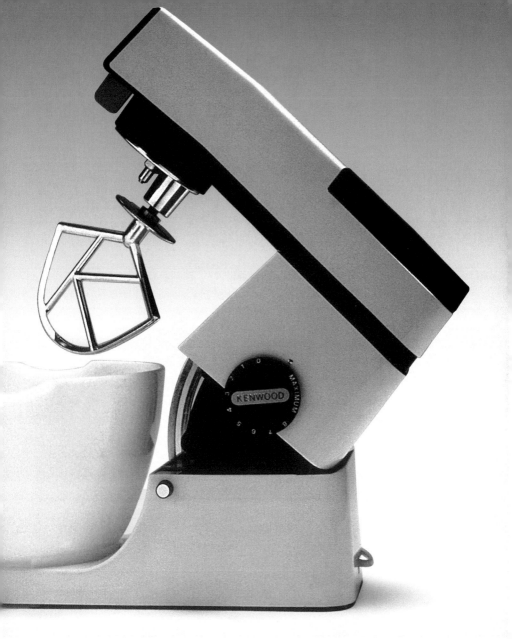

HABITAT
Home Furnishing and Furniture Manufacturer

Habitat UK Ltd., London

1964 first Habitat shop on Fulham Road, London, by **Terence Conran**

1967 shop in Manchester opens

1973 first shop outside of England and Paris (already eighteen shops in Great Britain)

1995 IKEA takes over Habitat

1998 **Tom Dixon** becomes chief designer

Products

1964 Chinese woks and Japanese futons

1977 *Country Kitchen*

1999 bed linen with *Black Leaf* design by **Lucienne Day** (design, 1960), *Mushroom* armchair by Pierre Paulin, and armchair by **Robin Day**; *Clam* ashtray by Alan Fletcher (design, 1968)

Page 193

top left: textile, around 1970

top right: nest of tables, collection 1999

bottom: sofa, collection 1999

Of all the post-war stores to sell modern design, Habitat is by far the best known by the British public. It came into being in the mid-1960s as the brainchild of **Terence Conran**, who was disillusioned with the way in which his own furniture designs were distributed. His aim was "to take the foot-slogging out of shopping by assembling a wide selection of unusual and top-quality goods under one roof." From the outset, the flagship store on London's Fulham Road catered to a young, style-conscious clientele that sought all its furniture and furnishings in one venue at a price it could afford. Habitat sold Italian furniture, French Provençal pottery, and Scandinavian textiles together for the first time and, as a result, helped make the British public design-conscious.

This mission was enhanced when the store spread to other parts of the country, with branches opening in Manchester, Liverpool, and on London's King's Road and Tottenham Court Road. The "lifestyle" philosophy that Conran embraced meant that the whole look of the store was modern. In the Fulham Road store in the early days, for example, the sales assistants had Vidal Sassoon haircuts. As the style the store projected spread through British society in the 1970s and 1980s, it became linked with the idea of young couples setting up home at a price they could afford, even though it meant taking everything with them at the time of purchase. Later the originality of Habitat was challenged by the arrival of the Swedish store, IKEA, which did to out-of-town sites what Habitat had been doing in city centers. The IKEA group bought Habitat from Conran who, in the early 1990s moved out of retailing almost completely. The heritage of the taste revolution brought about by Habitat from the mid-1960s onward remains an important phenomenon in the history of post-war Britain, however. **Tom Dixon** is now in charge of design at the stores and is carrying on the tradition of innovation that Conran established.

HEAL'S

Department Store, Furniture and Textile Manufacturer

Heal's & Son Ltd., London

1810 founded as furniture store by John Harris Heal

1893 Ambrose Heal enters the firm (since 1913)

1898 *Plain Oak Furniture* catalog according to style of **Arts and Crafts**

1915 Heal becomes cofounder of the **Design and Industries Association**

1983 takeover by **Habitat**/Mothercare

1997 goes public

Products

1899 simple bedroom furniture

1951 garden chairs made of steel by A.J. Milne for the Festival of Britain

1973 pop-wastebasket by Durlston Design

1990 shopping bag by Lewis Moberly

Page 195
top: textile
bottom: concentric textile

Shopping bag by Lewis Moberly, 1990

The family-owned Heal's furniture store was established in the early nineteenth century on London's Tottenham Court Road, and sold up-market, well-designed furniture to discerning customers throughout the twentieth century. It also manufactured items, among them hand-made beds in which it has always specialized. It is especially notable for two moments in its history. The first was in the early years of the twentieth century when a member of the Heal family, Ambrose, became a furniture designer and made the store a focus for retailing **Arts and Crafts** furniture. The second was in the years between the two world wars, and following World War II, when Heal's helped to bring the work of Scandinavian designers to the notice of the British public. Its influence was also particularly important in the area of modern textile design in this latter period, commissioning work from leading figures such as **Lucienne Day** and **Barbara Brown**. In the 1980s the Heals family sold the store to the Storehouse group, led by **Terence Conran**. Today it remains one of London's leading modern furniture stores, although without the dominant position it held a few decades ago as other stores such as the Conran Shop in South Kensington are strong competitors.

From the 1970s onward, there has been an enormous growth of interest in Britain's heritage and traditions. This has taken several different forms, many with implications for architecture and design, although not in the modern, progressive sense. As a cultural phenomenon, it is part of a search for a notion of "Britishness" that can be identified as a national morale booster and also as a focus for cultural tourism, which has become one of Britain's most lucrative industries.

The National Trust has played a key role. It was formed in the late nineteenth century, during the first wave of expanding popular interest in national heritage, with a brief to "preserve places of historic interest or natural beauty for the nation to enjoy." One of its most important roles has been to preserve the many English country houses that began to go into a state of decay around the time of the Trust's formation.

Throughout the twentieth century, but most noticeably in recent decades, the Trust has been able to preserve, and to make available to the public, large numbers of properties that would have otherwise ceased to exist. Petworth House in West Sussex, Stourhead Gardens in Wiltshire and Thomas Hardy's cottage in Dorset are among properties in the ownership of the Trust.

A huge expansion of popular interest in National Trust property has taken place over the last two decades. In recent years it has introduced a holiday cottages scheme, in which members can stay in one of its properties, decorated in an appropriate style. This idea had been pioneered earlier by

another organization, the Landmark Trust, which bought up buildings of architectural interest and then offered them for holidays.

The last few decades have seen many more houses open to the public and a widening of the scope of interest of the National Trust. Recently, for example, the architect Erno Goldfinger's home in Willow Road, London, designed in the 1930s, was opened to the public, the first modern house to be given a "heritage" label.

Even more recently, the 1950s council house in which the ex-Beatle, Paul McCartney, was brought up in Liverpool, has been added to the formal heritage list. This interest in the past, and in the preservation of its material culture, has had considerable spin-offs in terms of popular taste. People are more concerned to preserve aspects of their interiors than to destroy them, less inclined to throw out the old and start again.

While this does not lead to new design solutions, it has a considerable impact on the way in which people decorate their homes. Given the small amount of new housing stock in Britain and the dominance, in most of its urban centers, on housing from the Victorian and Edwardian eras, this can be seen as an appropriate way of thinking about decoration. It raises the "authenticity" debate, which become more and more frequent. Architectural salvage firms selling old fireplaces, mantelpieces, doors, moldings, and other architectural features are thriving.

Another aspect of the shift in taste in interior decoration that has resulted from the growing interest in heritage has been the success of the

"The people generally seem to understand more and more that, to put it in the words of the king, the fundamentals of a nation are laid in one's own home."

Catalog *Ideal Home Exhibition,* 1924

from left to right:
Cups with imprint by Paul Clark, 1967
Textile by Laura Ashley collection, 1980
Dodo designs, 1961

National Trust paint project. Farrow and Ball, a company that produces historic paint colors made from natural materials, used in the refurbishment of National Trust properties, has made its products available on the open market. The interest in them has been enormous and a whole new palette of subtle, muted colors is now being produced by commercial paint companies under range names such as "heritage."

There has also been a huge growth in the variety of products commissioned by the National Trust to be sold in their shops. This has significant design implications as the packaging needed for the jams, scarves, soaps, and other items thought to be appropriate has created a spin-off industry. Recently students at London's Royal College of Art were asked by the National Trust to design a range of more modern products for the Goldfinger house.

The other key player in the heritage industry is the public organization, English Heritage. Its function is more broadly historical than that of the National Trust and its properties cover a wider chronology.

It boasts the Stonehenge stone circle, created 5,000 years ago on Salisbury Plain, Tintagel Castle in Cornwall, and the oak tree in Staffordshire in which the future Charles II of England hid from Oliver Cromwell's soldiers in the seventeenth century. Like the National Trust, English Heritage also owns important twentieth-century buildings such as **Norman Foster**'s Willis Faber Dumas building in Ipswich. Recently The National Trust spent a large sum of money re-gilding the statue of Prince Albert on the Albert Memorial in London's Hyde Park.

Clearly there is a very strong tourist aspect to this industry. At the same time, however, it enhances the country's understanding of its own past and therefore plays an important cultural role. As British manufacturing declines, its heritage industry expands.

This has extended into manufacturing itself being seen as heritage, as English Heritage's involvement with Ironbridge and early industrial sites in and around Coalbrookdale make clear. It demonstrates Britain's control over its own environment and its own self-image in the twenty-first century. It is an industry of value abroad, which can be seen as a substitute for the decline of the country's manufacturing industry.

It is also an industry that encourages the British population to move away from the promise of modernity and from all that goes with it—new materials, new forms, etc.—and to see themselves as a citizens of a country with a past.

"The British couldn't shake off the values of the nineteenth century because those values made the country into what it was."

David P. Marquand

Matthew HILTON

Furniture Designer

1957 born in Hastings

1975 studies at Portsmouth College of Art — from 1976 on studies three-dimensional design at Kingston Polytechnic

1984 studio opens

Products

1985 *Oval Bowl*

1986 *Bow* shelf for **SCP**

1988 *Antelope* table and *Swan* candleholder

1991 *Balzac* armchair for SCP

1996 *Coleridge* bed and *Orwell* sofa for SCP

1998 *Mercury* sofa for Driade

Page 201
top: *Balzac* armchair, 1991
bottom: *Auberon* table, 1991

Kerouac sofa for SCP, 1993

Together with **Jasper Morrison**, Matthew Hilton is one of Britain's leading young furniture designers. It was the work of Morrison and Hilton, for instance, that the furniture company **SCP** (Sheridan Coakley Production) chose to promote first in Milan in the mid-1980s. SCP has continued to work with Hilton and the collaboration has resulted in a vast number of stunningly innovative furniture designs, among them the *Club* and *Balzac* upholstered seating ranges of the early 1990s and, more recently, the *Coleridge* bed, the *Flipper* table, and the *Ulysses* armchair. Hilton's work is characterized by its strikingly novel, yet restrained and highly sophisticated forms, some of which stress the curvilinear and the sensorial while others remain within the preserve of the rectilinear. In every case, he pushes the formal language just a little further than is predictable, while never sacrificing the constraints of practicality and use. He delights in the effects of the grain of different woods and loves to include legs that stand on pointed feet, like ballerinas. He describes his ideal design as being one full of seeming contradictions.

In addition to working with SCP, Hilton has collaborated widely with European manufacturers, among them Driade, Disform, Montis, and XO.

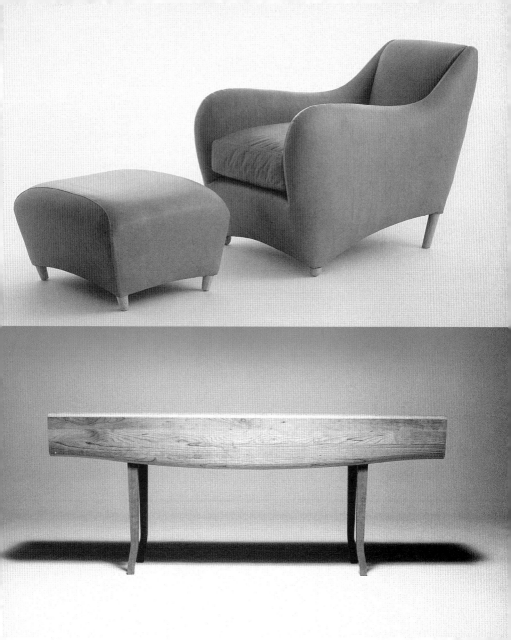

Geoff HOLLINGTON

Studio for Furniture and Product Design

1949 born in Essex

1974 graduates from **Royal College of Art**

1976 works for Milton Keynes Design Team

1978 founds Consulting Firm with Michael Glickman

1980 founds studio

1989 works for Hermann Miller

1990 Hollington Industrial Design opens

1992 wins Gold Award from Industrial Design Society of America

Products

1990 *Relay-Mobel* for Hermann Miller

1991 *Safes* for John Tann Ltd.

1993 *Sonnet* and *Frontier* fountain pen for Parker

1994 *MSC* Chair for **SCP**

1998 *Zephyr* and *Yoyo* chair for Lloyd Loom

Page 203

top left: *MSC* Chair for SCP, 1994

top right: *Trumpet* vase for Herman Miller , 1990

bottom: *Sonnet* and *Frontier* pen set for Parker, 1993

Remote control for Hermann Miller, 1989

This product design consultancy has been in existence for two decades. It has become one of Britain's leading groups providing a mainstream design service for international clients, prominent among them Hermann Miller, Parker, and Ericcson. In the company's own words, it concentrates on creating "compelling products" that are "economic to manufacture, attractive at point of sale, work well, are easy to use, and rewarding to own." The team, headed by its founder, Geoff Hollington, takes a conventional design approach in many ways. For example, it has gradually streamlined the Parker company's signature motif, the arrow clip, careful not to make the change too abrupt or disruptive. In other projects the group has taken a more actively innovative role, proposing entirely new products to manufacturers. Such was the case with the elegant little stacking chair for **SCP** (Sheridan Coakley Production), furniture pieces for Lloyd Loom, and vases and candleholders for Design Ideas. The group's work covers a wide spectrum of products, from decorative items to high-technology goods and interaction design. It is committed wholeheartedly to the future—"This is not a good time for nostalgia."

IMAGINATION

Studio for Interior Design and Event Design

Imagination Ltd., London
1978 founded
1988 moved to Store Street in London

Projects
1992 EU-Pavilion at the *Expo* in Seville
1994 Fantasy Factory for Cadbury
1998 stand for Ford at the Geneva Auto Show
1998 stand for Ericsson at the CeBit, Hanover
1998 Aurora project in Berlin

Page 205
top: *Journey Zone*, The Dome, 1999
bottom: *Talk Zone*, The Dome, 1999

The Imagination group was formed in the late 1970s by its current managing director, Gary Withers. In its two decades of operation, it has expanded dramatically and now has more than 300 employees. Describing itself as a "communications, design and project management agency," it has pioneered a new kind of British consultancy. It offers a very broad, conceptually led, multimedia service to clients in search of brand enhancement or a cultural spectacle. The design of spaces and environments is central to Imagination's work but is only part of the total experience it offers to its clients. Using music, sound styles and the moving image, among other things, they have become known for the highly sensorial, interactive spaces that they have created at exhibitions and at important promotional and cultural events. In the late 1990s, for instance, it created an exhibit for Ford in Geneva and, in the same year, a project with Ericsson for CeBit in Hanover. Imagination helped Ford launch its radical *Ka* and *Puma* models. One of its most successful projects to date was the *Aurora* launch, also for Ford. The team has also designed for London's Natural History Museum and London's BAFTA awards. No one style characterizes their work. Retail and leisure interiors are dealt with by their subsidiary Virgile and Stone. Imagination are committed to the idea of working beyond the constraints of a single discipline or medium. The team's most prestigious clients have included Ford, British Airways, British Telecom, Lego and Cadbury Schweppes. For Ford, at Geneva, they created a bridge out of 60 tons of sheet aluminum to represent the two-way dialogue between client and customers. For Cadbury they created a "Fantasy Factory" at the company's headquarters in Bournville, where children can experience chocolate-making. Their work represents an extension of the British design consultancies of the 1970s and 1980s and also adopts a completely new approach toward the manipulation of media in brand identification.

INFLATE

Studio for Furniture and Product Design

Inflate Ltd., London

1995 founded by **Nick Crosbie** and **Michael Sodeau**; wins *100% Design Award*

1996 nominated for the *BBC Design Award*

1997 Michael Sodeau leaves the group

1999 exhibition at the **Victoria and Albert Museum**, London

Inflate is one of the most successful of the new British design groups to emerge in the 1990s. As its name suggests, its has capitalized on the vogue for the style of the 1960s by reviving the idea of the inflatable vinyl object, taking it to new extremes and in new, hitherto unimagined, directions. Current inflatable designs include a flower vase, a picture frame, a fruit bowl, a screen, a postcard, a mirror, an eggcup and a light, as well as the more familiar furniture items.

The group's youthful ambition—"to build a popular, global brand that stands for original, fun, functional, affordable designs that make everyday living more enjoyable"—is clearly stated and sums up its approach to design.

The team was formed in the mid-1990s by three graduates from British design schools, **Nick Crosbie** and Michael and **Mark Sodeau**. Crosbie had shown inflatable furniture at his final-year college show, and the group

Page 207
Table lamp by Nick Crosbie, 1997

Digital Grass CD and letter holder by Mark Garside, 1997

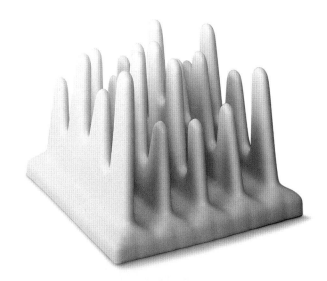

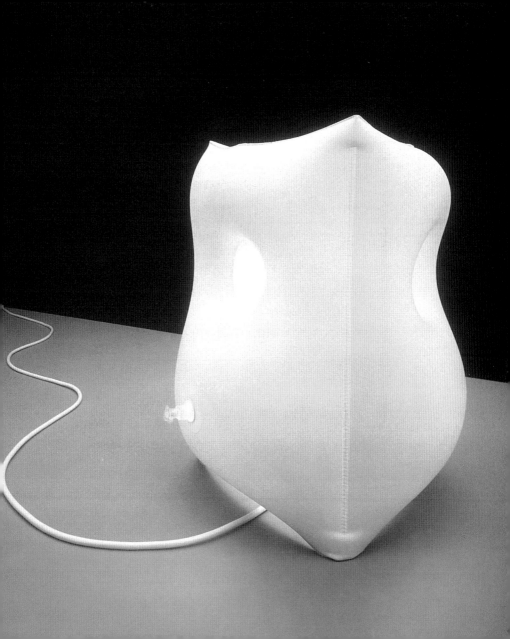

Products

1995 inflatable egg cup

1997 inflatable table lamp and inflatable armchair with steel frame, inflatable fruit bowl; *Luna* ashtray; *Mr. and Mrs. Prickly* salt-and-pepper shakers

1998 *UFO* hanging lamp; *Pod Bag* (with Craig Morrison)

immediately put together pieces to display at a London venue. The collection was well received and set them on their future path. The group rejected an offer from Alessi and decided instead to create its own brand. Since that point, it has concentrated on developing the brand with the help of a business manager, Nitzan Yaniv.

Quite quickly, Inflate decided to diversify and to extend its range beyond the inflatable product. It also began to think of itself as a production house and not simply as a design and manufacturing outfit. Steve Bretland, Mark Garside, **Michael Marriott**, and **Michael Young** were all approached to submit designs for a new collection in the late 1990s, which resulted in the launch of a dip-molded, PVC range of products, including a salt-and-pepper dispenser, a piggy bank, and a wine-bottle stopper. More recently, the company has made a range of bags from the same material. In the late 1990s Michael Sodeau decided to leave the group and branch out on his own.

Inflate represents contemporary British design at its most energetic, most imaginative, and most witty.

Page 209

top: *UFO* hanging lamp by Nick Crosbie, 1998

bottom left: pillow by Janine Trott, 1996

bottom right: *Pod Bag* by Nick Crosbie and Craig Morrison, 1998

Egg cup by Michael Sodeau, 1995

James IRVINE

Furniture and Product Designer

1958 born in London
1978 student of design at Kingston Polytechnic Design School, London
1981 studies at **Royal College of Art**
1984 works under Michele De Lucchi and Ettore Sottsass for Olivetti in Mailand
1988 opens own design studio
1993 partner at Sottsass Associate in Milan
1999 retrospective in Asplund, Stockholm

Products
1996 *Spider* armchair for Cappellini
1997 *Tubo* chair for BRF
1998 *Lunar* sofa bed for B&B
1998 *Luigi* bottle opener for Alfi Zitzmann
1999 *Ustra* city bus for Mercedes-Benz, Germany

Page 211
top: sofabed *JI* for CBI, 1996
bottom: *Ustra* City Bus for Mercedes-Benz, Germany, 1999

Spider armchair for Cappellini, 1996

He developed glass objects for Egizia and a bus for Mercedes-Benz, and he belongs to the generation of many-faceted industrial designers which allows Britain occasionally to call itself with pride the"world's creativity workshop." Indeed, this graduate of the renowned **Royal College of Art** primarily works outside of his home country, in Sweden or Germany for example, where his clients list includes such high profile companies as Interlübke, Vitra and WMF. Because of the disciplined language of his visual forms, this born Londoner ranks among the most important protagonist of the "new simplicity," although he has never become dogmatic. In the mid-1980's Irvine worked in the studio of Michele De Lucchi for several years. Intense collaboration with leading Italian manufacturers like Alessi and Cappellini— Irvin coordinated Cappellini's *Progetto Ogetto* collection together with **Jasper Morrison**—motivated the nomadic designer to move to Italy altogether. As a distinguished representative of the "new international style" he also made sure that visitors to the World's Fair in Hanover reached the fairgrounds in well-designed busses. The bus he designed for the city's municipal transportation system combines a modern graphic appearance with a love of functional detail.

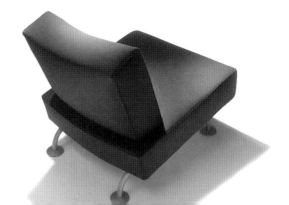

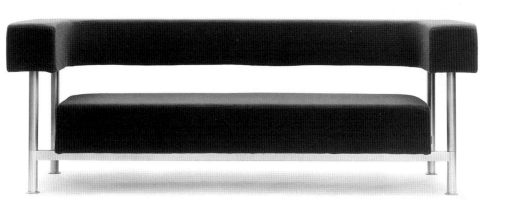

1931 founded by **Wells Coates**,
Graham Maw, Molly
Pritchard, **Jack Pritchard**,
and Robert S. Spicer

1932 *Lawn Road Flats* project,
opens 1934

1933 apartment at the exhibition
*Industrial Art in Relation to
the Home*

1937 Isobar Club opens

1939 **Arthur Korn** becomes
coworker, firm closes

1963 newly founded by Jack
Pritchard

Products

1933 stacking stool

1934 electric heater by Wells
Coates

1936 end table by
Walter Gropius; children's
furniture, dining table and
Long Chair by
Marcel Breuer

1939 wooden furniture by
Egon Riss

Page 213

top: *Isokon Long Chair*, 1936

bottom: *Isokon Dining Table/Isokon
Dining Chairs*, 1936 all by Marcel
Breuer

Isokon Electric Fire by Wells
Coates, 1934

Much British design of the inter-war years was backward-looking in nature. There were, however, a few instances when it seemed as if Britain was aware of the more progressive developments in continental Europe. **Jack Pritchard**'s Isokon venture was one such instance. With his wife, Molly, and the architect, **Wells Coates**, Pritchard formed Isokon with the intention of producing modern furniture and architectural fittings for the British market. Unlike Germany and France, which used tubular steel, Pritchard was aware that British taste was much more conservative than that of Europe and, as a consequence, he stayed with bent plywood. The firm produced, nonetheless, some highly innovative pieces designed by the ex-Bauhaus immigrants to Britain, **Marcel Breuer** and **Walter Gropius**. Breuer created what has since become classic designs for Isokon, among them his famous chaise longue (a plywood version of earlier models he had designed while still in Germany), which were executed in tubular steel. They played a prominent role among the small handful of progressive designs to emerge from Britain at that time and remain highly desirable objects today.

Alec ISSIGONIS

Engineer and Automobile Designer

1906 born in Izmir, Turkey

1922 immigrates to Great Britain

1927 studies engineering in London

1928 technical drafter at Rootes Motors, Coventry

1934 engineer at **Morris** Motors, Oxford

1953 chief engineer

1957 technical director

1961 development chief for British Motor Corporation (later Leyland)

1964 becomes Royal Designer for Industry

1972 chief designer

1988 dies in Birmingham

Products

1948 *Morris Minor* small car

1959 *Morris Mini Minor* and *Austin Seven* small car

1962 *Morris 1100* compact limousine

1967 *Morris 1800* compact limousine

Page 215

top: *Morris Mini* small car, 1959

bottom: *Morris Minor* small car, 1948

Born in 1906 in Smyrna, Turkey, Issigonis was educated formally at Battersea Polytechnic in London, but his real training came when he worked as a draughtsman with Rootes Motors in Coventry. After his experience with Rootes, he went on to work with **Morris** Motors and became its chief engineer. The *Morris Minor* of the late 1940s was his first big breakthrough and was to transform British motoring. As the case with all his key designs, Issigonis's main innovation was technological in nature. The unified construction technique that he chose for the *Minor* was revolutionary, and the type of suspension for which he opted resulted in an entirely new kind of car for British manufacturing. The curved body styling made reference to U.S. forms of the period but the diminutive size of the car gave it a completely new identity. Instead of looking aggressive, the *Minor* was a "friendly" little vehicle, and the British nation rapidly adopted it as the new family car. Issigonis's next major achievement came a decade later with another revolutionary design — *Morris Mini*. Once again, its engineering was radically new. It had small ten-inch wheels, front-wheel drive, a transverse engine, and rubber suspension. All these features, and others, were new to British cars and Issigonis offered the British public a truly innovative design; a really small car that offered a generous amount of interior inside. The *Mini* was a kind of utilitarian, neutral box that could be given an identity by whoever sat behind its wheel. Its low price appealed to young and old alike, and to both men and women. Issigonis's third major design success came with the *Morris 1100* a couple of years later. This was yet another engineering feat but the car was not as culturally radical as the two designs which preceded it. By the early 1960s Issigonis became chief engineer and technical director of the British Motor Corporation. His achievements coincided with the last years in which the British mass-production car industry had an international reputation and was seen as innovative.

JAGUAR

Automobile Maker

Jaguar Cars Ltd., Coventry

1922 Swallow Sidecar Company founded

1945 Jaguar Cars Ltd. founded

1951 first of seven victories at the 24-Hour race in Le Mans

1966 fusion with the British Motor Corporation

1984 Jaguar is privatized

1985 takeover by Ford

2000 returns to Formula 1

Products

1938 *Coupe SS Jaguar* 100

1956 *MK I* limousine

1961 *E-Type* sports car and *Limousine MK10*

1968 *XJ6* limousine

1979 *XJ* limousine by Pininfarina

1998 *XJ8* limousine

1999 *S-Type* limousine

2000 *F-Type* sports car

S-Type limousine, 1999

Page 217
top: Sportscar *Sk 120*, 1948
bottom: *XY 12* limousine, 1972

Page 218–219
left: *Cabriolet E-Type Series III V12*, 1974; right: *Cabriolet F-Type*, 2000

Although aggressively modern in form and spirit, Jaguar's cars have come to stand for the traditional British aristocratic ideal. In the early 1920s, William Lyons, the founder of Jaguar Cars, co-created the Swallow Sidecar company, which went on to become Jaguar Cars. The Sidecar company grew during the interwar years to become a significant force in British manufacturing, making its first appearance at the Motor Show in 1929. In the mid-1930s the company produced the *SS100 "Jaguar"*; the name stuck. At the end of World War II, Jaguar Cars leapt into the new postwar marketplace. The emphasis at that time was on sports cars, and at the end of the decade a number of new, highly successful models were developed. The *Mark VI* of 1951 was the first of a family of saloon cars to earn Jaguar its reputation for quality and sophistication. In 1961 Jaguar launched one of their most well-known "classic" cars, the *E-type*. Based on the design of their racing cars, it was aimed at a non-racing audience. It was probably their most overtly modernistic and desirable design to date. It remains one of Jaguar's most seductive cars and marks a high-point in British car design. By the mid-1960s Jaguar's reputation was riding high and it had bought the Daimler company, but it was soon to become part of British Leyland. The company was privatized again in the mid-1980s and was bought by the Ford car company in 1989.

JAM DESIGN

Studio for Furniture and Product Design

JAM Design &
Communication Ltd.,
London

1994 founded by **James Anley**,
Matthieu Pallard, and
Astrid Zala

1998 invitation from the Queen

1999 featured on **BBC**-TV

Products

1994 *Robostacker*

1995 *Drum Stool* and *TV Stool*
both for Whirlpool

1997 *Freeforms* for Zotefoam

1996 *Ladder Chair* (with SGB
Youngman)

1998 *Bulb* vase for Mencap

Formed in the mid-1990s, JAM is an example of a new model of design group in Britain. It covers a wide range of activities—product design, fine art, architecture, exhibition design—and also collaborates on projects that touch the areas of fashion, film, graphics, and music. This open-ended approach has produced some of the decade's most daring and innovative work. The group describes itself as a "design and communications agency that explores the potential of existing technology and materials as the starting point for collaborative projects." Work to date has included a collaboration with Whirlpool on a range of domestic designs—a storage cabinet, a stool, and a table—made from stainless-steel washing-machine drums; a project with Zotefoam developing a range of products from free-standing furniture to desktop accessories, showing the versatility and eco-friendliness of the firm's materials; the design of a range of seating using lightweight aluminum ladders, manufactured by SGB Youngman; and, in collaboration with Philips, the design of a vase created from a spotlight.

from left to right:
Ladder Chair, Ladder Stool, Ladder Bar Stool (with SGB Youngman),
1996

Interior Architect

Eva Jiricna is among the small handful of women who run architectural and design practices in London. Czechoslovakian by birth, she has worked in England since 1968 when she came over to Great Britain to work with the Greater London Council. Since then she has become a key figure in the British neomodern, or "high-tech" movement of the 1980s and 1990s, playing a key role in the design of retail environments and well-known for her interiors for the chain of Joseph stores in London. Jiricna's work is characterized by her use of glass and steel, and her respect for the structural and functional possibilities of these materials. Trained as an architect and engineer, she favors a minimal, technologically sophisticated aesthetic that respects the human scale but relishes, and indeed exploits, the possibilities offered by using exclusively modern materials. Before setting up in practice on her own, she was employed in the Richard Rogers team for the interior of the Lloyds Building in London. She is especially recognized for her work for Joseph Ettedgui in the mid-1980s and for the interior of the Legends nightclub.

1939 born in Prague
1968 immigrates to Great Britain (since 1976 British citizen)
1978 partnership with David Hodges
1982 works for Richard Rogers
1985 opens own studio
1991 becomes Royal Designer for Industry

Projects
1980 Joseph Store in South Mouton Street
1984 Way-In Store for Harrods
1988 Joseph Store on Fulham Road
1996 interior for the Legends nightclub

Spiral steps made of glass and steel for Jardine Insurance, London

Ben KELLY

Interior Architect

1949 born in Great Britain
1974 graduates from the **Royal College of Art**
1977 founds Ben KellyDesign
1996 participates in the exhibition *BBC Design Awards* in Glasgow

Projects

1977 Howie fashion store in London
1982 The Hacienda nightclub in Manchester
1989 The Dry Bar in Manchester
1991 The Waterfront restaurant complex in Norwich
1994 American Retro Shop, London
1995 basement at national Museum of Science and Industry, London
1998 retail concept for Halfords Ltd.

Ben Kelly defines his work as an interior architect as follows: "Interior design is a transformative practice based on the principles of breathing new life into existing spaces." Best known for his radical transformation of the fashionable Hacienda Club in Manchester in the early 1980s, where he introduced imagery deriving from the **Punk** movement into a nightclub for the first time, he is one of Britain's leading creators of dramatic interior spaces. Bars, shops, nightclubs, and museums have all been given a "new life" by Kelly and his team. His signature is a combination of unusual materials, shocking juxtapositions, and an innovative use of color. As he explains, "Our palette of materials has combined slate from the Lake District with recycled plastics."

Recent work includes an exhibition, *True Stories*, showing British culture to a Japanese audience; a reworking of the Children's Gallery in London's Science Museum, which earned Kelly numerous awards; converted offices for the **Design Council**; and a concept for flagship stores for the Halfords retail group.

The Haçienda, Manchester, 1982

Danny LANE

Interior Architect and Furniture Designer

Although he was born in the United States and didn't come to London until the mid-1970s, Danny Lane is considered a key figure in the group of furniture designers who worked in Britain in the 1980s. His dramatically expressive furniture creations in metal and glass fitted right at the center of the movement, associated with London and with the breaking down of barriers between the areas of art, craft, and design.

This movement emerged from London's art schools and the co-existence of students working across these areas. It can also be seen as a response to the fact that there was no longer a thriving British furniture manufacturing industry. **The Crafts Council** played a key role in supporting many of the individuals who worked in this area.

Alongside **Ron Arad**, **Tom Dixon**, **André Dubreuil**, and a handful of others, Lane helped to break down existing disciplinary boundaries and to create, in the interstices between the conventional areas, a range of furniture pieces that were both shocking and exciting. Typically he did not

1955 born in the United States
1975 moves to Great Britain
1980 graduation from the Central School of Art and Design
1981 founds studio in London
1983 glass manufacturing begins
1986 collaboration with **Ron Arad**
1988 products for Fiam, Italy

Emerald Table, 1997

Products

1986   bar made of steel and glass for the Moscow Bar, London; *Etruscan Chair*

1988   *Soloman Chair*, table *Shell and Atlas* for Fiam

1992   sculpture for the Borehamwood Synagogue

1994   glass stairs for the **Victoria and Albert Museum**, London

1995   cross for St. Paul's Church

1997   *Esmerald Table*

1998   *Split Wall* object

1999   *Archangel* and *Stands to Reason* object; *As Above So Below* table

emerge from within design itself but began his career as an apprentice to the well-known stained-glass craftsman, Patrick Reyntiens.

After his apprenticeship, he became a fine art student at London's Central School of Art and Design, and established a studio in the East End of London in the early 1980s before founding his own company, Glassworks, which functioned as a cooperative. It was here that he began to create, with his coworkers, a series of pieces of glass furniture that were all "one-offs." The business had expanded considerably by the mid-eighties and he took on a number of large-scale architectural projects. He became involved with **Ron Arad** at this time, exhibiting designs in his Covent Garden showroom, One-Off, and collaborating with him on a number of interior commissions. His output increased by the end of the decade and numerous tables and chairs emerged from Glassworks, made from uneven pieces of cut glass and etched and sandblasted with strong, abstract patterns. He recently created the glass staircase for the new Glass Gallery in London's **Victoria and Albert Museum**.

Page 225
left: *Etruscan Chair*, 1986
right: *Stands to Reason* object, 1999

Angaraib object, 1987

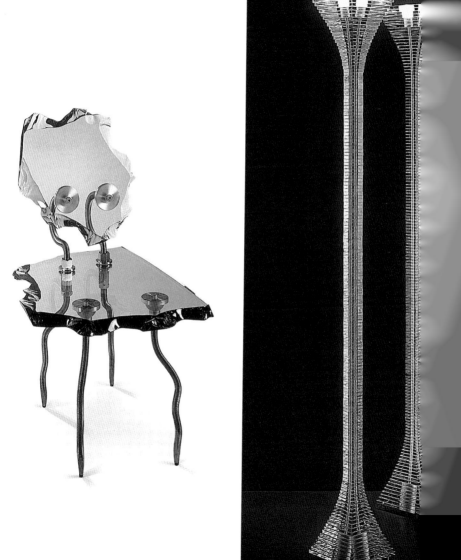
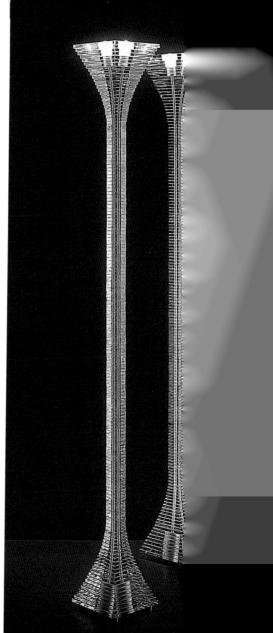

LIBERTY

Department Store and Textile Manufacturer

Liberty Public Ltd.
Company, London

1862 founded by Arthur Lazenby Liberty

1874 products by artists such as Dante Gabriel Rosetti and **William Morris** at Sortiment

1875 department store

1888 Japan trip by Arthur Lasenby Liberty

1890 Archibald Knox becomes chief designer

1975 exhibition at the **Victoria and Albert Museum**, London for one hundredth anniversary

Products

1910 flower-patterned fabric becomes known as *Liberty Print*

1930 partially synthetic textile *Sungleam Crepe*

1939 textile collection by Paul Poiret

1952 *Tudor* and *Fritillary* textiles by **Lucienne Day**

1967 *Lanthe* fabric by Rene Beauclair (design 1902)

Page 227
top left: textile by L.P. Butterfield, 1891
top right: candleholder by Archibald Knox, 1903
bottom left: *Ella* textile, 1940
bottom right: *Cosmic* textile, 2000

Liberty's department store on London's Regent Street is one of a number of interesting retail outlets that have played a key role in the development of British design and visual culture in the twentieth century. It was founded by Arthur Lazenby Liberty at the end of the nineteenth century and, from the outset, embraced the idea of innovative design. In particular, in the early days, it sold goods imported from Japan, which were highly fashionable at that time. A number of designers—among them Archibald Knox and Arthur Silver—worked for Liberty's, producing Celtic-style pieces that appealed to the store's aesthetically discerning customers. In the early years of the twentieth century Liberty's furniture could be bought widely in Europe and, in turn, modern European designs, by the German designer, Richard Riemerschmid for example, were imported into London by Liberty. So fashionable was the store in Europe that Italy dubbed its version of the Art Nouveau style in architecture and the decorative arts "Stile Liberty."

In more recent years Liberty's has become particularly well-known for its fabric designs, which it commissions and then produces itself; names such as Susan Collier are linked with the best-known designs. The store acknowledges its heritage as a turn-of-the-century influence on British visual culture and as a bastion of traditionalism. The building itself is an icon of the inter-war Tudor Revival movement in British architecture and is on the tourist route for foreign visitors to London. It still plays a role in the promotion of international contemporary design. It hosts exhibitions of modern design, including one, in the early 1990s, of progressive plastic products.

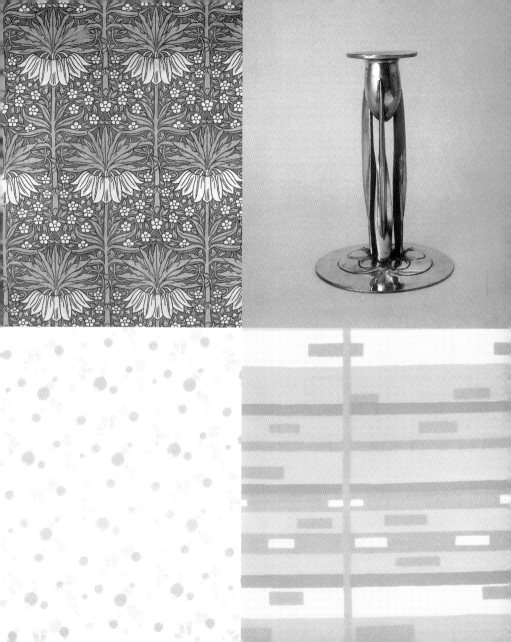

LONDON TRANSPORT

Traffic and Transportation Business

1863 first subway line opens

1907 introduction of the uniform Underground logo

1916 typographer Edward Johnston develops lettering

1925 poster series by Edward McKnight; Kauffer *Pleasures by Underground*

1930 double-decker buses introduced

1933 takeover of the public traffic by the London Passenger Transport Board; Frank Pick becomes chief and creates a uniform corporate identity

1939 advertisement poster by Man Ray

1998 introduction of new station shelters and electronic displays for travel information

The London Transport organization can be numbered among the most important patrons of British modern design in this century and, although it was at its peak as such in the 1930s, the effects are still visible in such details as the London Underground map, emulated around the world. London Transport took on this important role in the 1930s with the guidance of Frank Pick, who was the vice chairman and chief executive from its establishment. He saw his role as bringing the best of contemporary British design to the British public. To this end, he commissioned a number of key creative individuals to produce work for him.

In the area of corporate identity, Pick had asked Edward Johnston to develop a typeface before London Transport was formed, and it remained in use for many years. Harry Beck's map for the Underground was a revelation and much emulated abroad. Numerous posters were commissioned in the 1930s from leading graphic designers and artists of the day, Hans Schleger among them.

The rolling stock of the trains and buses was also given a modern face-lift under Pick. Later the industrial designer, Douglas Scott, was involved in the design of the revolutionary Routemaster bus, launched in the late 1950s, which subsequently became a classic and still graces the streets of London in large numbers. In the 1930s, Pick commissioned leading designers—Enid Marx, Marion Dorn, and Paul Nash in particular—to work on fabrics for bus and train interiors. The final area where the organization made a visual impact was in architecture—and here it was the architect, Charles Holden, who was the creative force.

This thorough-going approach toward the design of its objects and equipment remained a characteristic of London Transport for a while after Pick left at the beginning of World War II, and since then some attempts have been made to sustain those energies. The lasting icons and imagery that still surround us in contemporary London mostly stem, however, from an earlier period.

Cockfosters station, 1935

Ross LOVEGROVE

Furniture and Product Designer

Since he graduated from the **Royal College of Art** in the early 1980s, Ross Lovegrove has become one of Britain's most successful product designers. He has a particular fascination with traditional British craftsmanship, as manifested in goods such as leather saddles. This constituted an important theme in his final-year college show and has gone on to underpin a number of his subsequent designs.

Lovegrove is best known for a number of outstanding designs such as his *Coachline* luggage for the traditional British company, **Connolly**; his *Eye* camera for Olympus; his organically curved *Figure 8* plastic chair for Kartell; and his brightly colored acrylic *Basic* thermos flask for Alfi (designed with **Julian Brown**). His work is recognized for his unique language of form and materials, and for an approach toward the designed artifact, which combines the ergonomic with the sensory. His objects are always elegant and sophisticated, but never showy. They display a sensitivity toward the user that is unmatched in contemporary British design.

As one writer has explained, for Lovegrove, "everyday and familiar acts like eating, brushing one's hair, typing data into a computer or pouring out a cup of coffee, provide food for thought and at the same time for action." He is keen to link tradition with modernity wherever possible, and to find forms appropriate to each project he undertakes without imposing a stylistic formula upon them.

Lovegrove left England immediately after his graduation and spent some time in the office of Frogdesign in Germany before moving on to Paris as a consultant to the American-based company, Knoll International, where he produced the highly successful Alessandri Office System. During his stay in France he was invited, with Jean Nouvel and Philippe Starck, to join the Atelier de Nimes and worked with French manufacturers, among them Cacharel, Louis Vuitton, Hermes, and Dupont. He returned to London at the

Products

1991 *Basic* thermos for Alfi Zitzmann (with **Julian Brown**)

1992 Pottery Barn cutlery; *Coachline* bag series for **Connolly**

1993 *Elastomer* photo camera (prototype) for Olympus

1994 *FO8* chair for Cappelini

1995 *Crop Chair* for Fasem

1996 *Eye* camera for Sony; laptop—*Ammonite* prototype for Apple

1997 *Apollo* sofa and *Spin* chair for Driade; *Magic* chair for Fasem

1998 *Solar Bud* light for Luceplan; *Landscape* sofa for Frighetto; *Teso* table for Driade

end of the 1980s and based himself in a converted warehouse in Notting Hill, although his clients are internationally located. They have included Cappellini, Driade, and Luceplan in Italy; Sony and Olympus in Japan; and Apple Computers and Hermann Miller in the United States. Many international awards and honors have come Lovegrove's way, and his work is in a number of permanent museum collections.

Ammonite laptop (prototype) for Apple, 1996

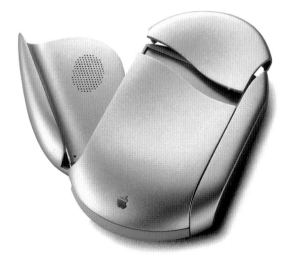

Architect and Furniture Designer

Scotland's most notable contribution to twentieth-century British design is, without doubt, the work of the turn-of-the-century Glaswegian architect/ designer, C.R. Mackintosh. With his wife Margaret MacDonald and the other two members of the "Glasgow Four," Herbert MacNair and Frances MacDonald, he developed a modern style equivalent to Europe's Art Nouveau, which was in advance of anything else emerging in Britain at that time. His work made a huge impact upon other major centers of progressive design, especially in Germany and Austria.

Mackintosh's creative originality lay in the way he combined a modern, abstract approach toward the structure of his designs and the spatial arrangements in his architectural compositions with a stylized decoration that was rooted both in nature and in ancient Celtic imagery. The striking rectilinear forms of his pieces were frequently softened by abstract roses and sinuous plant stems, and female forms that blend into the structures they embellish. Above all, his furniture pieces and decorative items all played spatial roles within the interiors he constructed so meticulously. Every detail counted, from the handles on a chest-of-drawers to the light fittings. Every Mackintosh interior was a total work of art controlled by his eye.

Mackintosh started out as an architectural apprentice in the Glasgow office of Honeyman & Keppie. He met his "Glasgow Four" colleagues at evening classes at the School of Art, and they worked together on a number of poster projects in the 1890s. Mackintosh began designing simple furniture items in the same decade and came to the notice of the Viennese designers when he exhibited in Vienna in 1900.

Josef Hoffmann was particularly influenced by his work. A few key architectural projects dominated the first years of Mackintosh's mature career. A house named Windyhill provided Mackintosh with his first challenge. Another commission followed, from the publisher Walter Blackie,

1868 born in Glasgow

1884 works for the architect John Hutchinson (from 1890 for Honeyman & Keppie)

1896 exhibition in London with Herbert J. MacNair and his sisters Frances and wife Margaret as "the Four"

1897 construction of the Glasgow School of Art (until 1909)

1900 participates in the eighth exhibition of the Vienna Secession; marries Margaret McDonald

1901 travels to Belgium, France and Italy

1902 participates in the International Art Exhibition in Turin

1903 Hill House, Helensburg

1916 moves to London, 1923; moves to France; dedicates himself to painting

1928 dies

Products

1896 chair with high back;
     furniture for Guthrie and
     Wells
1899 furniture for a director's
     bureau
1901 furniture and lighting for
     the School of Art
1902 white commode with
     colored glass
1904 furniture and lighting for
     the Hill House,
     Helensburgh
1903 Willow Tea Rooms,
     Glasgow

Page 235
left: *Ingram* chair, 1901
right: *Hill House* chair, 1904

Page 236–237
left: *G.S.A.* table, 1900, and *Argyle*
chair, 1897 (remake by Cassina)

which resulted in Hill House in Helensburgh. In both houses Mackintosh drew on Scottish baronial traditions, creating structures, which determined the external appearance by the plan and spatial requirements of the interior. The architect designed the complete interiors and fittings of the two houses. His best-known architectural work, however, is the remarkable Glasgow School of Art, which he began working on at the turn of the century. The site was unusual as it was on a steep hill, but Mackintosh studied it very carefully and planned a building that utilized it effectively. As in all his buildings, the details were all-important. The windows on the front façade, for instance, had what looked like pieces of decorative ironwork attached to them. They were, in true Mackintosh fashion, however, not mere gratuitous decoration but served to support the ladders of the window cleaners. The front façade was strikingly asymmetrical and the interior was equally dramatic. The library, for example, with its high ceiling, hanging lights, and dark wood built-in furniture, was a very powerful space, and the huge windows of the painting studios introduced a sense of light into the building, which was strikingly modern.

Mackintosh made an enormous impact in the city of Glasgow in the years around the turn of the century. Nowhere was this more obvious than in the series of tea-rooms he designed for Miss Cranston. Taking tea was an important social ritual at this time and the environment in which this activity took place was important, especially to the ladies of Glasgow who participated in it.

Several of Mackintosh's most striking furniture designs were created for tea rooms, notably one of his early high-backed chairs, which had four back pillars and an oval headrest. It was created for the Argyle Street tea rooms, the exaggerated height used to enhance the spatial qualities of the interior. He used his dramatic ladder-back chairs to similar effect in his houses.

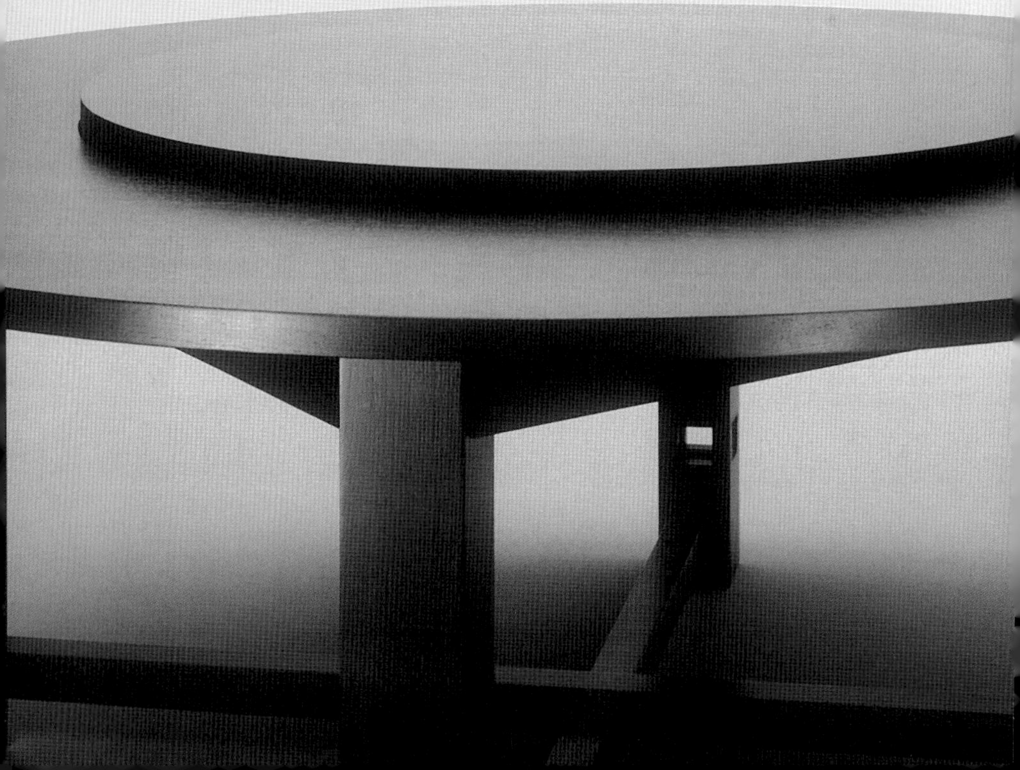

1905 *Berlino* table
1920 furniture for Derngate House, Northampton
1916 fabrics for Foxton's & Sefton's
1917 grandfather clock for Bassett-Lowke
1918 *Busnelli* chair

Unlike his **Arts and Crafts** contemporaries, however, Mackintosh was not interested in fine craftsmanship for its own sake nor in the "truth to materials" maxim to quite the same extent. Many of his wooden surfaces were painted, often with white paint. His priority was always the decorative and spatial impact of the components of a total environment—the parts all belonged to the whole.

Other important interiors he created included 120 Mains Street, Glasgow, the house he made into a home for himself and his wife, Margaret. Once again the emphasis was on the interplay between horizontal and vertical lines and the muted colors of the interior—white, cream, soft gray, and a touch of purple—were characteristic of many of his creations in these years.

In this interior, as in many others, Mackintosh created the structural framework while Margaret worked on the decorative detail. Their partnership showed itself once again in the stunning "Rose Boudoir" shown in Turin a couple of years later.

Although Mackintosh's work made a strong impact at the time, his career as an architect and designer was relatively short-lived. He left Glasgow for London just before the World War II and only undertook a few more commissions, the most notable being the interior of a house for the industrialist, W.J. Bassett-Lowke. In the 1920s he worked on floral designs for textiles and watercolors. He died at the end of that decade in the South of France. Mackintosh's presence is still with us, however. The Italian company, Cassina, has, since the 1960s, been reproducing a number of furniture designs; the tea rooms in Glasgow have been restored; the Glasgow School of Art is still very much in operation; the interior of 120 Mains Street has been moved to the Hunterian Museum in Glasgow; and, recently, Mackintosh's sketch entitled "House for an Art Lover" has been transformed into a completed building just outside the city.

Page 239
top left: *Rose and Teardrop* textile, 1902
top right: *Barrel-shaped chairs*, 1897
bottom: *Berlino* table, 1905 (remake by Cassina)

Alex MACDONALD

Furniture Designer

1965 born in Cheltenham
1983 studies at Parnham
College, Beaminster
1989 founds studio for furniture
design
1994 own furniture
manufacturing

Products

1997 *Tilt Top* table; *Dining Chair*
1998 sofa; *Small Tables*
1999 *Pegasus* dinner table

Before he went into pop videos, at which he has been enormously innovative and successful, Alex McDowell was a record-sleeve designer working with rock music groups and singers attached to independent labels at the height of the punk movement in the 1970s. His strikingly original work (the best of which, perhaps, was created for Iggy Pop) was highly influential, affecting the subsequent direction of designers such as **Neville Brody** who picked up on the way he used symbols and emblems. McDowell set up his own design company, enigmatically called Rocking Russians, moving on from there to create groups with similarly "funky" names—State Arts T-Shirt Company, the 3 Kliks video firm (once he had moved into that arena), and, more prosaically, Direct Hit Records. He brought the same original eye to pop videos, where he worked as a director from the early 1980s. Pop-video production was a hybrid phenomenon, bringing together the skills of filmmakers, photographers, graphic designers, and advertising people, and as such was a hot-bed of creativity and innovation. McDowell thrived in this context, making some videos of lasting significance, among them one for the group Everything But The Girl, entitled "When All's Well," for which an elaborate underground set was constructed.

Page 241
top right: *Tilt Top* table, 1997
top left: *Dining Chair*, 1997
bottom: *Pegasus* table, 1999

Small Tables, 1998

John MAKEPEACE

Furniture Designer

1939 born in Solihull

1957 learns furniture carpentry from Keith Cooper; studies abroad in Scandinavia (1961 North America, 1968 Italy, 1974 West Africa)

1972 wins Kitchen Design prize from magazine *Observer*

1977 founds college for furniture design in Parnham, Dorset

Products

1964 dining room chair for **Habitat**

1970 *Desk with a View*

1975 *Sylvan Chair*

1977 *Mitre Chair*

1982 *Oriental Cabinet*

1992 *Whale* table

1993 *Brasserie Chair*

1994 *Living Table*

1995 *Lean-on* bookshelf

1998 *Serendipity* chair (limited series for the millennium)

1999 *Ripple* wardrobe

Page 243

top: *Whale* table, 1992

bottom left: *Mitre* Chair, 1977

bottom right: *Thron Swaledale*, 1994

"For industry, wood is a piece of lumber" he once said, "but for me it's a marvelous medium like no other." Almost single-handedly, the Englishman John Makepeace saved the virtues of furniture making in the **Arts and Crafts** movement by carrying them over from the 19th Century into the present, thereby ensuring the continuation of a century-old tradition of aesthetically demanding artistic woodworking in England. This modern design Druid who chose a career in furniture making over one in theology, dedicated his life to but one purpose, namely the greater appreciation of wood as a medium. In just under four decades Makepeace had made a name for himself in major areas of accomplishment: in the design and production of almost impossibly expensive one-off pieces of furniture; as a prominent advocate and teacher of the fine art of furniture making; and as a pioneer of ecologically based design and manufacture. He also sought the collaboration of other artists such as Andy Goldworthy. Makepeace's own works are modern antiques. Toward the end of the 1970's, he founded a college as a trust in an Elizabethan manor in Parnham in southern England. It is the only school in the world to offer an integrated curriculum of design, the craft of cabinet-making and business management. Hooke Park College, which he opened several years later, combines scientific research in the field of ecological building techniques and their practical application to the construction of homes and furniture. More than almost anyone else, England's Lord of the Woods succeed in bringing about a renaissance for this material, and not only in the field of finely crafted furniture. Makepeace designs range from a practical folding chair to a filigreed chest of drawers, and from playful pieces like the *Dancing Circle Table*—with stylized figures as legs—to expressive objects like the cabinet *Obelisk*, a mark of distinction for any dwelling.

Michael MARRIOTT

Furniture Designer

1963 born in London

1985 graduates from the London
College of Furniture

1993 graduates from the **Royal
College of Art**

1994 studio founded

1996 works for Sheridan
Coakley Production;
participation in the *Design
of the Times* exhibition at
the Royal College of Art

1999 participation in the
Stealing Beauty exhibition,
ICA; *Jerwood Furniture
Prize*

Michael Marriott is probably the most original of the new generation of internationally acknowledged young British furniture designers, and his reputation as an important innovative force continues to go from strength to strength. He is committed to making the banal beautiful and to using existing objects in new ways to create new forms and meanings, as well as developing sophisticated design solutions. There is a natural quirkiness and sense of irony and resourcefulness in his work—for example, his appropriation of a glass lemon squeezer with a bulb replacing the lemon to create a floor-lamp called *Max*.

His highly creative, fresh approach does not result in a single style but rather in a range of possibilities. While many of his pieces are batch-produced—by **SCP** (Sheridan Coakley Production) and **Inflate**, for example—others are hand-made in his East End of London studio and function as "one-off" pieces for exhibition.

The concept is usually the most important part of a Marriott design, but it is always combined with form and technique to result in a satisfying artifact. The *Skittle Table* for SCP, for example, so named because it has four skittles for legs topped by a sheet of glass, is both a light-hearted gesture and a beautifully simple and resolved piece of design. Marriott describes his own approach as being "friendly and logical," while Sheridan Coakley thinks that Marriott's approach comes out of the same school of classic functionalism as the other SCP designers, but adds the designer's individual eccentric twist. He delights in evocative titles—his simple wooden coat stand for SCP is entitled *Hi Honey I'm Home*, while his highly minimal leather and chrome daybed for the same company is called, simply, *Missed*. He is not interested in novelty for novelty's sake, however, and would rather see an existing object used in a new way than a new object created just for the sake of it. In this attitude there is a characteristically 1990s ecological quality in that

Page 245

top: *Missed* couch for Sheridan
Coakley Production, 1998

bottom: glass *Skittle* table for **SCP**,
1996

Products

1990 *Seven Series* shelf

1992 *XL1* chair

1994 *Postcard Light*; *Fez* stool

1995 *4x4* table series

1996 *Skittle* glass table for SCP

1997 *Drop* vase; *Fast Flatback Table*

1998 *Missed* couch for SCP

1999 *Ruth de Luxe* table

materials are not wasted and recycling is common. But there is nothing about Marriott that is doctrinaire or sanctimonious in this respect. His recycling is an aesthetic response first and foremost.

Marriott trained at the London College of Furniture, followed by London's Royal College of Art. He works from his own studio and began his collaboration with SCP in the mid-1990s, although he has also produced designs for Inflate. He teaches at Kingston University and at the Royal College of Art.

Page 247

left: *Regal Seven Series*, 1990

right: *Postcard Lamp*, 1994

Alexander MCQUEEN

Fashion Designer

When the Scottish fashion designer, Alexander McQueen, showed his Bumster collection in Paris a few years ago, consisting of low-waisted trousers showing the wearers' bottoms in the style of workmen, this was just another opportunity for this enfant terrible to shock his audience out of complacency. Since his graduation from St. Martins School of Art and Design in London in the early 1990s, McQueen has moved from one shocking sartorial venture to the next, using tactics of horror, aggression, and sordid sexuality. His graduating show was entitled *Jack the Ripper Stalking His Victims* and contained slashed items of clothing designed in a post-punk idiom. His autumn 1997 show contained a headdress with antlers mounted on it, and another collection included a vinyl dress complete with rivets. His infamous *Highland Rape* collection contained lace dresses covered with blood.

McQueen is no amateur designer, however. From the age of sixteen he worked with a pattern cutter for a Savile Row tailor in London, then went on to work for Koji Tatsuma and Romeo Gigli in Milan before returning to London to take up formal training in fashion design. These apprenticeships stood him in good stead, enabling him to move straight into establishing his own business after graduating.

In spite of his reputation for designs that stand at the margins of the mainstream, McQueen's skills and imagination have brought him into the limelight and in the mid-1990s he moved to Paris, taking over from John Galliano as the head designer for the house of Givenchy. As a result of this move, his designs have become more mellow and more overtly elegant, but they still bear all the hallmarks of a designer with a highly original eye and a deep knowledge of the way clothes are constructed and made.

David MELLOR

Furniture and Product Designer

1930 born in Sheffield

1946 studies at Sheffield College of Art; from 1950 on at **Royal College of Art**

1953 studies at the British School in Rome

1954 works for cutlery manufacturer Walter & Hall

1962 becomes Royal Designer for Industry

1965 design consultant for the transportation department

1969 opens shop in London

1980 opens shop in Manchester

1982 becomes director of Crafts Council

1990 own cutlery production

1998 solo exhibition at **Design Museum**, London

Products

1951 *Pride* cutlery

1957 bus stop

1963 *Embassy* cutlery

1966 mailbox for the British Post Office

1982 *Café* cutlery

1998 *City* cutlery

David Mellor is a key member of the generation of designers who emerged from the Royal College of Art in the 1950s, the first to benefit from the post-war training intended to create a bridge between craft and industry. Mellor works in the area of metalwork and has created several classic sets of flatware in stainless steel, among them *Pride*, *Embassy*, and *Thrift*, which echo the simplicity and elegance of Scandinavian examples and rank among the most timeless of British post-war designs. He has also created a number of other lasting designs, including a bus shelter for the Ministry of Transport, cookware, textiles, and wooden goods. He has set up his own manufacturing establishment and created a number of important and influential retail outlets that have made it possible for consumers to buy top-quality kitchen utensils in Great Britain.

Born in Sheffield, the home of the British cutlery industry, Mellor has remained loyal to that part of the country, establishing his workshops there first in a restored historic building, Broom Hall, and later in a purpose-designed and constructed building that won him numerous awards.

Throughout his long career as one of Britain's leading designer retailer manufacturers, Mellor has held on to the same rigorous principles of "good design" that he formulated in the 1950s, providing a level of consistency and commonsense that has made a lasting impact. His close involvement with the work of the **Design Council** and the **Crafts Council**, as well as his maintenance of standards in design, has earned him a lasting reputation.

Page 251

top left: *Abacus chair 700*, 1973

right: *Pride* cutlery, 1951

bottom left: tea kettle, 1963

MG

Automobile Manufacturer

Rover Group, Warwick

1924 founded by Cecil Kimber and William Morris as Morris Garages

1931 victory in the Ulster Tourist Trophy

1933 victory in its class with the Mille Miglia

1968 takeover by British Leyland

Products

1925 Number One race car

1928 *18/80 HP* and *Midget M-Type* sports car

1936 *Midget T-Type* sports car

1937 *EX 135* record model

1950 *TD* sports car

1955 *MGA* sports car

1962 *MGB* sports car

1976 *Midget 1500* sports car

1992 *RV 8* sports car

1995 *MGF* sports car

Today it would be called "customizing." When pioneers William Morris and Cecil Kimber began to design automobiles, the latter specialized in revamping his companion's production-line vehicles as sports cars. In his day the enthusiast Kimber won the Land's End Trail on the southwestern tip of England in the legendary Old Number One. The car was a modified **Morris** Bullnose he had assembled with his own hands. Under the name of MG, which stands for "Morris Garages," they earned a reputation for fast two-seaters, especially the open models. The cars were compact and maneuverable as the name *Midget*, one of the most successful model series, implies. Small sports cars of this type became a British specialty, represented also by other auto makers like **Aston Martin** and **Morgan**. At the 1955 Auto show in London the firm introduced its new model the *MGA*. Among other things, the aerodynamic body construction by Sid Enever made this 160 km/h speedster the first serially-manufactured sports car to exceed a production run of 100,000. Like Porsche, MG created a true sports car prototype with this post-War model. It continues today and has even survived the company's many fusions and management changes.

right: *MGF* roadster, 1998

Page 253
top: *MG B* convertible, 1962
bottom: *MG A* convertible, 1955

MINALE TATTERSFIELD

Studio for CI, Product and Packaging Design

Minale Tattersfield
Partners Ltd., London

1964 founded by Brian
Tattersfield and Marcello
Minale

1968 Alex Maranzano becomes
a partner

1983 exhibition at the Padiglione
d'Arte Contemporanea in
Milan, Italy

1988 exhibition in the Axis
Gallery, Tokyo, Japan;
Nobuoki Ohtani becomes a
partner

1998 *All Together Now* is
published; the eighth book
on design strategy

2001 Marcello Minale is
murdered in France

Page 255
top: milk bottles for Express, 1998
left: bottom oil bottles and cans for
BP, 1987
bottom right: plastic bottles for San
Pellegrino, 1999

One of the first sights to greet arriving passengers at London's Heathrow Airport is a row of blue pigeons depicted in various stages of flight which guide visitors to the pedestrian passageways. The pigeons are one many baffling creations of Minale Tattersfield, a design agency responsible for innumerable original projects over the last three decades, ranging from pure graphic art to packaging, CI's, furniture, articles for mass production, architecture and public spaces. A recent example is the agency's work on the gigantic Hammersmith Underground station in London. Equally superb are the elegant furniture designs created over the years for the Italian Zanotta company, packaging for Harrods, and prepared meals for the Tesco supermarket chain. The broad array of accomplishments, however, does not imply that Minale Tattersfield is a large anonymous design consultancy. On the contrary, through all of its various projects it has maintained a sense of individualism based on a combination of wit and intelligence, as personified by agency founders Marcello Minale and Brian Tattersfield. The two men met in the mid-1960's at the Young & Rubicam advertising agency. Their differences in approach were to produce remarkable results. While Tattersfield was trained in graphic arts at the **Royal College of Art** and brought experience in the USA to the mix. Minale had a more European orientation and combined Italian temperament with a penchant for Scandinavian purity.

In the 1960's and 1970's the group stayed small and concentrated its efforts on graphic arts, from letterheads to logos, and from brochures to book publishing. The goal was always to combine commerce with art. Over the years various partners joined the agency, such as Alex Maranzo in the late 1960's , Nobuoko Ohtani, a Japanese industrial designer, who came on board in the late 1980s, followed by Nigel James MacFall a short time later. Minale Tattersfield faced one of its greatest challenges in the early 1980s when British design studios—**Pentagram** or **Wolf Olins**, for example—transformed

Products

1967 logo for Harrod's

1978 packaging for Johnnie Walker Whisky

1980 Corporate Identity for Central television

1987 oil container for British Petrol

1989 Hammersmith subway station in London

1992 Corporate Identity for the English Premier League

1993 logo for the Olympic Games in Sydney; redesign of British Petroleum gas stations; gas stations for Repsol, Spain

1999 packaging for San Pellegrino mineral water

Page 257

top right: poster for exhibition *British Airports at the Design Center*, 1974

top left: logo for the F.A. Premier League, England, 1992

bottom: logo for Exedo, 1997

Logo for Olympic Games in Sydney 2000, 1993

themselves into sizeable companies and began to command international attention. In many respects, the agency had an advantage over the others because its orientation had been global from the start. Ideas rather than styles were the determining factor. For this reason, the company was able to master the transition and become one of Great Britain's leading design groups. Within only a short period, the studio made a name for itself in Italian ice cream circles by creating an image for the Sammontana brand. Later on, the Italian fashion enterprises Coin Spa and Giorgio Armani came knocking at their door. Minale Tattersfield made headlines in the early 1990's with its redesign of BP service stations. The bone of content was not so much the quality of their work, but their exorbitant fee.

SYDNEY 2000

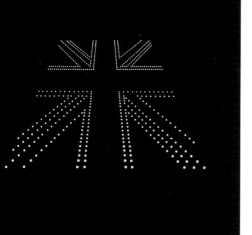

British Airports at The Design Centre
Haymarket, London. June 19 – July 21. Open Monday – Saturday 09.30 – 17.30. Wednesday & Thursday until 21.00. Admission free

THE F.A. PREMIER LEAGUE

Bill MOGGRIDGE

Product Designer

1943 born in Great Britain

1966 graduates from the Central School of Arts and Design in London

1969 studio in London

1977 moves to California

1988 becomes the Royal Designer for Industry

1991 founds **IDEO** Product Development in San Francisco (with David Kelley and Mike Nutall)

1996 IDEO becomes the *Design Group of the Year* (design center Nordrhein-Westfalen, Germany)

Products

1982 Compass portable computer for Grid

1988 mouse for Microsoft

1996 sunglasses for Nike

1997 1+1 furniture system for Steelcase and children's keyboard for Yamaha

1998 Palm V and electronic Softbook

Bill Moggridge is a member of the generation of industrial designers, which also includes David Carter and Nick Butler, who emerged in the 1960s and who set up in private practice at the end of that decade. He now runs a huge operation, named **IDEO**, which is based in California and London and which specializes in the design of high technology goods, especially computers. His firm was responsible, for example, for the first portable computer—the 'Compass' of the early 1980s—which was manufactured by Grid. Like many of the products emerging from Moggridge's company it is a highly minimalist design which combines technological sophistication with a strong visual elegance.

Like many of his successful peers Moggridge studied at London's Central School of Art and Design. He spent about a decade working with his firm Moggridge Associates creating scientific and consumer products for clients such as Hoover and Pitney Bowes before moving to the USA where his business flourished dramatically and his number of employees expanded accordingly. The move was timed perfectly to coincide with the expansion in the market for well-designed computer equipment.

Page 259
top left: mouse for Microsoft, 1988
top right: *Softbook*, 1988
bottom: *Compass* portable computer for Grid, 1982

Radio (prototype), 1998

MORGAN

Automobile Manufacturer

The Morgan Motor Company Ltd., Malvern Link

1906 Henry F.S. Morgan opens his own car garage

1910 auto manufacturing begins

1954 introduction of the angular front wall cooler

1976 sales start in the United States

1990 *Plus 8* equipped with catalyst

Products

1910 three-wheel car

1928 *Super Sport* three-wheel car

1935 *4-4* sports car

1950 *Plus 4* sports car

1965 *Plus 4 Plus* sports car

1968 *Plus 8* sports car

2000 *Aero* sports car

Morgan *Aero*, 2000

Page 261
Morgan *Plus 8*, 1968
Morgan *Plus 8* (assemblage)

At the turn of the millennium the time was ripe. When the tiny automaker from Worcestershire County celebrates a genuine debut—which only happens about once every thirty years—the automotive world turns an attentive ear. On the outside, the new *Aero 8* is an interpretation of the classic *Plus 8* model from the late 1960's, but with a 286 PS engine and an aluminum body it's a high tech coach. As the name implies, the new Morgan received a streamlined retro design, a quantum leap for an automaker whose reputation is founded on a tradition of individually hand-made sports cars. Even when other auto makers like **Aston Martin** or **MG** developed new models after the war, Morgan remained loyal to its pre-War body styling, demonstrating an unshakeable sense of tradition which is considered typically British. The result was the brand's unmistakable profile and a community of unwaveringly loyal fans. The fenders, the boxy grill and the protruding head lamps became Morgan trademarks. Only once, in the mid 1960's, did the company enlist the services of a designer for the *Plus 4 Plus* model. The *Aero 8* with its cock-eyed lights was developed in-house by Charles Morgan and Technical Director Chris Lawrence.

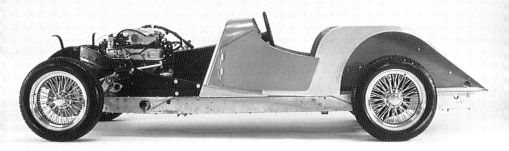

William MORRIS

Social Reformer, Furniture and Textile Designer

1834 born in Walthamstow

1843 visits the Academy for Young Gentlemen, Arundel

1853 studies at Exeter College in Oxford

1855 journey to France

1856 works for the architect George E. Street; becomes painter after encounter with Dante Gabriel Rosetti

1859 marries Jane Burden

1860 moves into Red House

1862 cofounder of the furniture company Morris, Marshall, Faulkner and Co. (from 1875 on Morris and Company)

1865 moves to London

1871 purchases Kelmscott Manor in the Cotswolds (1978 moves to Kelmscott House in Hammersmith, London)

1877 founds Society for the Protection of Ancient Buildings; furnishes own weaving mill

1881 workshops in Merton Abbey

Page 263
Tulip and Willow textile, 1873

If one single name stands out in the history of British design, it is that of William Morris. Today he is best known for his hand-made decorative wallpapers and textiles covered with stylized, intricate bird and flower patterns, his furniture designs, his embroidery, and his printing. He is respected as far afield as Japan. His reputation is also that of a design reformer who raised standards and injected a social agenda into what had hitherto been governed by commercial principles alone. A giant among designers, the name of Morris acts as a beacon even today—and his designs still grace many living rooms in search of a rural ideal. His influence has been felt throughout this century, from the German Bauhaus to the Crafts Revivals of the 1970s and 1980s. His name stands for integrity in design. If Morris's ideas about design and society continue to have currency today, so do his designs, which convey a somewhat different message. His decorative textiles and wallpapers, still in production today, evoke an England of an aristocratic, rural past in which the craftsman's hand dominated. The powerful images of flowers and birds, and the muted colors of his designs, stand for a particular idea of "Englishness." Their use as curtains and upholstery in comfortable middle-class homes suggests a level of civilization and taste that comes from the past. Morris himself looked back to the world of the medieval craftsman, whose activity was not compromised by the advent of the machine and who could enjoy his labor as a complete task. For Morris the division of labor that came with industrialization destroyed that idyll as far as the craftsman was concerned, and rendered meaningless and inauthentic the results of his work.

Morris suggests different things to us today but, above all, he stands for the idea of authenticity in design. His designs went back into production in the 1960s, when the faith in new technology had run its course and people were in search of something else from the material world. Morris, with his emphasis upon continuity and beauty, filled the gap.

1882 reads *Das Kapital* by Karl Marx

1884 founds Socialist League

1888 first exhibition of the Arts and Crafts Society

1891 founds Kelmscott Press, makes public *The Works of Geoffrey Chaucer*

1896 dies

Products

1856 chair with high back (with Dante Gabriel Rosetti)

1862 *Legend of St. George* closet (with Philip Webb); *Trellis* wallpaper

1863 *Sleeping Beauty* tiles (with Edward Burne-Jones)

1865 *Sussex Chair*

1867 *Green Dining Room* in the **Victoria and Albert Museum**, London

1868 first embroidery of fabric

1871 interior furnishing for Kemscott Manor (until 1896)

1889 *Bullerswood* carpet

Page 265

top left: *Artichoke* wallpaper, 1899

top right: three-paneled standing screen by J.H. Dearle for Morris Co., 1885–1890

bottom left: *Sussex Chair*, 1865

bottom right: *Rose and Thistle* textile, 1881

During his own lifetime William Morris was active on a number of different fronts, principally as architect, designer, businessman, poet, writer, and political activist. He studied theology at Oxford University but moved into the architectural office of George Edmund Street in Oxford with the intention of making architecture his career. A turning-point came after his marriage to Jane Burden, when he commissioned a family house from the architect Philip Webb but could find no suitable furniture and fittings available on the market with which to furnish it. With Edward Burne-Jones he set about designing his own items, which resulted in the formation of his own company, Morris, Marshall and Faulkner. The firm designed stained glass, tiles, and embroidery to commission. At this time, Morris designed some of his early textiles, among them *Daisy*, *Fruit*, and *Trellis*. Over the next decade the firm strengthened and included furniture and interiors in its work. By the 1870s Morris had expanded his efforts to become a poet, writer, and lecturer. He changed the name of the firm to Morris and Co. and began to learn weaving, setting up the Merton Abbey Mills to put his own designs into production. The 1880s was a decade of political activism and alliance with socialism, while in the 1890s he set up the Kelmscott Press and concentrated on printing handmade books. Morris was prolific as a designer across a range of media. His textile and wallpaper patterns were radical in the context of the Victoriana that surrounded them. His maxim was "truth to materials," a guide he followed throughout his creative career. As a result, in spite of his commitment to craft and to the spirit of medievalism, his work looked extremely modern. Morris was highly influential. Together with the writings of John Ruskin, his work was a mainstay of the Arts and Crafts Movement, the leading architecture and design movement of the latter half of the nineteenth century in England. The major irony of his life and work was that while he stood for a new democracy in design, claiming that he didn't want "art for a few," his preferred manufacturing method— hand-production— meant that his work was expensive and therefore exclusive.

Jasper MORRISON

Furniture and Product Designer

Page 267

top: *Three Sofa de Luxe* for Cappellini, 1991

bottom left: *Plychair* for Vitra, 1988

bottom right: tray with *Op-la* stand for Cappellini, 1998

Jasper Morrison is a key figure in current British design. Perhaps more than any other single individual, he has succeeded in showing an international audience that there is still some truth in the idea that the combination of understatement, quality, respect for materials, and thoughtfulness constitutes a lasting image of "Britishness," especially where design is concerned. His simple, unostentatious designs mirror a personality that is equally modest and non-assertive.

Over the last two decades he has represented these qualities in an impressive collection of work that spans furniture, products, and transport. His highly individual voice has become an important one at a time when the excesses of 1980s consumerism have resulted in demands for a more humble, restrained approach and a search for lasting solutions to everyday problems. From his simple *Laundry* hardboard and wing-nut chair of the mid-1980s (a graduation piece at the **Royal College of Art**) to the tram he designed for the German city of Hannover, he has shown that his design skills can be extended to a wide range of product types with international appeal. Morrison owes much of his early visibility to the London-based furniture company, **SCP** (Sheridan Coakley Production), which picked up his designs before he had finished his studies at the Royal College of Art. In the early 1980s, SCP manufactured his simple *Handlebar* table, while the Italian company, Cappellini, was also quick to adopt his *Flowerpot* table, a pile of pots topped by a circular piece of glass. By the time of his fêted graduation show, Morrison was already in the design periodicals—and his reputation established. Over the last decade and a half he has furthered this reputation by becoming one of today's leading designers.

In Morrison's early *Laundry* chair, the imaginative transference of a material and a construction technique from a well-known everyday object used to transport laundry to a chair was ingenious. He organized the batch production of the piece, showing his commitment to the manufacturing process as well as to the concept and form of his design. A year later the

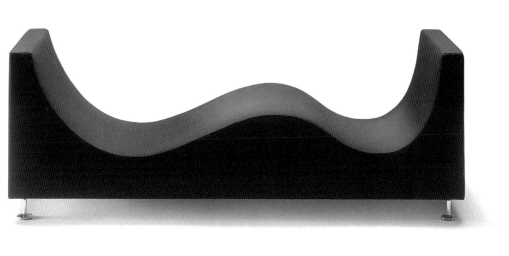

Products

1981 *Handlebar* table

1983 *Flowerpot* table

1984 *Wingnut Chair* and *Ribbed Table* for Aram Designs

1985 *A Rug of Many Bosoms* carpet

1988 *Plywood Chair* for Vitra and *Thinking Man's Chair* for Cappellini

1990 *1144* doorknob for FSB

1991 *Three Sofa de Luxe*

1993 *Three Sofa Regular*

1994 *Bottle* rack for Magis

1995 *Lima Chair* all for Cappellini

1997 *TW 2000* tram for the city of Hanover, Germany

1998 *Tin Family* cans for Alessi

Page 269

top left: Tin Family for Alessi, kitchen cans made of high-grade steel, 1998

top right: *Bottle* rack, 1994

bottom left: *Three Green Bottles* for Cappellini, 1988

bottom right: *Sim* salad cutlery for Alessi, 1998

Pages 270–271

Universal system for Cappellini, 1989

interior of his west London flat appeared in various magazines, and commissions flooded in from Italy and Germany, the most important ones being from the door-handle company, FSB, and the furniture manufacturer, Vitra. As well as working to commission, Morrison has also undertaken important work for exhibitions, among them Documenta 8 in Kassel, and Design Werkstadt, part of the "Berlin, Cultural City of Europe" program.

Morrison's designs from the late 1980s include the *Thinking Man's Chair*, a lounge seat constructed in metal with pads for the hands, which has become a familiar icon in modernist interiors; the witty *Rug of Many Bosoms* with its light, semi-circular motifs; and the *Ribbed* table for Aram Designs, characterized by curved metal supports for the glass tops. Numerous furniture pieces for Cappellini, SCP, Vitra, and others from these years are all characterized by a simple, sleek sensuousness achieved by his control of line and form, and his rigorous use of materials—plywood and aluminum, in particular—that are suited to mass manufacture. The design critic Peter Dormer said, "Morrison makes it plain that the impetus behind design is manufacturing: there can be no design without production. Without production, design becomes something else." His colors are always neutral and his forms subtle, creating a quiet backcloth for his simple yet stunning innovations—the gentle curve of the chair back in the simple plywood chair designed for Vitra in the late 1980s, or the "keyhole" openings in the drawers of his *Universal* storage system designed for Cappellini in the same period. Such creative instances of attention to detail are what make Morrison both a "designer's designer" and someone whose work is available to everybody.

In the 1990s Morrison continued to be one of the stars of the furniture fairs, both in Italy and Germany, as well as moving into new territory such as that of the Hannover tram, launched mid-decade. He has continued to exhibit as well, organizing with James Irvine Progetto Oggetti for Cappellini and, at the end of the decade, participating in an exhibit showing the interaction between design and film for the Milan Furniture Fair. He continues to be one of Britain's most "thinking" and influential designers.

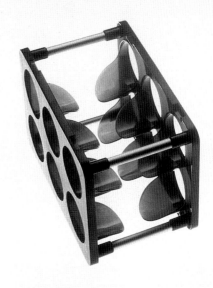

Alex MOULTON

Bicycle Constructor, Designer

1920 born in Bradford-on-Avon

1958 founds Moulton
Developments Ltd.

1962 Moulton Bicycles

1974 hired after takeover by
Raleigh Production;
founding of the Moulton
Bicycle Club

1983 continuation of the
production process

Products

1962 *Moulton Standard*

1970 *MK3* model

1983 *AM GT* model made of
plain high-grade steel

1998 *New Series*

Page 273
top: Moulton Standard, 1962
bottom: AM GT bicycle, 1982

The Moulton bicycle was an icon of the 1960s. Its novel form caused it to stand out from conventional bicycles and marked out its riders as progressives. It was the product of the creativity of the designer/engineer, Alex Moulton, and its design was a radical step forward for an object that had not changed significantly for well over half a century. It was also a classic example of a strongly British phenomenon—the invention, design, and development of a new product by a single individual. Often this process did not lead to commercial success, but in this instance the Moulton bike caught the public's imagination and, for a short time at least, became a visual landmark in the urban environment. It was launched at a time when people were beginning to become disenchanted with the car and its effect on the urban environment. The Moulton bicycle was seen as a viable alternative for the journey to work.

The essence of Moulton's design was the development of a new suspension system that allowed for smaller wheels. They were stronger and lighter than regular wheels—therefore less energy was required to make them turn and move the bicycle forward. The querkiness of the appearance of the new bicycle was part of its appeal and part of its undoubted "Britishness." It has not really lasted, although enthusiasts still use them. It remains a "classic" British object, belonging to the same era as Alec Issigonis's "Mini" car. Along with a handful of others, Moulton and **Issigonis** belong to a British engineering tradition that began with Brunel in the nineteenth century and that goes beyond mathematical calculations into the sphere of aesthetics and the pursuit of beauty through function.

Peter MURDOCH

Furniture Designer

1940 born in Great Britain

1964 studies and graduates from the **Royal College of Art**

1967 *Design Council Award* for the series *Those Things*

1969 studio in London

Products

1964 *Spotty* cardboard chair for Kinder

1967 folding chair made of plypropylene

1968 logo for the Olympic Games in Mexico City (with Lance Wyman)

Peter Murdoch's "paper" chair is one of the most lasting icons of the "Swinging Sixties." Incorporating flexibility, ephemerality, youth, and fun, it was created for his final-year show at the Royal College of Art, where he studied furniture, and was put into production by him immediately afterward.

The chair was a perfect evocation of the values of the sixties and represented the death (or so it seemed at the time) of solid wooden furniture that was made to be indestructible and to last forever. In reality, the "paper" chair, which was bought in a flat pack and assembled at home, was relatively strong, made from thick cardboard covered with plastic. Symbolically it was meant to be a "pop" object whose meaning was temporary. Murdoch covered its white surface with large dots—red, blue, or green—to enhance the fact that its surface was everything, that its form was transient. This was in keeping with the many other objects—mugs, carrier-bags, trays, etc.— that were given a bright, strong-impact surface treatment in this decade. Strong surface pattern, it was felt, meant that an object had an immediate effect upon its viewers but a temporary one. Decoration was more important than form because its meaning was more short-lived and suited the fast pace of the changing imagery that youth surrounded itself with in the sixties.

Spotty children's cardboard stool and packaging, 1964

Ceramic Designer

Keith Murray was a designer who aligned himself with the European Modern Movement in design, during the interwar years. He is best known for his elegant, stepped vases for **Wedgwood** and his lightly engraved glass for Stevens & Williams. A New Zealander by birth, he trained as an architect at the Architectural Association in London. Murray became an industrial designer in the 1930s, specializing in ceramics and glass. Murray was introduced to the Midlands-based glass manufacturer, Stevens & Williams, in the early 1930s. At the same time, he began a collaboration with the ceramics firm, Wedgwood. He dedicated the rest of that decade to designing items for both companies. His glass ranged from mass-production to hand-blown pieces, and he developed, strong shapes and a style that depended upon cutting and engraving the material to produce light, decorative effects. The ceramics that Murray designed for Wedgwood were monochrome pieces in a range of greens, blues, grays, whites, and beiges that depended upon their structure for their visual impact.

1892 born in Auckland, New Zealand

1915 studies at the Architectural Association in London (until 1918)

1930 works for **Wedgwood**

1932 works for Stevens & Williams

1935 participates in the exhibition *British Art and Industry* at the **Victoria and Albert Museum**, London

1936 architecture bureau with C.S. White

1940 architect at the Wedgwood factory in Barlaston

1981 dies

Products

1930 cup and pot made of clay

1933 clay bowls for Wedgwood

1935 *Cactus* vase for Stevens and Williams

1948 *Commonwealth Service* for Wedgwood

Bowl and vase for Wedgwood, 1933

1948 born in Great Britain

1972 BFA degree in ceramic
and glass

1974 MA degree in glass

1976 becomes director of the
Glasshouse firm in London,
Covent Garden

1998 design consultant for
Moser, Karlsbad

Products

1975 *Winged Cup* and *Winged Bowl*

1988 triangle-shaped cup

1997 *Honeycomb* bowl

1998 one-of-a-kind *Three Pearls of Wisdom*

left: *Many Hand Make Light Work* glass bowl, 1994
right: glass carafe, 1978

The recent design boom in Britain focused on areas such as product and furniture design, graphic arts and fashion, but was by no means limited in this respect. Ceramics is a field, for example, which for decades was dominated by legendary figures like Bernhard Leach and **Keith Murray**.

Then, in the 1980's and 1990's, a new, innovative generation came of age, which drew among other things on modern tendencies in British interior design. The same holds true for glass design, were good technique and decorative surfaces were no longer sufficient in themselves, but had to be augmented by a sense of the medium itself. One designer who is at home in both areas but has excelled in glass, is Steven Newell, director of the Glasshouse company since the 1970's. The simplicity, restrained playfulness and upbeat colors of his vases and carafes are harbingers of tendencies which only emerged at the beginning of the 21st century. Since the late 1990's Newell has been a consultant to the exclusive high-end Czech Moser brand.

A born Australian who worked in Japan for several years, Newson opened a studio in Paris in the early 1990's and, by the end of the decade, founded his own company in London. Renowned international producers of lighting and furniture number among his clients, including Alessi, Cappellini, Flos and Magis. As an example, he designed a TV-seating combination with a chair and sofa of steel and foam rubber for Moroso. Worldwide, Marc Newson has designed numerous restaurants and places of business such as the Pod Bar in Tokyo, the Crocodile Boutique in Hong Kong and the restaurant Coast in London. His other projects include the retail chain W&LT owned by Belgian Walter van Bierendonck and the redesigned interiors of all Apple stores in the U.S. Although Newson's 1984 degree from Sidney was in sculpture, he has since become known as one of the most talented and most successful all- round designers. The only reason this acknowledged eclectic deserves to be considered English is because his work draws so freely on a wide range of historical design epochs. The result is an amalgamation in which

1962 born in Sydney, Australia

1984 studies art in sculpture and jewelry in Sydney, Australia; receives design prize of the Australian **Crafts Council**; displays own exhibition in Sydney

1987 lives and works in Tokyo, Japan (until 1991)

1991 founds studio in Paris

1993 *Designer of the Year*, Salon du Meuble in Paris

1994 merges his furnishing company Pod with the Swiss watch maker Ike to Ikepod

1997 founds Marc Newson Ltd. in London with Benjamin DeHaan; retrospective in Villa Noailles in France

Orgone table for Cappellini, 1991

Products

streamline from the machine age, amoebas from the 1940s and '50s and a futuristic element all combine in a miraculous fashion to form a wholistic unit. A good example is his Lockheed chaise which uses visible rivets to parody aircraft aesthetics. Like **Ron Arad**, with whom he collaborated for a period of time, this universal talent belongs to the cadre of new enlightened designers who play with the feelings and fantasies of consumers by transforming daring visions of the past into articles of the present. Many of Newson's products look as if they were taken right out of a science fiction movie. It is not surprising that Italian automaker Fiat hired him to research automobiles of the future. One of his more recent projects is a collection of mechanical wrist watches for which his own furniture company, Pod, joined the Swiss manufacturer Ike to form the Ikepod brand. Objective: "design consciousness in the fast-paced world of watches."

Page 279

top: *Wood Chair* for Cappellini, 1992

bottom left: dish rack for Magis, 1998

bottom right: *Felt Chair* for Cappellini, 1997

Relations glass collection for littala, 1999

Vaughan OLIVER

Graphic Designer

1957 born in Sedgefield

1979 completes studies in graphic design at the Newcastle-upon-Tyne Polytechnic

1980 works for 4 AD Records (with Nigel Grierson from 1987 on with Chris Bigg)

1988 founds studio V23

1996 solo exhibition tours through Great Britain

Products

1984 *X-mal Deutschland* cover

1987 *Xymox* cover

1988 *Le Mystere Des Voix Bulgares* cover

1989 *Pixies* cover; *Doolittle* all for 4 AD

1990 *Soviet Design* poster

1993 CI for the Spanish TV station Documamia

1994 *Lush* cover

1999 *Gus Gus* cover; *VIP* all for 4 AD

X Mal Deutschland cover, 1984

Page 281
top: *Pixies* cover, *Bossanova*, 1991
bottom: *Gus Gus* cover, *VIP*, 1999

At the beginning of a new millennium, contemporary British graphic design is highly innovative with an open-ended approach, its protagonists as happy to work with the moving as with the still image. Much of its inventiveness stems from attitudes that were born in the **Punk** revolution of the 1970s. Vaughan Oliver is one such designer. His roots are in Punk music and his highly textured, fine-art–oriented work, which delights in the "found" image, was first seen on the covers of albums and accompanying posters for groups such as the Cocteau Twins, the Pixies, and Lush. In the early 1980s, with Nigel Grierson he was part of 23 Envelope, the design team working for 4AD Records. In the middle of the eighties his collaboration with Grierson ceased and he began to work with Chris Bigg, who is currently his partner. Later in the decade he became freelance, calling himself v23. In that capacity he has continued to work for 4AD, as well as taking on commissions from, among others, David Sylvian, the Psychedelic Furs, and Venture Records.

As well as working with the music business, Oliver has undertaken a wide range of other projects for different clients.

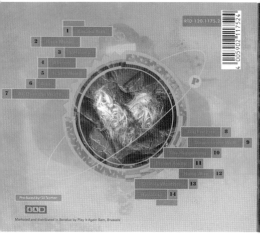

OMK

Furniture Design Studio

OMK Design Ltd., London

1966 founded by Jerzy Olejnik, Bryan Morrison, and **Rodney Kinsman**

1969 wins *Observer Design Award*

1972 works for Bieffeplast, Italy

1990 Kinsman becomes Royal Designer for Industry

1991 Kinsman made a fellow of the Royal Society of Arts

1996 Kinsman becomes a professor at the London Institute

1998 participates in the Design Council Millennium Product

Products

1967 *T1* Chair

1972 *T System* bureau furniture and Omkstak Chair

1974 *Cassis* armchair and sofa

1976 *Ritz* lighting series

1979 *Angolo* table

1984 *Orbit* mirror

1987 *Detroit* table

1989 *Trax* seat

1992 *Seville* bench

Page 283
top left: *Tokyo Chair* for the Expo in Seville, 1985
top right: *Transit* bench system, 1981
bottom: *Graffiti* shelf system, 1981

OMK was formed in the mid-1960s at the height of the pop revolution. The cool neomodernist furniture in tubular steel and black leather that its founder, **Rodney Kinsman**, produced at that time was a far cry, however, from the throw-away aesthetic associated with "Swinging London." Instead, OMK evolved a sophisticated, modern furniture style that presented Britain to the rest of the world in a different light. Since then OMK, using Kinsman's designs, has sustained this achievement. It is best known for its striking public seating created for the British Airways Authority and British Rail.

Kinsman formed OMK in partnership with Bryan Morrison (the financial side of the company) and Jerzy Olejnik, after graduating from the Central School of Art and Design in London as a marketing company to manufacture his designs in the UK. In the early 1980s he created Kinsman Associates to handle the licensed production of his designs internationally. The company's earliest designs such as the *Melon* chair by Olejnik, and the *TI* by Kinsman (the latter strongly influenced by **Marcel Breuer**'s work at the Bauhaus in the 1920s) appeared in *Vogue* magazine and were sold through **Terence Conran**'s shop, **Habitat**. Kinsman was quick to expand his market, however, and was soon selling to the United States. Through the 1970s and 1980s he created a number of seminal seating items, among them the *Omkstak* chair of the early 1970s, a light stacking chair with a pierced metal back and seat, and the *Transit* seating, also in metal. The mid-1980s saw the *Tokyo* chair, created for London's Groucho Club, and at the end of the decade came *Trax*, another successful example of public seating. The *Seville* bench appeared in the early 1990s.

PENTAGRAM

Studio for Corporate Identity, Product and Packaging Design

Pentagram Design Ltd.
London

1972 founded by Theo Crosby, Alan Fletcher, **Kenneth Grange**, Colin Forbes, and Mervyn Kulansky in London

1978 expansion of the firm in to New York

1986 bureau established in San Francisco

1990 Peter Saville works for Pentagram

1993 Consists of seventeen partners

Products

1961 *Chef* electric kitchen mixers for Kenwood

1966 Kodak *Instamatic* camera for Kenneth Grange

1986 poster for Daimler Benz

1988 redesign of the daily newspaper *The Guardian*; logo for the **Victoria and Albert Museum**, London

Page 285
top: electric shavers for Henry Milward and Sons, 1963
bottom: *Discovery* iron for Kenwood, 1995

Watering cans for the garden for Geeco, 1988
all for Kenneth Grange

Pentagram has a special place within British design of the last thirty years. It is one of the oldest of the group design consultancies still in operation today, combining graphic, product, and environmental projects, and it boasts some of the most significant and long-lasting achievements, including identity schemes for Whitbread's brewery, British Telecom, and the Museum of Modern Art in Oxford. It is also very well-known internationally.

The consultancy came into existence in the early 1970s when the existing graphic partnership of Fletcher, Forbes, and Gill joined forces with the industrial designer, **Kenneth Grange**, and the architect, Theo Crosby. They initiated a system, still in existence, whereby the individual designers work independently as far as their finances and clients are concerned. However, when particular projects cover a range of disciplines—such as that for British Rail, which required both product and graphics—they collaborate. The team has grown, and has been joined by designers such as

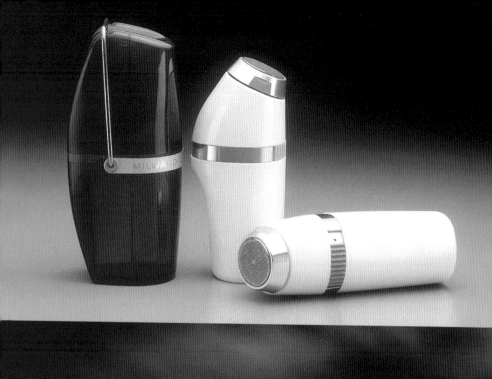

1985 *CI* for the Boots store chain

1989 tour poster for *New Order* by Peter Saville

1990 children's car seat for Takata Corporation, Japan

1992 book cover for the book *Ansel Adams* by Neil Shakery

1992 Protector razor for Wilkinson

1994 plastic packaging for the CD *Very* by the Pet Shop Boys

1995 *Discovery* iron for Kenwood

1997 design for the Swatch store Timeship in New York by Daniel Weil

Page 287

top left: annual report for Reuters by Mervyn Kurlansky, 1986

top right: redesign *The Guardian* by David Hillman, 1988

bottom left: book cover for *Phaidon* by David Hillman, 1991

bottom right: logo for Faber and Faber by John McConnell, 1981

Packaging for children's medicine by John McConnell, 1991

Mervyn Kulansky, John McConnell, **Daniel Weil**, and **Peter Saville**. Some of Pentagram's best-known design achievements include McConnell's re-design of *The Guardian* newspaper; Kenneth Grange's work on the high-speed train for British Rail; and Alan Fletcher's collaboration with the architect Norman Foster on the signage system for Stansted Airport. Its identity is constantly changing, even more so now as the original members retire from the group. It continues, however, to represent a standard of excellence within the world of British design consultancies and to play an important role within the London design community by supporting exhibitions and sponsoring open lectures and other events.

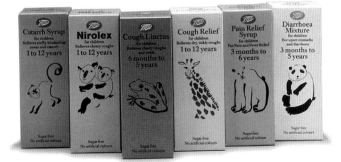

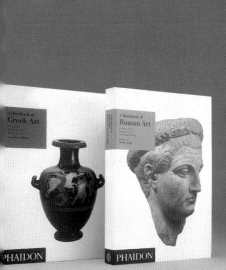

POP DESIGN

In the 1960s London became the youth cultural center of the world. It was a revolution that affected everything, including design. Suddenly a new energy came into being, centered upon pop music, but extending also into the goods the new, young consumers chose to surround themselves with as markers of their newfound freedom. The new culture arose from a number of changed circumstances—the consumer boom of the late 1950s and early 1960s was largely responsible, together with the growing influence of American mass culture and the emergence of a new generation of British youth eager to express itself and to distinguish itself from that of its parents.

By the early 1960s, pop music had thrown off its American roots and found a place within British urban culture. Groups such as the Beatles emerged from Liverpool, while others such as the Rolling Stones were London-based. By mid-decade London had the epithet "Swinging" attached to it and had become the "mecca" of pop culture.

Following close on the heels of music, fashion played a vital role in this new phenomenon. Designers such as **Mary Quant**, Foale and Tuffin, and Ossie Clark graduated from London's art schools to provide the new style-conscious consumers with clothes that suited their young, energetic image. Miniskirts, black-and-white geometric patterns and Op Art imagery were prevalent and soon fashion magazines were filled with British designs worn by the new "child" models such as Jean Shrimpton and Twiggy.

Male fashion was available as well, through retail outlets established by

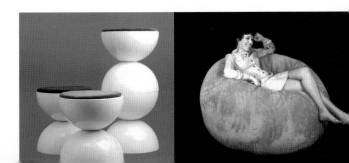

the Glaswegian, John Stephen, on London's **Carnaby Street**, the heart of youth culture. Fashion boutiques—Mary Quant's Bazaar on King's Road, Barbara Hulanicki's Biba in Kensington, and Lord John and Dandy Fashions on Carnaby Street among them—dominated the picture and soon became pop objects in themselves. On King's Road, for example, Granny Takes a Trip featured an American automobile protruding from its front window into the street, and the interior designer, Jon Wealleans, created a dramatic, Disney-inspired pop interior for Mr. Freedom in Kensington. Shopping for clothes and other lifestyle accompaniments was the means of entering into pop culture and designers were quick to respond to this, creating both appropriate objects and sympathetic environments in which to consume them.

Pop design meant more than just clothes, however. The movement's emphasis upon ephemerality and the idea of the "throw-away" extended beyond clothing and shop interiors into the more seemingly "permanent" world of furniture. **Peter Murdoch**'s "paper" chair was a supreme example of this, its polka-dotted surface emphasizing the importance of image, and the fact that it was bought in a flat-pack and assembled at home reinforced its inherent flexibility.

Other experiments moved in the same direction—Hull Traders, for example, manufactured a series of chairs and tables, designed by Bernard Holdaway, made from thin plywood, and painted in bright "pop" colors, while, by the second half of the decade the "inflatable" chair had become a

"I find latex interesting because it is the only authentic material of the twentieth century and the only one that is still regarded as a taboo."
Alan Jones

from left to right:
Stacking stools by Richard Miles
Sea Urchin seat by Roger Dean, 1968
Prude shirt by Mary Quant, 1964
Logo for BIBA by John McConnell, 1968
Inflatable sofa by Quesar Khanh, 1969

1967 *Sergeant Pepper* album for the Beatles by Peter Blake and Ian Haworth; Hapshash and the Coloured Coat design poster for the UFO Club; Union Jack becomes pop icon

1968 the *White Album* by the Beatles by Richard Hamilton; *PH 5 Plexiglass* armchair by Peter Hoyte

1969 inflatable sofa with colored, gas-filled PVC by Quasar Kanh; armchair, table, and coat rack by **Allan Jones**; *Fur Chair* by **Roger Dean**

1970 *Here Tomorrow* exhibition with furniture prototype at the **Design Center**

1973 pop wastebasket by **Heal's**

ubiquitous object in teenagers' bedrooms and fashionable interiors. Terence Conran's newly formed **Habitat** stores sold inflatables and the **Hille** company produced a chair covered in synthetic fur, designed by Roger Dean.

Graphic design was inevitably touched by pop's impact in this fast-moving decade. Nowhere was this more apparent than in the area of record covers and other music-related fields, where a new freedom emerged. The fine artists, Peter Blake and Richard Hamilton, both worked on record covers for the Beatles—Blake creating the famous *Sergeant Pepper* album cover and Hamilton the "all-white" cover—and for a while it looked as if the barriers between the worlds of fine art and design were finally going to be broken in this revolution of youth.

The emergence of new music and dance clubs in London in the 1960s stimulated designs for posters and items of graphic ephemera that were all marked with the new spirit. In the second half of the decade a popular poster movement emerged. Designers such as Martin Sharp, who created the famous Bob Dylan poster image, and the Hapshash and the Colored Coat design team, consisting of Michael English and Nigel Waymouth, created vast numbers of drug-inspired, psychedelic posters that became familiar appendages of the everyday environment. In contrast to the hard-edged style of the early 1960s, the posters of 1966 onwards were much more backward-looking and nostalgic, influenced by a wide range of visual sources from Alphonse Mucha and Aubrey Beardsley to Red Indian and Buddhist imagery.

Pop design did not respect distinct media categories, however. Above all, it sought to unite the environment stylistically so that the dictates of utility were overruled by those of expression. In the first half of the 1960s, for example, images such as the flag and the target were applied to a vast range of goods, including mugs, carrier bags, clothing, and furniture. The image was deemed far more important than the object, and simple icons and bright, primary colors became messengers of the new lifestyle. The Union Jack became an ambivalent messenger at this time, however, standing both for Swinging London as an export and also as an anti-nationalistic gesture on the part of rebellious youth.

In the end, these subtleties were subsumed by the over-arching power of commerce and the dominance of style over everything else. On one level, pop design was highly influential both at home and abroad throughout the 1960s, but it can also be seen as a temporary commercial exercise, an attempt by manufacturers and retailers to appeal to the new youth market and to encourage it to part with its money, not just once but over and over again.

As the fashionableness or the physical properties of their purchases wore out. It was a victory for commercialism, using design to keep the flow of goods moving and the economy healthy. On another level, however, it represented a real liberation for designers. Trained as they were in the ideas of "form follows function," the philosophy of an earlier age, the invitation offered by pop culture to break the rules and evolve another approach in which expression was to the fore provided an opportunity to move toward a new definition of modern design. Pop design, seen from this perspective, made possible the shift from modernism to postmodernism in British design. The work of the British architectural group, **Archigram**, was seminal in this context. Although they were never realized in physical form, the ideas behind their comic-book–inspired visions, which were directly linked to pop culture, offered a new way forward.

"We live in a throw-away society. It is obviously absurd to burden things that have a short, useful life with eternal values."
Reyner Banham

Julian POWELL-TUCK

Interior Architect

Page 293
above: Metropolis Soundstudios, London, 1990
below: Lund Osler Knightsbridge London dental clinic by Angus Shepherd and Steve Gittner, 1998

When Beechwood Investment Holdings Ltd. wanted to make their **Arts and Crafts** house in London's Cheyne Walk into a single dwelling, it turned to the interior design team, Powell-Tuck Associates. The sensitivity needed to work on this interior, designed by **C.R. Ashbee**, was all too obvious. This was, however, an unusual project for Julian Powell-Tuck and his team, who work across a wide range of interior projects, most of them requiring a modern sensibility—from recording studios to dentists' surgeries, 1920s modern houses, loft conversions in New York City, and a graphic designer's studio in California. Since the beginning of the 1990s the team has undertaken projects such as these, applying the same level of design integrity to each one, however different.

Powell-Tuck, who was previously a director with Powell-Tuck, Connor and Orefelt Ltd., graduated from the environmental design course at the **Royal College of Art** in the mid-1970s and has been one of Britain's most consistently rigorous designers ever since. He has ventured into product design as well. Soon after graduating, he designed a wooden chair that had a strong postmodern feel to it. Since the early 1980s, the Concord Lighting Company has retained him as a consultant (he has the Myriad and Optics ranges to his name). Powell-Tuck's style is spare and modern, with a strong commitment to new materials.

POSSESSING A WELL FUNCTIONING MOUTH IS IMPORTANT BOT
SLIGHTLY UNDER HALF THE ADULT POPULATION REPORT THAT THEY HAVE NOT VISITED A DENTIST IN THE LAST SIX MONT
NEARLY ALL THE DEATHS OF ORAL HEALTH ARE THE RESULT OF LIFESTYLE, AND ARE MOSTLY AVO
IF PROPER CARE IS TAKEN OVER TEETH AND GUMS EVERYONE SHOULD EXPECT TO HAVE A HEALTHY

PRIESTMAN GOODE

Product Designer

Priestman Goode, London

1986 founded by **Paul Priestman** and **Nigel Goode**

1998 *IF Industriedesign* Prize for Hitachi video recorder

1998 *UK Millennium Product Award* for Hotspring Radiator (also receives awards in 1999 and 2000)

Products

1997 *Hotspring Radiator*, digital video camera for Vision; *Soft Fan* ventilator

1998 *Refrigerated Display Cabinet* for **Marks and Spencer**

1999 *Mobile Video Phone* for Orange; *Isascope* medical scanner for Astronmedica; West and Cross Country trains for Virgin

Page 295

top left: *Soft Fan* ventilator (prototype) by Paul Priestman, 1997

top right: *Mobile Video Phone* for Orange by Priestman Goode, 1999

bottom: West Coast high-speed trains for Virgin by Priestman Goode, 1999

Priestman Goode, the partnership of Paul Priestman and Nigel Goode, is among the most successful of the product and development design teams to have emerged in the mid-1980s. Priestman emerged in the early eighties from the **Royal College of Art**, designing a megaphone in his final year that won him a trip to Japan, while Goode graduated from Central St. Martins, having worked in the offices of Frazer Designers and Allied International. The pair has been responsible for a number of remarkable designs that are destined for a long life and which, while full to the brim with personality and humor, are well engineered and supremely functional at the same time. A case in point is a highly successful design of the mid-1990s, *Cactus*, an electric convection heater inspired by industrial elements seen in an Italian factory. *Bisque*, a hot spring radiator created a couple of years earlier, had the same combination of character and function and quickly became a favorite, earning the group a *Design Week* award. While large-scale international clients such as Hitachi keep the team going financially, it is the self-generated projects such as the *Soft Fan*, made of fabric, and the *Tamagochi Baby-sitter*, which hit the design press headlines. One of the most prestigious projects of recent years is the new fleet of West Coast and CrossCountry trains for Virgin. Priestman Goode has always been committed to working across a wide range—digital cameras, audio-visual equipment, domestic appliances, telecommunication products, aircraft seating, the car industry, retail products, stationery, and sporting goods. In their words, the company strives for "inspired effective design that has both wit and simplicity." Recently the duo has extended their activities and set up Plant, which they describe as "manufacture management."

PSION

Computer Manufacturer

1980 founded by David Potter
1982 production of *Hand-Computers* begins
1996 Exporter prize of the Year (also in 1997)
1999 *IF Design* prize for Series 5

Products
1984 organizer
1991 *Palmtop Series 3*
1997 *Palmtop Series 5*
1999 *Revo* organizer

This company specializes in making tiny computers. In England it is one of the infrequent examples of a congenial relationship between designers and producers. In the mid 1980's a collaboration was begun with Martin Riddiford, who at the time was still employed by Frazer. Riddiford is no design star but rather a consultant in the best British tradition. Psion's clientele still consist primarily of professionals who have today grown so accustomed to typically spare designs that it's easy to forget how innovative they were. When the company embarked on developing an electronic pocket calendar for people with complicated schedules, the software existed first—then came the name. Psion invented the jacket pocket sized *Organiser*, which was to replace another British invention which was enjoying great popularity at the time, the **Filofax** of leather and paper. A decisive step forward was the sophisticated hinge mechanism developed for *Series 3* models, resulting in a drastic reduction in size. *Series 5* went a step further: it was a miraculous thing with a drawing application, infrared communication via mobile phone and—perhaps the greatest advantage—a touch type keyboard and a touch-sensitive screen that make the many-faceted product run as fast as a real notebook.

All pictures are of the *Revo* organizer, 1999

For many people Britain is strongly associated with the various youth subcultures that emerged in the post-war period. The cultural influence of these groups has been enormous, affecting everything from music to design. Teddy boys, rockers, mods, hippies, and punks have all had a strong stylistic influence on British culture at large. Rooted in various different moments in pop music, they each evolved a manner of dress and a visual style that expressed their rebellious stances and helped to identify them. While rockers and hippies were strongly influenced by American subcultures, mods and punks were much more exclusively British. They have come to stand for one face of "Britishness," which is recognized internationally—the countercultural, anti-establishment force that accounts for much of the energy present in British design and culture over the last few decades.

The youth movement known as "Punk" emerged in the mid-1970s, hitting the media in a dramatic way in 1976. As usual, it came to the fore through pop music with groups such as the Sex Pistols and the Clash leading the way. From the start it was one of the most outrageous subcultures in terms of its language, dress, and gestures. It adopted a defiant, subversive and aggressive attitude toward the establishment, which was extremely shocking to many people, as it was intended to be. It first became visible in London, manifesting itself musically in certain clubs and in street fashion (or anti-fashion) worn by young, primarily working-class people who paraded their unconventional dress on the King's Road.

From the outset the Punk style was a mixture of individual customizing

and commercial manipulation. It was characterized by dyed hair in bright, luminous colors, shaved and sculpted heads, "Mohican" haircuts, tattooing and body piercing, torn and worn-out clothing often held together by safety pins, chains and other elements of bondage, synthetic materials such as black dustbin liner, and Doc Marten's boots. These items had become key elements of the punk uniform by the second half of the decade. They combined to create a strongly anti-commercial, anti-aesthetic, nongendered self-image. **Malcolm MacLaren** and **Vivienne Westwood**'s various retail outlets on King's Road catered for this new direction in dress from the mid-decade onwards. Pop groups such as the Sex Pistols wore T-shirts with huge tears and slogans scribbled across them, and torn trousers, the two legs held together by chains. The same imagery featured in punk graphic material such as fliers, album covers, and "fanzine," were created by a new generation of graphic designers. Notable among these were **Neville Brody**, **Peter Saville**, **Malcolm Garrett** and Barney Bubbles. Bubbles (formerly Colin Fucher) had been active within the "alternative" climate of the 1960s. His main contribution to punk was to include 1920s modernist imagery, thereby introducing a more self-conscious, self-referential note to the brash quality of punk. Punk regalia grew more and more extreme as it was personalized and moved into the 1980s, becoming a familiar sight in urban and suburban centers throughout Britain. It was a strong visual indicator of one part of a disenchanted youth culture, for whom personal display had taken over everything else.

"No other subculture shows more clearly how important theft and transformation are in the development of style."
Helen Rees

from left to right:
Buzzcocks record cover, *Another Music in a Different Kitchen* by Malcolm Garrett, 1978

Buzzcocks record cover, *A Different Kind of Tension* by Malcolm Garrett, 1979

Fac2 record cover, *A Factory Sample* by Peter Seville, 1978

Sid Vicious, guitarist for the group Sex Pistols (pictures from the punk fanzine *Scum*), 1977

Cover for the magazine *The Face* by Neville Brody, 1986

Mary QUANT
Fashion Design

Mary Quant was the best-known and the most influential of the British fashion designers to emerge in the 1960s in the context of pop culture. She made the miniskirt popular and invented the "Swinging London," "dolly bird" look, which was essentially young, free, playful, and modern. With her businessman partner/husband, Alexander Plunkett-Greene, she designed huge numbers of clothing items and created a successful retail outlet, Bazaar, which was the model for the sixties "fashion boutique" that marked London out as a retail fashion center in this energetic decade.

Quant opened her first retail outlet on London's King's Road in the heart of Chelsea and "Swinging London." She later opened a second Bazaar boutique in Knightsbridge, designed by **Terence Conran**. From the start, she presented a new image of fashion that appealed to a younger, more independent consumer than had existed before. The previous generation had worshipped French haute couture and favored a "grown-up," sophisticated look. Quant, in contrast, wanted to make shopping for clothes enjoyable and kept the boutiques open late so that people could shop in the evening. She adopted a simplified black daisy motif as her logo, in keeping with the stark black-and-white "Op" imagery that was so popular in that period.

It was soon applied to a wide range of merchandise, including dress, accessories, tights, etc., and eventually to make-up which she still produces today in large quantities. Quant's most lasting contribution to British 1960s culture was the miniskirt. Worn with tights—essential accessories as skirts got shorter and shorter—it provided a completely new look. It was compatible with the dominant image of the flat-chested, tall, skinny-legged, pre-pubescent girl-child featured in fashion magazines at the time.

Many of Quant's early garments were childlike in nature, including dungarees, pinafore dresses, tunics, and an outfit for rainy weather called Christopher Robin after A.A. Milne's children's book character. One

Page 301
left: collection, 1963
top right: collection, 1964
bottom right: dress *banana split,* 1967

Products

Page 303
left: collection, 1965
top right: collection, 1966
bottom right: cosmetics, 1965

pinstriped pinafore was named, playfully, Bank of England. Quant essentially created outfits in which girls could play at "dressing up," taking on a new identity for as long as it appealed to them. In photographs, the poses of her models were playful and active, many of them leaping into the air for joy. In spite of the young image she conveyed her clothes were still relatively expensive, appealing to the more affluent of the new young consumers. Barbara Hulanicki's BIBA catered, in contrast, to a less affluent audience.

Quant's lasting influence was to free women from the constraints of tiny, nipped-in waists and the need to be corseted. The look she created went perfectly with the short geometric hairstyle created by Vidal Sassoon, and with the heavily emphasized eyes of the period. It was a look London exported internationally in the 1960s, earning it a reputation for fashion design that it had not experienced before. It was also a look that Quant sported herself. She can be seen, in fact, as an example of a designer, like **William Morris** earlier and **Terence Conran** currently, who designed like she did because there was nothing available on the marketplace that she could find to buy for herself.

In the early 1960s the success of Bazaar encouraged Quant to expand and through the creation of her company, the Ginger Group, she began to distribute her designs widely. Her empire grew through the sixties, and her successful foray into makeup brought her more international recognition. Japan was especially responsive to her message, and she now has a chain of retail outlets there and is hugely admired.

Queensbury Hunt Levien,
London

1966 founded by David
Queensberry and Martin
Hunt

1977 Robin Levien becomes
partner; *Design Council
Award*

1983 Martin Hunt becomes the
Royal Designer for Industry

1987 *BBC Design Award*

Products

1976 *Concept* tableware for
Hornsea Pottery

1981 *Trend* tableware for Thomas

1987 *Trend* cutlery and *Studio*
bathroom for Ideal
Standard, United States

1988 portable telephone for
British Telecom and vase
for Mikasa

1989 *Tournee* porcelain for
Thomas and *Domi*
bathroom faucet for Ideal
Standard

1990 *Rondo* bath series

1998 *Space* bath series for Ideal
Standard

Rondo bathtub, 1990

Page 305
top: *Domi* bathroom faucet, 1989
bottom: *Space* washbasin series,
1998
all by Robin Levien for Ideal
Standard

"The craft approach to design is highly relevant to the ever more technical world we live in." So wrote Robin Levien, a partner in the English design consultancy, Queensbury Hunt Levien, one of the few to have been going since the mid-1960s and to be as much in demand as ever. The success of the group lies in its distinctive contribution to modern British design. All three of the group's prime movers—David Queensbury, Martin Hunt, and Robin Levien—have their backgrounds in the traditional materials of ceramics and glass and, while they are all deeply committed to mass production and industrial manufacture, they retain something of the craft ethic in all their projects. Thus their designs for ceramic and porcelain tableware items for the German company, Thomas China, and others, are a result of their belief in a soft, elegant aesthetic that has its roots more in the Scandinavian design ideals of the 1950s and 1960s than in the mechanistic approach of more technocratic cultures. This softness is extended to more functional items such as bathroom furniture and taps, designed for Ideal Standard, as well as to more overtly technological projects such as their proposal for a portable telephone for British Telecom in the late 1980s. One of their most long-lasting designs is the *Concept* tableware for Hornsea Pottery, first created in the mid-1970s, which has become a classic item of British design.

Ernest RACE

Furniture Designer

1914 born in Newcastle

1935 graduates from the Bartlett School of Architecture, London

1945 founds Ernest Race Ltd. (until 1954)

1964 dies

Products

1945 *BA Chair* (1991 newly introduced)

1948 stacking stools

1951 *Springbok Chair* and *Antelope Chair* made of plywood and steel pipe

1953 *Steamer Chair* made of laminate birch tree

1957 *Heron* armchair

1961 *Shoppery Range* cushioned furniture

In the 1950s Ernest Race was one of a number of British designers to gain international recognition for their achievements. His reputation is based on his designs for three highly innovative chairs, firstly the aluminum-framed *BA* chair, designed just after the war—a strikingly novel little chair that was well received at the *Britain Can Make It* exhibition—and secondly two chairs made of steel rod—*Springbok* and *Antelope*—created for the Festival of Britain. They all captured the modernistic mood of the moment and are still admired as icons from that optimistic moment in the story of modern British design.

Race not only created innovative forms for furniture and exploited the possibilities of new materials, he also succeeded in bringing his designs to manufacture. Through Ernest Race Limited, which he created with an engineering colleague, J.W. Noel Jordon, at the end of the war, Race was able to bring his ideas to the marketplace. He was a director for a decade and then continued to work for the company on a freelance basis until his death. His designs remain of interest today and are collectors' items. The *BA* chair has recently been put back into production.

Steamer Chair (Neptune), 1953

Page 307
top: table and stool, 1955
bottom left: *Springbok Chair*, 1951
bottom right: folding chair, 1961

Jamie REID

Graphic Design

1940 born in Great Britain

1962 studies at the Wimbledon Art School (from 1964 on at the Croydon Art School)

1970 cofounded the magazine *The Suburban Press*

1979 art director for the movie *The Great Rock 'n' Roll Swindle*

1980 works in Paris (until 1982)

1986 retrospective solo exhibition *Chaos in Cancerland* in London

Products

1973 stickers for *Suburban Press*

1974 publisher for the *Suburban Press Poster Book*

1976 graphic for the group Sex Pistols

1977 record cover *Pretty Vacant* and *God Save the Queen*

1978 graphics for the group Dead Kennedys

Page 309
Record cover for the Sex Pistols, *God Save the Queen*, 1977

Jamie Reid is widely acknowledged to be **Punk**'s most significant graphic designer. The combination of his anarchic approach to life, his highly original eye, and his ability to draw inspiration from a wide range of popular sources—such as ransom notes, graffiti, and other forms of "ready-made" material—and his use of overtly "shocking" images and language brought into being a whole new, and highly subversive, approach to graphics, which is still being felt today in young British graphic design. Reid trained at Croydon Art School in the 1960s (with the guru of punk, **Malcolm MacLaren**), where he set up a paper called *The Suburban Press*, whose use of cut-out lettering, torn paper, and recycled material sowed the seeds for his later work. He began his professional career working with independent record companies and creating fanzines for punk events. He is best known, however, for his designs of the mid-1970s for the Sex Pistols group's promotional material. Best known of all, perhaps, is an image with a safety-pin stuck through the Queen of England. The Royal Jubilee of the late 1970s provided an opportunity for his anarchism and anti-royalism to express itself fully in his work, and his *God Save the Queen* record cover for the Sex Pistols was among the most successful of his ironic images produced in that decade.

Above all, Reid managed to make graphic design available to many. As Catherine McDermott explained, "All you needed was a newspaper, some scissors, and possibly, a bit later on, an airbrush." After the demise of punk at the end of the 1970s, Reid moved into the area of film. His contribution to contemporary graphic design was recognized in an exhibition at London's Hamilton Gallery in the mid-1980s.

GOD Save THE QUEEN

Sex PisTOls

RETAIL DESIGN

For centuries Britain has been known as a "nation of shopkeepers" and it has maintained that reputation in recent years. Indeed as British manufacturing has gone into decline, so the country's retail sector goes from strength to strength. Many of the innovations of the 1980s that were recognized abroad were in the area of retail design, with consultancies such as **Fitch** & Co., **David Davies**, and **Din Associates** making big breakthroughs with the interiors of lifestyle retail outlets such as Next and **Habitat**.

Before that, however, Britain had also led the way in the area of supermarket and chain-store design. It had played a key role in the move away from the independent stores and department stores, and in the introduction of corporate identity in the context of retail. With the advent of self-service in the 1960s, the Sainsbury's supermarket chain pioneered the idea of having a consistent design policy and a unified approach toward branding and packaging design. The **Marks & Spencer** chain was also aware of this at a relatively early stage, conscious that visual consistency was important. In the 1960s, the chain store idea of integrated design was becoming visible little by little in a few groups such as Boots, W.H. Smith, and Dixons. They had not yet extended into the idea of lifestyle (that came in the 1980s), although the pioneering work of **Terence Conran**, whose first Habitat store opened in 1964, was nearly two decades ahead of its time.

The big breakthrough in lifestyle retailing in Britain came in the 1980s. It was encouraged by the consumer boom of that decade and responded to the needs of expanding customer demand. Following the model provided by

Conran, a number of stores brought in designers to create their interior environments. George Davies's Next store was a guiding light in this respect. A fashion store in essence, it expanded to offer interior furnishings as well.

David Davies worked on some of the early stores, and Din Associates's Next stores were among the most sophisticated and seductive of the interiors commissioned by the chain. The other groupings of stores developed during this decade that took the lifestyle concept to an extreme were those owned by the Moroccan, Joseph Ettedgui. Using **Eva Jiricna** for a number of his outlets and the architect **Norman Foster** for his fashion flagship on London's Sloane Street, Joseph created a sophisticated, high-tech look for his stores. Like Davies, he moved from fashion to interiors and on to restaurants, taking his sophisticated clientele along with him. The pioneering work of Ettedgui in his upmarket stores and of Terence Conran quickly trickled down to the High Street. Conran expanded his retail empire through the 1980s, taking over the children's clothing outlet, Mothercare, and the chain store, British Home Stores. His expansion was too rapid, however, and he had to take time out at the end of the decade before refocusing his attention, and his meticulous eye, on restaurants.

Few retail outlets, whether in the urban centers of Britain or in suburban High Streets, have remained unaffected by the lifestyle design revolution of the 1980s. Its influence can be found everywhere and its creators are in demand internationally.

"Shopping is like a never-ending cocktail party."
Mary Quant

from left to right:
Peter Robinson's Oxford Circus, 1953
Display case for the Swatch Timeshop, New York, by Daniel Weil, 1996
Nicole Farhi Showroom, London, by DIN Associates, 1994
Entrance of Next Dept. X, London by DIN Associates, 1988

ROVER

Automobile Manufacturer

Page 313
top: *Rover P5*, 1959
bottom: *Rover 75*, 1999

The Rover company once stood for the concepts of quality and class that were the lasting characteristic features of British car design. Unlike Italian cars, which have a reputation for stylishness and flair, and Germany's reputation for high-quality engineering, Rover's leather upholstery and walnut veneers evoke a commitment to tradition and craftsmanship, which put these cars into a league of their own.

The Rover name was first used two centuries ago in the context of bicycle manufacture. The company turned to cars in the early years of the twentieth century, producing an eight-horsepower model. From the 1920s it moved into the area of high-quality, middle-class cars that conveyed an air of luxury linked with the traditional arena of the "gentlemen's club." The solid, pressed-steel coachwork, combined with the use of wood trimming and leather, created a lasting image of "Britishness." The basic, solid form of the Rover sedan cars developed in the second half of the 1940s remained in place until the 1960s, earning the company a reputation for sturdy cars aimed at the well-to-do businessman. The two-litre *P6 2000* created for the executive market in the early 1960s remains an icon of British middle-class culture. Designed by a member of the family that owned Rover, Peter Wilks, it continued the spirit of "Britishness" which, with the expansion of pop, was fast disappearing. Although Rover was bought by British Leyland five years after the launch of the 2000, it remained in production for almost a decade.

In addition to its famous sedan cars, the Rover company was also responsible for one of Britain's most lasting icons in this field, the 4x4 Land Rover, which was launched three years after the end of the war. The raw, utilitarian character of this model caught the imagination of many and became closely associated with the idea of rural Britishness. It was created by Maurice Wilks, the owner of the company, because he felt angry about having to use a Jeep, an American design, when he was driving across the fields of his country estate. He was determined that there should be a British-

Products

bottom: Land Rover,
Freelander, 1998

Page 315
top: Land Rover *Defender TD5 110*,
1999
bottom: Land Rover *Discovery*, 1999

made car that could be used in this context, and he commissioned a design from Gordon Bashford. The result was a car with a military appearance for use in peacetime. The rugged image of Land Rover gave it an instant appeal in rural settings, and its popularity soon transferred to the urban context as well. By the 1980s it had acquired a level of urban chic that Wilks could never have anticipated. The basic Land Rover was joined, in the mid-1970s, by the much more stylish 4x4 Range Rover, which rapidly became a powerful status symbol both in the country and in the city.

In the 1970s Rover ceased to be the British company that it had always been and entered a new phase of its history. At first it was linked with the Japanese company Honda but in the mid-1990s it was taken over by the German company BMW. In 1998 came the launch of the model *75*, which succeeded, to some extent, in reclaiming the earlier reputation for the name of Rover and linked it once again with the ideas of solidity and quality. Words such as *stately* and *understated* were used by critics, echoing the acclaim expressed four decades earlier. But it was too little, too late, and in spring 2000 this once-great British company finally closed. The more lucrative Land Rover name was sold to the Ford car company.

Gordon RUSSELL

Furniture and Product Designer

1892 born in Cricklewood
1906 works in his father's restoration workshop
1910 first furniture designs
1922 furniture exhibited in Cheltenham
1927 founds Gordon Russell Ltd.
1929 first mass-produced dining room furniture in Great Britain
1939 participates in "Utility Scheme," the Government's furniture program
1947 becomes director of the Council of Industrial Design
1980 dies

Products
1924 reading lamp
1926 *Tallboy* closet
1934 *Cabinet* radio
1942 apartment designed for Utility Lines Furniture

Page 317
Cabinet radio, 1934

Of the handful of key establishment figures who were influential in British design in the twentieth century, the name of Gordon Russell stands out for at least three reasons. First, he was active as a furniture maker and designer through his firm, Gordon Russell Ltd., in the Cotswolds in the first half of the century, and was an important advocate of the idea of "truth to materials" that had been promoted by the **Arts and Crafts Movement** a century earlier; secondly, he was in charge of the Utility Furniture scheme during World War II, which facilitated the manufacture of a restricted range of well-designed, functional, standardized pieces; and thirdly, he headed the Council of Industrial Design, an offshoot of the Board of Trade established to control standards in British design and encourage exports, soon after it was set up in 1944. He was also the first editor of *Design* magazine when it was launched five years later. In all these capacities, he was a highly influential figure and was well-known abroad. His high-minded yet conservative approach characterized the image of British design that dominated at least until the 1940s. At the same time he was not against mechanization, and in many ways in his formulation of what he called "good design," he helped design in Britain to move away from the backward-looking nineteenth century and into the twentieth century.

Peter SAVILLE

Graphic Designer

1955 born in Manchester

1976 cofounder of the record label Factory Records

1983 Peter Saville Associates in London founded

1990 works for **Pentagram** (until 1996)

Products

1978 *Unknown Pleasures* cover for Joy Division (1989 *Substance*)

1980 *Thieves Like Us* cover for New Order (1981 *Ceremony*, 1985 *Low Life*)

1980 *Orchestral Manoeuvres in the Dark* cover for Dindisc (with **Ben Kelly**)

1987 program and posters for the Whitechapel Gallery

1989 posters for the New Order, United States tour and commercial for Yohji Yamamoto

Page 319

top left: New Order's *True Faith* cover, 1987

top right: Joy Division's *Unknown Pleasures* cover, 1978

bottom: *Orchestral Manoeuvres in the Dark cover*, 1980

New Order's *Ceremony* cover, 1981

This often-decorated image designer created campaigns for fashion houses of renown such as Christian Dior, Yohji Yamamoto, Jil Sander, **John Galliano**, Hugo Boss and **Vivienne Westwood**. Temples of culture like London's famous Whitechapel Gallery or the Centre Pompidou in Paris also enlisted his services. But for his most noted campaign, Peter Saville had no employer: he invented the "corporate identity" of British Pop music. To the point, he founded the Factory Records label in Manchester, and its cult bands Joy Division and New Order, for which he created a total graphic identity from covers to T-shirts. Subsequently he became Art Director at Virgin subsidiary Dindisc Records before founding Peter Saville Associates in the mid 1980's together with typographer Brett Wickens. In the early 1990's the stylist of pop culture switched to **Pentagram**, a major agency, and participated in the rejuvenation of such venerable institutions as the Natural History Museum (with architect David Chipperfield) as well as the visual identity of television station Channel One in Los Angeles. In the meantime, CI expert Saville offers his graphic services as a free-lance consultant.

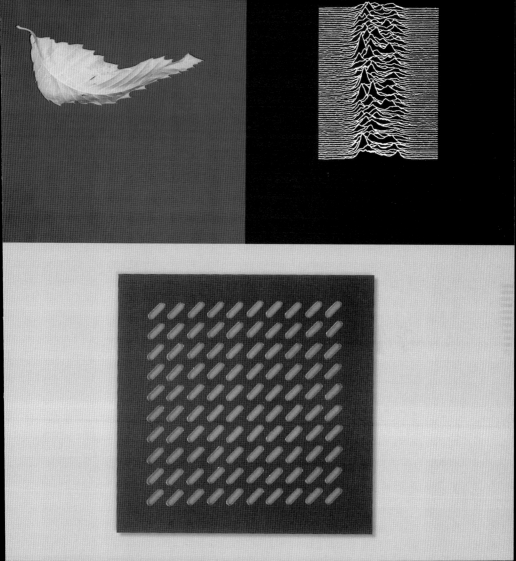

SCP

Furniture Manufacturer

SCP Ltd., London

1986 founded by Sheridan Coakley; first presentation at the Milan Furniture Fair

1992 receives first public orders

1998 expansion of the showrooms on Curtain Road

Products

1984 Side Table by **Jasper Morrison**

1986 Bow shelf by **Matthew Hilton**

1988 sofa by Jasper Morrison

1989 Flipper table

1991 Club Armchair; armchair with Balzac foot rest

1995 Reading Chair all by Matthew Hilton; Analogue wall clock by **Konstantin Grcic**

1997 Woodgate sofa system by **Terence Woodgate**

1998 Hoop sofa by **Tom Dixon**

1999 Stafford armchair by Andrew Stafford

One of the most important factors behind the strong international profile of many of Britain's innovative furniture designers since the mid-1980s has been the role that the small furniture company SCP has played in supporting and promoting them, and in making their products available. Without SCP, there is no question that **Jasper Morrison**, **Matthew Hilton**, **Michael Marriott**, Terence Woodgate, **James Irvine**, **Geoff Hollington**, **Konstantin Grcic**, and others would have found it much harder to address the right audience and to be heralded as quickly as they were.

Coakley began his career in Notting Hill, in west London, dealing in twentieth-century furniture and manufacturing early modern classics. He has played this unprecedented role by selecting a stable of young designers whom he believes are creating "contemporary classics" that are not governed by the whims of fashion. He has a highly discerning eye and has been quick to realize the potential of several young designers before

anybody else. He established a showroom at 135-139 Curtain Road, in London's East End, in the mid-1980s, and dedicated its first show to the work of the French designer, Philippe Starck, whose designs Coakley was the first to import into England. This was followed by the manufacture of a collection of work by Morrison and Hilton, which was shown at the Milan Furniture Fair a year later and received with much acclaim. Production of pieces by these two designers was quickly followed by items by **Nigel Coates**, another member of the generation of designers to benefit from Coakley's support.

Coakley's strategies have been consistently long-term in intention. He has always been more interested in taking on a small group of designers whose work he considers to have lasting qualities, than taking on a larger number whose popularity may be fleeting. In the early 1990s, SCP moved into the arena of furniture for public spaces, and later began to display pieces by other European manufacturers.

from left to right:

Hoop couch by Tom Dixon, 1998

Reading Chair by Matthew Hilton, 1995

Analogue clock by Konstantin Grcic, 1995

SEYMOUR POWELL

Studio for Product Design

1984 founded by **Richard Seymour** and **Dick Powell**

1990 Design Week Award for *Norton F1* motorcycle

1991 *D&AD Silver Award* for the *Technophone* telephone

1994 *BBC Design Award* for *MZ Skorpion* motorcycle

1998 **Richard Seymour** becomes president of the D&AD Association

Products

1986 wireless water boiler for Tefal

1987 hair dryer for Clairol

1994 *Bantam* motorcycle for BSA

1999 *Designs on Your...* was broadcast

Page 323
top left: *Acadamy* faucet for Ideal Standard, 1998
top right: *Esterna* wristwatch for Casio, 1998
bottom: *BSA Bantam*, 1994

Sports cameras
for Minolta, 1996

Seymour Powell is one of Britain's most successful design partnerships. The combined talents of **Richard Seymour**, who began his professional life in advertising, and **Dick Powell**, who was trained as a product designer, have resulted in a plethora of designed goods—hair dryers, kettles, guitars, radios, lawnmowers, and motorcycles—that have had a significant impact on the everyday environment. The group numbers about twenty-six people and works from The Chapel studio in west London. Since the mid-1980s, when the partnership was first formed, it has helped change the image of British product design in foreign eyes. The sleek, "high-tech," modern forms of the body shells developed for the wide range of goods that the team has created compete favorably with those from Germany, Japan, and elsewhere. Indeed some of Seymour Powell's most notable designs—the *Freeline 1* cordless kettle for the French company, Tefal; radios for Philips in Holland; and lawnmowers for the Japanese firm, Yamaha—have been commissioned by foreign manufacturers.

As well as producing innovative and important designs, Seymour and Powell have as individuals played a key role in the world of British design culture in general. Both have been involved with journalism and broadcasting. Most recently, they appeared on a series of TV programs entitled *Designs on Your...* which looked, in turn, at the issues involved in designing a bra, a toilet, and an electric car.

Paul SMITH

Fashion Designer

Page 325
Spring collection, 1999

The first thing the fashion designer and retailer, Paul Smith, ever sold was a Union Jack handkerchief. As an object that evoked a national past but was also a key symbol of contemporary British pop culture, it was a sign of things to come. The contribution that Paul Smith has made to British contemporary culture is much more than that of a fashion designer. By combining British male sartorial tradition with a new approach toward clothes that has a worldwide appeal, especially in Japan, he has become a symbol of the new British look of the last two decades.

He has achieved this by paying attention to the fabric, color, and structure of conventional items such as suits, shirts, and ties, giving a new twist to old themes. Smith's eye for quality and his ability to create a bridge between the conventional and the new is not restricted to clothes, but evokes a complete lifestyle. In the early 1970s, for instance, he sold "classic" objects such as traditional fountain pens, old enamel toys and leather-bound **Filofax** personal organizers, as well as men's clothing, from his Covent Garden shop, demonstrating his total commitment to the way in which the best of the old can be adapted to the demands of contemporary life. It was a vision that appealed — and continues to appeal — to many people in Britain and elsewhere.

Smith did not come from the usual fashion designer background but has his roots in manufacturing and retail. He set up his first shop in Nottingham in 1970, selling designer clothes as well as garments he had made himself. His clothes appealed to young men who were seeking something different but not too excessive or flamboyant. His suits were well-tailored and used interesting fabrics in unexpected ways, and appealed to a market of young professional men who wanted to be both smart and fashionable at work and at play. A few years later he had come a long way and was showing his first collection of menswear in Paris. From the mid-1970s onwards British male

Products

1976 Paul Smith men's collection introduced

1986 cosmetic line introduced

1990 Paul Smith for children introduced

1993 R. Newbold collection introduced ("traditional styles with a modern twist")

1994 Paul Smith women, Paul Smith eyeglass collection, Paul Smith watch (under license), Paul Smith bag (under license) introduced

2000 *Small World* collection

Page 327

left: *Small World* collection, 2000

top right: *Jaguar* and *Shannon* shoe collection

bottom right: Thomas Goode

fashion went from strength to strength, with Paul Smith playing a key role within the growth industry. By 1983 the way had been prepared for an English Menswear Designer Collection in Paris, in which Smith played a key role. He was joined by more recent arrivals on the scene, among them Scot Crolla, a member of what was called at the time the "Peacock" movement in men's clothing. His use of decorated fabrics, such as one with a traditional rose pattern on it, showed that male clothing had taken a new turn. In line with Paul Smith's approach, however, it paid as much attention to tradition as it did to innovation.

Through the 1980s and '90s, although it grew significantly in size and the area around it has become much more fashionable, Smith has continued to use his Covent Garden shop as a retail base in England. He has recently opened a second shop in London's Notting Hill. The size of his manufacturing and export operation has expanded enormously, however, from his early Nottingham days and Smith himself has become a key figure in British design culture. A recent exhibition of his work at the **Design Museum** showed just how important a part he has played in the growth of international understanding of modern British design.

Smith's understated, well-made approach toward male clothing was extended into the feminine sphere a few years ago. The suits and other articles of clothing he creates for women are androgynous in nature, reflecting the same interest in traditional materials—wools with checked patterns, classic gray wool flannel, etc.—and good cut as in his men's clothes. It is a smart look that appeals to professional women and has been extremely successful.

Michael SODEAU

Furniture and Product Designer

1969 born in London

1995 cofounder of **Inflate**

1997 leaves Inflate and founds Michael Sodeau Partnership with Lisa Giuliani

Products

1997 *Satellite* end table; *Charlie* for Asplund carpet

1998 *Macassar* fabric; woven lights; *Single* and *Twin* vases

1999 *Duo* shelf

Michael Sodeau is one of the most exciting designers to have emerged in London in the 1990s. After graduating in product design from London's Central St. Martins, he went on to form **Inflate**—a company that made its reputation through the design and production of a wide range of inflatable goods—with three partners. After three years he left to form his own design studio, the Michael Sodeau Partnership, with Lisa Giuliani. Their first collection, entitled Comfortable Living, consisted of woven cane lights, ceramic homeware, tables, rugs, and a lounge chair, and was received with rapturous applause. Sodeau has a strongly materials-based approach to design, which is also committed to organic forms and natural colors. Rosewood and aluminum are combined in his Satellite side tables, and his use of woven cane to create modern sculptural forms in his designs for lights has suggested a wholly new aesthetic for the 1990s. Ceramics are used for his vases and ashtray. His rugs take their patterns from the cane and ceramic objects, showing Sodeau's commitment to the sensory wholeness of any environment.

Page 329

top: *Satellite* end table, 1997

bottom left: woven lights, 1998

bottom right: *Single* and *Twin* vase, 1998

Charlie for Asplund carpet, 1997

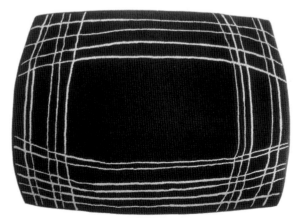

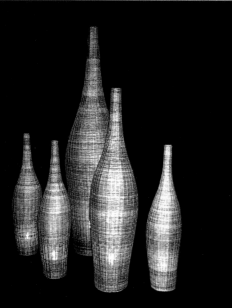

One of the most notable characteristics of post-war British design has been its strong relationship with youth subcultures. The term "street style" describes the way in which imagery and ideas from within subcultures are appropriated by the design profession, and transformed into designs that then enter into mainstream culture. This interaction first flourished in the 1960s, when ideas emanating from pop culture filtered through into the work of designers looking for a way out of the impasse of "good taste." The "throwaway" chairs of furniture designer Peter Murdoch, and the ideas of the architectural visionary group **Archigram**, which drew heavily upon comic-book imagery, were examples of this process.

The dissemination of images through the mass media has become quicker and quicker, making it increasingly difficult to say where new ideas and styles come from. It is a circular process in which subcultural consumers and customizers are constantly sending messages to designers and vice versa.

The punk movement of the mid-1970s showed that street style was something that designers could offer to members of a subculture, as well as the other way round. **Punk** culture found its way into a number of other design areas, especially graphics. The main demand was for record covers and ephemeral notices advertising the appearances of punk bands. Several designers started out in punk but later moved into a more mainstream context.

The links between art schools and pop music had been in place since the 1960s and they became strong once again in the late 1970s. Trained graphic designers such as Jamie Reid identified with the anarchic tendencies of punk, seeing it as an opportunity to break all the rules and to experiment freely. Their work was produced rapidly and intended for the street rather than for the art gallery or museum. Inevitably, however, it ended up in museums as mainstream culture struggled to keep up with the level of experimentation that was going on at "street" level.

The fanzine was another major achievement of the punk movement. Many came and went but the most notable one was *Sniffin' Glue*, which only lasted for twelve issues in the mid-1970s. The raw appearance of its photocopied sheets, with graffiti-style scribble and tears, summed up the anarchic face of street style and, simultaneously, transformed British graphic design beyond all recognition.

Other graphic designers to emerge at this moment of radical change included **Neville Brody**, Barney Bubbles (whose career was cut short by his suicide in 1983), **Peter Saville**, and **Malcolm Garrett**. The record company, Stiff records, was responsible for commissioning work from several of them at one time or another, and for encouraging their innovative proposals. Illustration, photography, and typography were brought together in highly original ways in the service of the young generation for whom these images were intended.

from left to right:
Bob Marley, London, 1980
Mod (revival), Kensington Market, 1980
Commercial for Doc. Martens shoes, 1981
Punk, 1978
I-D magazine, 1991

1974 the group Sex Pistols is founded

1976 **Punk** spreads in the London Underground; the fanzine *Sniffin' Glue* is published

1977 **Ben Kelly** designs Paul Howies Shop in Covent Garden, London

1980 the magazine *i-D* is published; the first concert by Bob Marley in London; the first New Romantic Clubs

1981 Vivienne Westwood presents the collection *Savage*; **Neville Brody** becomes art director of *The Face*

1982 **Powell-Tuck**, Connor, and Orefelt design the apartment of Adam Ant; Skinheads and Doc. Marten shoes brand come into fashion

1985 *Gamma City* exhibition of the group NATO

1989 Camden Market in London becomes a flea market of styles; House Nights in Fridge Club, London

1993 Apache Indian releases his first album

By the early 1980s, it was clear that a new British design movement had been born from the punk explosion. Not only graphic designers but fashion , furniture, and interior designers had responded to the new sensibility that had risen to the surface. The style magazines, *i-D*, established by Terry Jones, and *The Face*, which made Brody, its art director, internationally renowned almost overnight, served the function of coordinating the various design media and presenting a unified lifestyle-oriented vision to their readers. Characteristically, the designs that were produced were linked to the leisure requirements of youth, such as the interior of the Hacienda club designed by Ben Kelly in Manchester, which translated the familiar signs of post-punk graphics into three dimensions. The same applied to the shop fronts and domestic interiors that Powell-Tuck, Connor, and Orefelt created, for example, for the punk shop Seditionaries and a flat for Marco Pirroni. The work of the architect/designers **Ron Arad** and the NATO group (from which **Nigel Coates** emerged) derived from the same energy and sense of rebelliousness. The imaginative possibilities were endless and young British design became revitalized and recognized as such internationally.

An exhibition in Rotterdam held in the late 1980s bore witness to this new phenomenon, although by that time it was clear that the initial impetus provided by Punk had given way to a much more sophisticated art-school awareness that had moved street style once and for all away from the street and into the gallery. Nonetheless, the inspiration that had derived from the punk movement remained an important catalyst in reinforcing the important role that subculture has played in the most innovative achievements of British design over the past few decades.

"All the designer can do is to predict when the people notice that what they have is boring. It is simply a matter of becoming the first to be bored."

Mary Quant

"Skinheads wouldn't exist without the culture from Jamaica."

Roddy Moreno

Gerald SUMMERS

Product Designer

1899 born in Great Britain
1931 founds Makers of Simple
Furniture (until 1940)
1967 dies

Products
1934 armchair made of plywood
and chair with high back
1935 beds, tables, tea trolley,
and vases

Gerald Summers is one of Britain's modernist furniture designers of the 1930s whose work reaches high prices in auctions today. It is widely respected for its geometric simplicity and its commitment to a new, modern aesthetic. Typical of British design of that era, his pieces are executed in bent plywood rather than metal, thereby expressing a level of conservatism that runs through so much British design in the twentieth century. Summers founded his firm, Makers of Simple Furniture, in the early 1930s. He lacked the ability to promote himself as effectively as many of his contemporaries, and as a result not many of his designs were realized. Those that were included tables, beds, chairs, coffee tables, and some pieces of children's furniture. Summers was among the first to use bent plywood in Britain and created a stunning lounge chair from this material, which ranks as one of the "classic" British designs between the two world wars. His round coffee tables were exercises in geometric form, with their flat legs intersecting the curve of the top. He has been compared to Marcel Breuer and Alvar Aalto.

Page 335
Armchair, 1934

Cupboard, 1933

TIMNEY-FOWLER
Textile Manufacturer

Timney-Fowler Ltd.

1979 founded by Susan Timney and Grahame Fowler

1980 enter the Japanese market with graphic works

1983 started producing its own range of interior furnishings

1990 work for **Wedgwood**

1993 studio in West London opens

1994 textile consulting (with SR Gent) for **Marks and Spencer**

Products

1993 Produced prints and garments for Paul McCartney world tour

Textile design has played an important role at the innovative end of British design in the last two decades. One of the most notable examples in this area is the firm of Timney-Fowler, which started out as a textile-printing company in the late 1970s. It was formed by Susan Timney and Grahame Fowler, who studied together at the **Royal College of Art** in the latter half of the 1970s. They realized that there was a gap in the market for innovative fabric designs. Their work combines innovation with a feeling for the past, and a strong spirit of faded antiquarianism inspires their work. As one of their current brochures explains, "Architectural details and hand-drawn elements of nature combine with chalky colors to create a mood of antique cloth dusted with color."

The striking black-and-white patterns and extensive use of classical imagery, which characterized their early designs quickly became very popular, especially in Japan where the firm received orders from the fashion designers, Issey Miyake and Yohji Yamamoto. This rapid acceptance by the avant-garde fashion industry expanded through the 1980s, with links also established with Calvin Klein in the United States. At the end of the decade, Timney-Fowler began to manufacture fashion items itself, producing scarves, shirts, ties, and T-shirts made from their fabrics. Color was added to the original black-and-white palette.

In the early 1990s Timney-Fowler branched out into furnishing fabrics and wallpapers, rapidly gaining an enthusiastic following for them. Their impact on the fashionable British domestic interior was considerable and was reinforced when the company began to design products as well. A contract with **Wedgwood** took them into the area of table and gift wares. They consolidated their efforts with designs for jewelry. Their decorative stamp upon a whole range of surfaces and artifacts was recognized both at home and abroad by the mid-1990s.

Page 337
all illustrations:
Neoclassical collection, 1999

TKO Design, Clerkenwell

1988 TKO in London by Anne Gardiner and Andy Davey founded

1994 Commissioned to redesign what becomes the *Freeplay* radio

1996 *Freeplay* radio wins a *BBC Design Award* for Best Product

1996 Andey Davey becomes *Designer of the Year*

Products

1989 *Taurus* digital telephone

1991 *Submarine* portable CD-player for Sony

1995 *New Wave* microwave for Sanyo; typewriters for Hasbro

1996 *Freeplay* travel radio; *Crystal Mu* lighting

1997 Hasbro's *Deamphine*

1998 *Inca Microanalysis* lab equipment for Oxford Instr.

Page 339

top left: *Crystal Mu* lighting

top right: *Freeplay* travel radio, 1996

bottom left: *Titan* washing machine, 1999

bottom right: *Inca Microanalysis* lab equipment, 1998

Jewelry case for DeBeers, 1999

TKO, although small in size, is one of Britain's most successful design consultancies in the area of high-technology goods and services. It was formed in the late 1980s when the group's partners, Andy Davey and Anne Gardiner, graduated from the **Royal College of Art**. It has achieved its international reputation in a number of ways. In the mid-1990s, for instance, TKO won a **BBC** Design Award for the design of the Freeplay radio, a wind-up machine created by inventor Trevor Baylis for the developing world where batteries are in short supply. Davey gave it an appearance that was neither excessively stylish nor amateurish. He succeeded in creating a functional-looking machine that still had an element of Western appeal. Japan has also bestowed awards upon TKO, recognizing the worth of products such as the *New Wave* microwave oven designed for Sanyo, and the *Crystal Mu LCD* computer display for LEC. The latter has been described as a "music-stand with a touch screen," and looks like nothing else in existence. Indeed, TKO's success derives almost exclusively from its activities in the Far East, where it built up an impressive client range during the 1990s.

Like many of its contemporaries, TKO takes an open-ended approach toward product design, recognizing that graphics, branding, and interactive multimedia are related areas that can no longer be ignored, and that design consultancies have to offer an increasingly broad service to today's clients.

TOMATO
Studio for Communication Design

1991 set up in London by Steve Baker, Kirk van Dooren, Karl Hyde, Rick Smith, Simon Taylor, John Warwicker, and Graham Wood

Products

1992 *Project Faith, Hope, Love*

1995 Graphics for Channel 4

1996 Book *Process: A Tomato Project*; CD-cover *Underworld: Second Toughest in the Infants*

1999 Book *Bareback*; CD-cover *Underworld: Beaucoup Fish*

Adidas, Coca Cola, IBM, Levi's, MTV, Nike, Philips, Reebok. The client list of this project—established only in the early 1990's in London—reads like the Who's Who of globally successful brand name products. The Tomato group, founded by Steve Baker, Dirk van Dooren, Karl Hyde, Rick Smith, Simon Taylor, John Warwicker and Graham Wood can already point to an impressive array of design awards. Even respected institutions such as Britain's **BBC** and Channel 4 chose to freshen their images with Tomato, a company with a light touch and the ability to marry commerce and subculture in a typically British fashion. The recipe for success: combine creatives with widely disparate talents into one group and in this way service the ever quickening pace of the visual communications market. Tomato's work is playful and straightforward, raw and sophisticated. The company's rise is proof of the unbroken regenerative potential of Britain's graphic arts scene, which calls itself **Communications Design** in the 1990's and draws strength from a multimedia approach in a multicultural setting. The electronic pop group Underworld which contributed to the sound track for the movie *Trainspotting* also belongs to Tomato.

Page 341

top: Process book: *A Tomato Project*, Bangert Publishing House, 1996

bottom: Underworld CD: *Second Toughest in the Infants*, 1996

Book, *Bareback. A Tomato Project*, Gingko Press, 1999

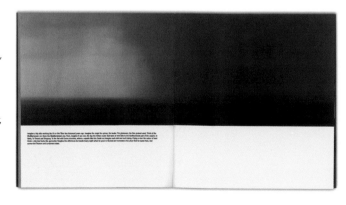

underworld : second toughest in the infants

WEDGWOOD

Ceramic Manufacturer

Josiah Wedgwood & Sons
Ltd., Barlaston

1759 founded by Josiah
Wedgwood in Burslem;
exhibition of a division for
"Modeller," which is
designing sketches

1769 studio for Emaille paintings
in London designed; black
Basalt in Sortiment

1770 sculptor John Flaxman
hired as "Modeller"

1795 Josiah II takes his father's
store

1812 first porcelain

1930 **Keith Murray** hired as
freelance designer

1935 first works by **Eric
Ravilious**

1945 multicolored lithography
introduced

1997 Rosenthal taken over

Page 343
Coffee set by Robert Minkin, 1979

Pages 344–345
Ceramic by Keith Murray, 1932

The name of Wedgwood stands for British fine china. Its reputation as a manufacturer of traditional goods—and at certain moments in its long history, of modern goods as well—from the eighteenth century to the present day cannot be equalled. Wedgwood's products are purchased with a level of ceremony that takes them out of the realm of mere utility objects into one where symbolism plays a key role. Its black basalt ware, in production after more than 200 years, is still a guarantor of good taste and quality, and other examples of its early production still add a note of elegance to any tea table.

More than anything else, Wedgwood stands for British traditions in manufacturing and design. The company was formed in Burslem in Staffordshire in the middle of the eighteenth century. It was an early example of the model of British industrialization, which influenced the rest of the world. Josiah Wedgwood's company was among the first to produce objects in bulk in a factory context, to make use of the new canal system to distribute its wares across the country, and to depend upon a divided labor system to create its goods. It was formed just at the moment when a new consumer society was emerging, keen to surround itself with the trappings of wealth and class. Nothing could express that more effectively than a ceramic tea or coffee service, designed in the fashionable, neoclassical style of the day.

From the outset Wedgwood manufactured cream-colored earthenware items in a neoclassical style that quickly became enormously popular. It followed this with what it called its "Queen's ware," so named because Queen Charlotte had become the factory's patron. This was available in an undecorated state or with a transfer-printed pattern. Some pieces were hand-painted with enamel colors and the firm opened an enamel painting workshop in Chelsea in order to keep up with demand. The popularity of Wedgwood's wares was such that earthenware soon ranked alongside porcelain, which had previously been in a class of its own.

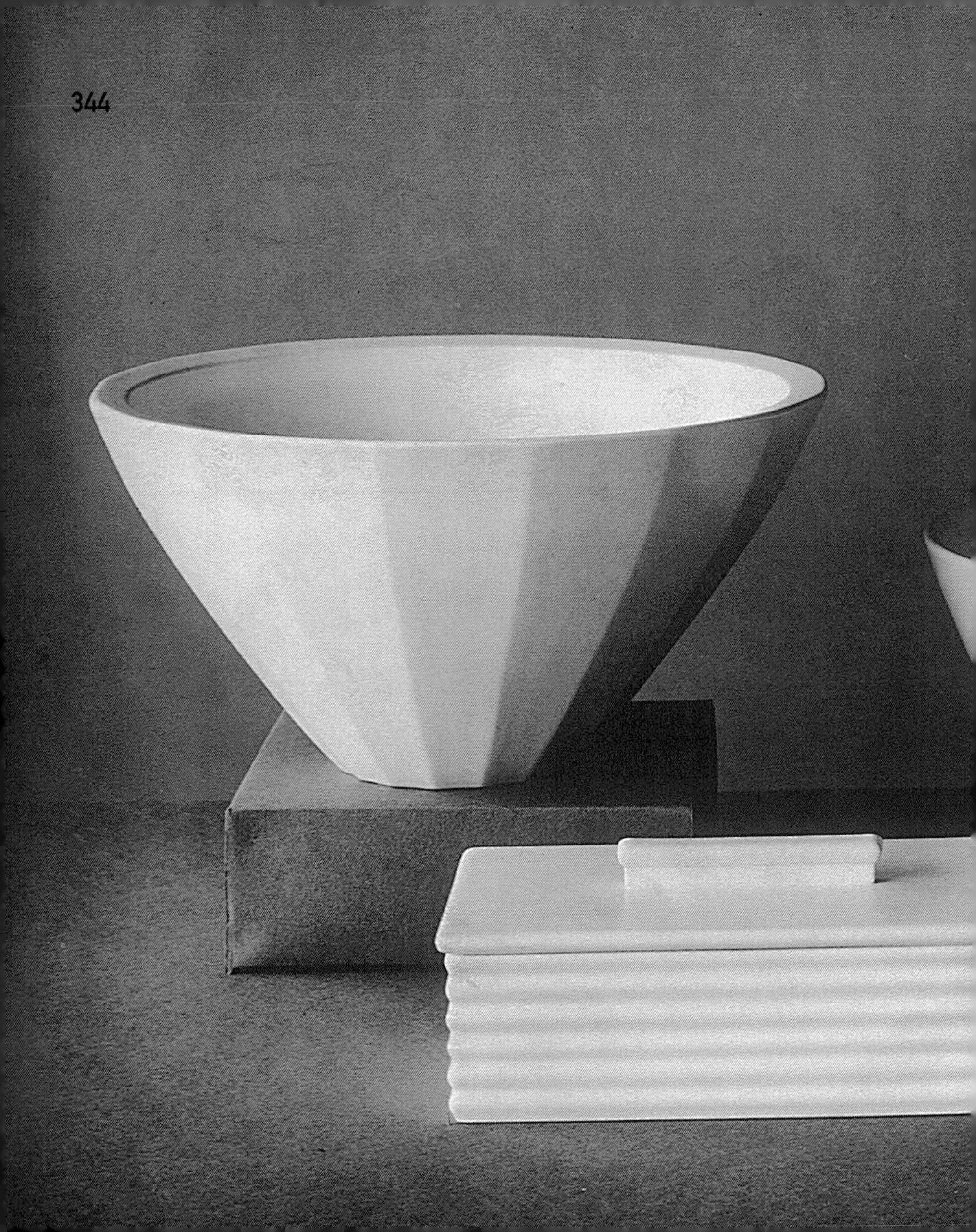

Products

For the rest of the eighteenth century Wedgwood went from strength to strength, producing exclusive hand-painted pieces alongside its mass-produced wares. The 1770s saw the creation of a lavish dinner service, covered with images of the English landscape, for Catherine the Great of Russia, so popular and fashionable had the name of Wedgwood become by that time. Well-known artists of the day such as John Flaxman and George Stubbs were commissioned by Wedgwood to create designs for the surfaces of his goods, which entered into the realm of "art" as a result. Most famous of all was his *Portland Vase*, a ceramic copy of the Roman glass original in the British Museum in London. Above all, Wedgwood was successful in making the neoclassical the dominant taste of the day in ceramics, thus aligning his wares with current fashions in architecture and interior design. As well as functional items, the company produced decorative busts and cameos, which proved highly popular in the burgeoning American market.

Service, 1955

At the end of the eighteenth century the firm went into the hands of Josiah the Second and it remained in the family until fairly recently. While little of note was achieved in the nineteenth century, the twentieth century saw the Wedgwood company make several attempts to modernize its wares, often with considerable success. The modernist designs of the architect, **Keith Murray**, from the 1930s stand out in this context, as do those of the artist and illustrator, **Eric Ravilious**. In the 1950s the company was outpaced by other ceramic manufacturers, Midwinter in particular, which were more receptive to avant-garde ideas from abroad. Without doubt, however, it is for the continued manufacture of its early designs that Wedgwood is now best known. They remain as popular as ever, memories of a time when British manufacturing was at its peak and it offered a lead to the rest of the world.

Vase, carafe, and bowl by Keith Murray, 1935

Daniel WEIL

Product and Packaging Designer

1953 born in Buenos Aires

1977 graduates from architecture studies in Buenos Aires

1978 receives his M.A. in product design from the **Royal College of Art**

1981 exhibits at the Memphis exhibition in Milan

1985 partnership with Gerard Taylor

1987 collaboration with Ettor Sottsass and Achile Castiglioni (Memphis)

1992 becomes partner at **Pentagram**

Products

1982 *Cambalache* radio; *China Wall Radio*

1983 Bag radio in plastic bag

1985 logo for Boots

1995 packaging for *Irony* watch for Swatch

1996 interior design for Timeship Swatch store, New York

logo for store chain Boots, 1995

Page 349
top left: packaging for Irony watch for Swatch, 1995
top right: packaging for Tretorn, 1999
bottom left: Pet Shop Boys CD cover: *Very*, 1994
bottom right: shoe box for Superga, 1996

In the early 1980's Daniel Weil created an innovative classic which is unfortunately no longer in production and is now known only among design cognoscenti. His *Bag* radio—a transistor radio sealed in transparent plastic—is based on a complex concept. On the one hand Weil draws on the anarchic aesthetic of **Punk**, while on the other he is already anticipating elements of fun design, which would gain popularity in the early 21st Century, when translucence finally became mainstream. This born Argentine with close ties to the Italian Memphis group was one of the few who succeeded in transforming the rebellious impulses of the early 1980's into actual design. By dissolving the radio's solid housing he not only threw into question the type of radio but simultaneously offered a new, expanded definition of functionality which already hinted at the implications of the digital age. Later, while employed at the **Pentagram** studio, he designed such widely diverse things as logos, album covers and shoe boxes. Finally this universal talent, who was now a professor at the renowned **Royal College of Art**, found success in retail design, the show piece of British design.

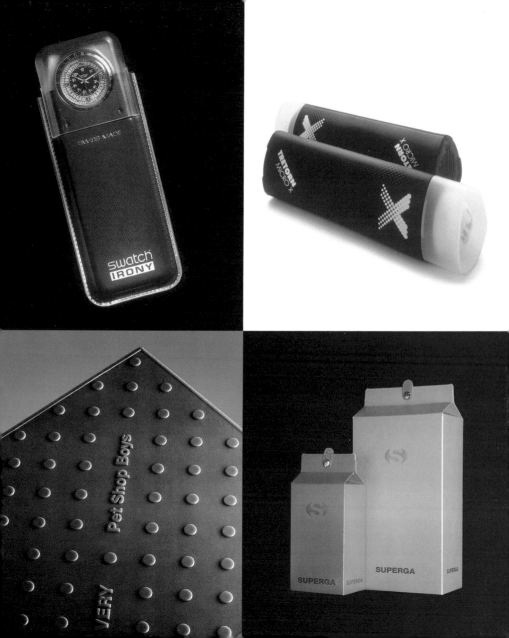

Vivienne WESTWOOD

Fashion Designer

Page 351

left: fall collection, 2000

right: spring collection, 1997

Pages 352–353

Summer collection, 1997

The fashion historian, Valerie Steele, has written that "Vivienne Westwood's clothes have been described as perverse, irrelevant, and unwearable. Westwood's creations have also been described as brilliant, subversive, and incredibly influential." Although she continues to be a highly debated figure, loved by some and hated by others, there can be little doubt that Westwood is among the most important fashion designers of this century. She is certainly a key figure within British post-war fashion. Like so many other innovative designers of her generation, she emerged from within the youth subcultural movement known as punk. Indeed, along with **Malcolm MacLaren**, Westwood can be seen as one of the actual creators of punk, at least in terms of the visual style through which it represented itself. From the outset she used dress subversively in a paradoxical, "anti-fashion" way, thereby becoming a highly controversial figure within British fashion.

Westwood did not come up through the conventional art-school background that characterized many of her peers. She did spend one term at Harrow Art School but then trained as a school teacher, a profession she followed until she became involved with MacLaren and the punk movement in the very early 1970s.

Their way of entering into subversive dress was by opening a series of shops that catered to this new audience. In true **Punk** fashion, ephemerality was the order of the day and none of their joint retail ventures lasted longer than a year or so. Between 1971 and 1980 they managed a total of five retail outlets on London's King's Road—in chronological order, Let It Rock; Too Fast To Live, Too Young To Die; Sex; Seditionaries; and World's End. The punk message was dramatic but short-lived and MacLaren and Westwood entered fully into this spirit, designing rapidly changing identities for punk's followers.

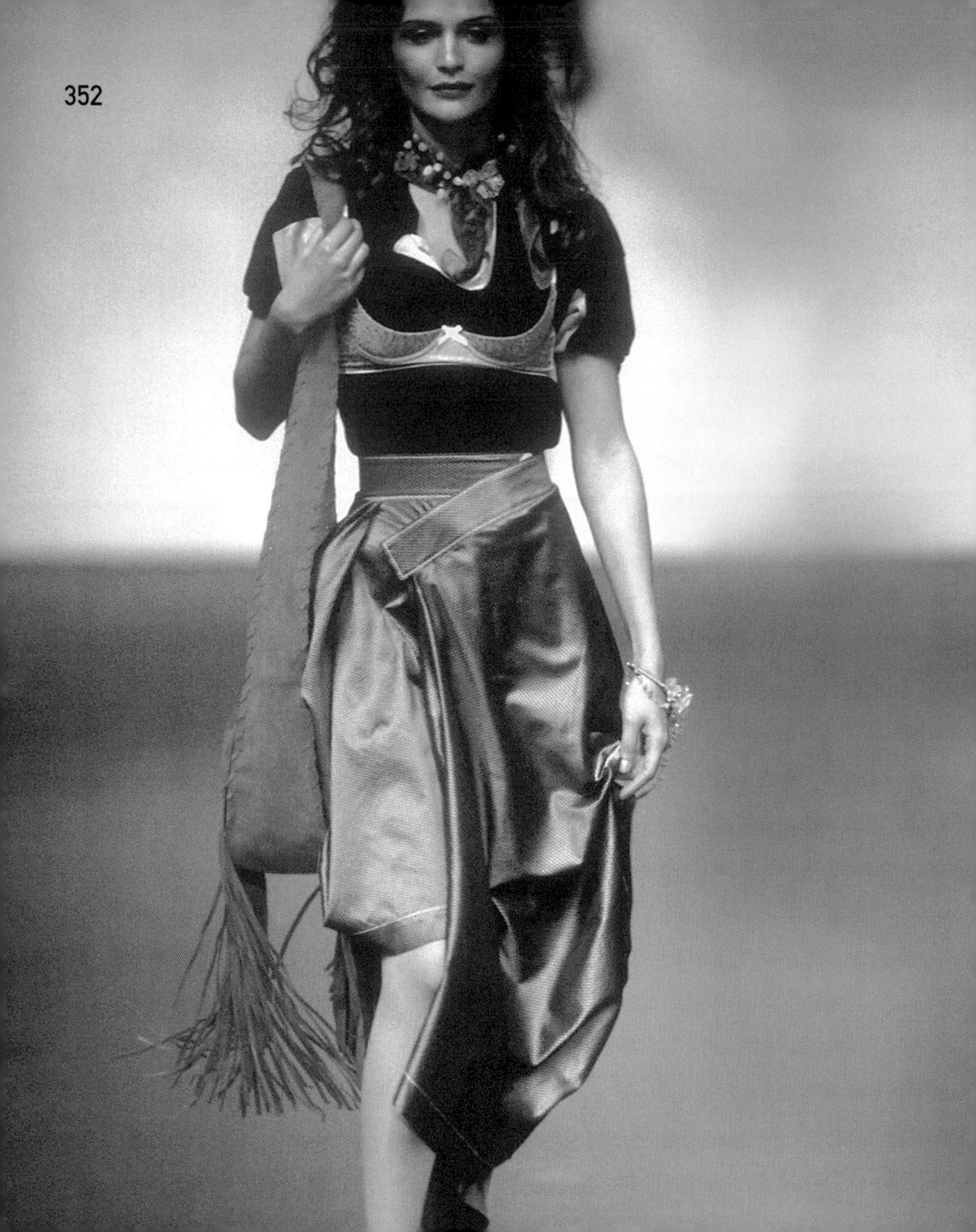

Products

The main themes of Westwood's designs moved from 1950s revival to leather clothing for bikers, and on to bondage apparel using leather and rubber with extensive use of buckles, strap, chains, and zips. Westwood explained, "I wanted to get hold of those extreme articles of clothing and feel what it was like to wear them."

The 1980s brought new directions for Westwood's career. Her style changed toward a more romantic, nostalgic direction, reflected in her *Pirates* collection. She began to show her designs in Paris under her own name for the first time, and quickly became recognized internationally as a designer of significance. Her collections of the first half of the decade were diverse and dramatic, with evocative names such as *Hoboes*, *Witches*, and *Punkature*. A major breakthrough was the *Mini-Crini* of the mid-decade, a hybrid of Victorian nostalgia and contemporary fetishism. A combination of past and future, of establishment values with subversive tactics, characterized much of her work from this time on through the rest of the 1980s and 1990s. She succeeded in remaining entirely independent from the world of haute couture, while simultaneously being lauded by the fashion world in general. She used her newfound power to become a public figure and to make her controversial views widely known. Her seemingly inexhaustible imagination, combined with her ability to remain transgressive even when working within a mainstream context, have earned her an important place not only in British fashion of the last few decades but within British cultural life in general.

Page 355

left: summer collection, 2000

top right: glasses King's Road for Filos, 1999

bottom right: summer collection, 1999

WHY NOT
Studio for Communication Design

Why Not Associates,
London

1987 founded in London by
Andrew Altmann, David
Ellis and Howard
Greenhalgh (current
partners are also Patrick
Morrissey, Iain Cadby, and
Mark Molloy)

1992 Greenhalgh leaves the
studio and founds Why
Not Films

1993 exhibition in the GGG
Gallery in Tokyo

1995 exhibition at St. Martins
School of Art

1997 book on ten years of work
by the studio is published

Products

1989 campaign for Smirnoff
Vodka

1993 *Doddy* lettering

1997 book *Why Not*

Page 357
top: double-page layout for
magazine *U&lc*, 1996
bottom: book cover *Why Not*, 1997

Advertisement campaign for
Smirnoff Vodka, 1989

Positioned in the energy field surrounding **Street Style**, advertising industry
and pop, Why Not is a typical product of Britain's new creative culture. But in
this case the impulse came from without. Andrew Altman, David Ellis and
Howard Greenhalgh who founded the programmatically named group
immediately after their graduation, were inspired by the work of a Dutchman,
Gert Dumbar, who had a short engagement as a professor at the **Royal
College of Art** in the mid 1980's. The trio succeeded primarily by utilizing the
potential now offered by Apple computers, whether in advertising
campaigns, identity brochures, posters or extraordinary books. Through
collage-like combinations of different typefaces, distorted or superimposed
on each other if necessary, they created a contemporary typographical
cosmos. Their commercial breakthrough came with an advertising campaign
for Smirnoff vodka and the catalog covers for the fashion chain Next in the
early 1990's. Shortly thereafter Greenhalgh founded Studio Why Not Films
which produces music videos for well known pop labels.

WHY NOT ASSOCIATES

WOLFF OLINS

Studio for Corporate Identity

Wolff Olins, London

1965 founded by Michael Wolff and **Wally Olins** in Camden Town, London

1968 office in Hamburg, Germany

1985 publishing of *The Wolff Olins Guide to Design Management*

1988 office in Spain

1996 *Design Effectiveness Award* for Orange-CI

1999 office in New York opened

Products

1984 CI for the oil company Q8

1989 CI for the oil company Repsol

1994 CI for the telephone company Orange

1997 media design for Channel 5

1998 Heathrow Express

Page 359
top: logo for British Telecom
bottom left: logo for Orange, 1994
bottom right: logo for the Bank 31, 1986

The Wolff Olins design consultancy, originally formed by Michael Wolff and **Wally Olins**, has been in operation for more than thirty years. Today it still has a very high international profile in the area of corporate identity and branding, and works with a wide range of clients. Indeed it ranks among the top three in the world in its field, with offices in London, Madrid, and Lisbon, and multidisciplinary project teams working in many different parts of the world. A total of 150 people—among them consultants, graphic designers, interior designers, architects, multimedia experts, and project managers—work for the consultancy, helping it to maintain its reputation as a leader in its field.

Wolff Olins has played a key role in pioneering this area, starting out with a relatively simple idea of designing corporate identity schemes, but moving over the last few decades toward a much more abstract, more sophisticated notion that is only partly visual in nature. Back in the 1960s, it came to the fore with highly original graphic schemes such as Michael Wolff's little hummingbird image for the construction company, Bovis, and his fox for Hadfields Paint. They explain that their aim is to "work closely with our clients to understand their concerns, issues and business objectives. We then help them to define what it is that makes them unique and stand out from their competitors." Wolff Olins's most important clients over the years have included ICI, Pilkington, BT (British Telecom), Renault, Unilever, and General Motors. Most recently, it has created identities for First Direct, Britain's first telephone banking company, and Orange, another company working in the same area. The consultancy's strikingly simple logo for Orange is characteristic of its continually innovative approach. The design of the new Heathrow Express train is also a Wolff Olins achievement, marking its continued impact on the everyday environment of today's Britain.

BT

orange™

Terence WOODGATE

Furniture Designer

1953 born in London

1985 studies furniture design at London's Guildhall University

1988 founds studio in London

1991 moves to Brussels, Belgium

1995 wins *IF Design Prize* Hanover, Germany

1996 returns to England

Products

1992 bench seating system for the public

1996 shelf system

1998 *Woodgate* table and sofa both for Sheridan Coakley Production; *Joe bench* seating system

Page 361
top: bench seating system, 1992
bottom: sofa system, 1997

Bench seating system, 1992

Terence Woodgate is among the group of young British furniture designers who have made an international impact in the last decade. He is best known, perhaps, for his public seating system for **SCP** (Sheridan Coakley Production), which has been installed on the platforms for the new Heathrow Express at Heathrow Airport, and for his work for the Italian company, Cappellini. His work displays a simple, geometric elegance reminiscent of early modernism, which maximizes his engineering skills. Woodgate is a little older than his fellow members of the SCP stable, having been trained initially as a design engineer before returning to study furniture design at London's Guildhall University in the mid-1980s. He established his first design studio in London at the end of that decade from where he designed his public seating for SCP, his *River* series of modular cabinets for the Spanish company, Punt Mobles, and a number of lighting objects for Concord Lighting. A move to Brussels in the early 1990s put him firmly in a European context with commissions coming from, among other firms, Cappellini and the Spanish manufacturer of office furniture, Casas. His time there helped him to establish a reputation for himself, which he brought back to England five years later. This time he established his studio in East Sussex, from where he continues to work for a wide range of European furniture manufacturers.

Michael YOUNG
Furniture Designer

Michael Young says that his work is about "F's—fun, frivolity, form, fervor, fucking, function, freedom, fame, and farting"— suggesting that a somewhat anarchic, or at least independent, thinking has inspired the highly original furniture designs he has produced over the last few years. The work does not look anarchic, however. It exhibits, instead, a cool elegance and a neomodern feel with a strong respect for the materials being used. Early pieces, for instance, were made from woven steel, while the elliptically shaped *Paris* light of the mid-1990s also used steel in a highly sculptural and sophisticated way. Young himself thinks that the simplicity of his work, and that of his British contemporaries, appeals to a large audience "because it is not caught up in tortuous concepts. Its strength is in the object and in the way that the designer has imbued it with his personality without being too self-indulgent."

After graduating in the early 1990s from Kingston University, Young made a rapid and dramatic impact on the contemporary scene, with prestigious companies such as Cappellini, Sawaya, and Moroni putting his pieces into production. He has exhibited widely and produced a significant body of work.

Products

While still at Kingston University, he began to work in **Tom Dixon**'s workshop, Space, producing his steel furniture and his *Smarty* cushion. Like Dixon, Young's designs were batch-produced until a manufacturer decided to take things further. Smarty went into production with Cappellini a few years later.

In the mid-1990s Young set up his own concept and production studio, MY022, but it ceased operating only a couple of years later. During its existence he designed furniture pieces for the Japanese company E&Y, launched his *Magazine Sofa*, and created his *Honeycomb* screen, which won a prestigious German prize. His next venture was the launch of the *Fly* collection and carpets for Christopher Farr. At the turn of the century Young moved to Iceland with his wife, where he began working with her on jewelry designs for Smak.

Bar stool for Cappellini, 1998

Page 365
Victoria and Albert Museum, London; glass stairs by Danny Lane, 1994

Guide

British Design Addresses

Design Council

34 Bow Street, London WC2E 7DL. Nerve center of British industrial design. In addition to providing information on a daily basis, this bustling institution publishes an annual report on the design-state of the nation. The new premises, across from the opera, is itself a showpiece of good design.

Crafts Council

44a Pentonville Road, London N1 9BY. Represents crafts in Great Britain. The attached shop advertises itself as the largest artistic crafts gallery in England. Crafts magazine is published monthly.

ALTHORP, NORTHHAMPTONSHIRE

Museum & Visitor Center Althorp

Althorp, NM7 4HQ. Commissioned by Earl Spencer, the studio Din Associates designed this award-winning memorial to Princess Diana. The exhibits are taken from her life and reflect both British fashion and recent history.

BARLASTON, STAFFORDSHIRE

Wedgwood Museum

Stoke-on-Trent, ST12 9ES. This company museum is a must for all fans of porcelain and fired clay. It is the country's largest collection of industrial ceramics and provides a comprehensive overview of the famous manufacturer's product and design history, from the legendary Portland vase to contemporary designs.

BATH, AVON

Circus

Circus, BA1 2EW. This masterpiece by John Wood, Sr., is a neo-classical circus dating from 1754. Number 4 houses the Fashion Research Centre, the scientific team of the fashion museum that also issues expertises for pieces of historical clothing.

Museum of Costume

Bennett St, BA1 2QH. A recently renovated collection of chic attire for aristocrats and the bourgeoisie spanning four centuries of fashion. The museum is located in the basement of the Assembly Rooms, which were built in 1771 for concerts, balls and meetings.

Bath Industrial Heritage Centre

Julian Road, BA1 2RH. A lovingly conserved store of a Victorian workshop.

BEAMINSTER, DORSET

Parnham House

Beaminster. Furniture school of John Makepeace. A Tudor manor house which serves as the creative center of a new generation of artistic "design makers," whose works are occasionally exhibited. Two miles from Beaminster, in the middle of a forest, Makepeace erected a modern, tent-like workshop of ecological materials, earning international acclaim for himself.

BIRMINGHAM

Birmingham City Museum and Art Gallery

Chamberlain Square, B3 3DH. A collection with an emphasis on the Pre-Raphaelites, Arts and Crafts creations by Morris & Co., as well as on contemporary art.

BRIGHTON, EAST SUSSEX

Brighton Museum and Art Gallery

Church Street, BN1 1UE. This house opened in 1873. It mounts exhibitions of decorative art, especially in the Art Nouveau and Art Deco styles.

Design History Research Centre

68 Grand Parade, BN1. Houses a University of Brighton department devoted to researching the history of design. The affiliated Design Council Archive maintains one of the largest collections of photographs in the field.

Royal Pavilion

Old Steine, BN1 1EE. This royal villa built in the "Indian Style" and completed in 1822 is the epitome of historicism and exoticism.

CAMBRIDGE

Jesus College Chapel

Jesus College, Jesus Lane, CB5 8BL. The stained-glass windows and ceiling frescoes by Morris & Co. date from 1866.

CHELTENHAM, GLOUCESTERSHIRE

Cheltenham Art Gallery and Museum

Clarence Street, GL50 3JT. Permanent exhibition of Arts and Crafts furniture with emphasis on the movement's founder, William Morris.

Pittville Pump Room Museum, Gallery of Fashion

Pittville Park, GL52 3JE. A stroll through fashions of the glorious days when noble visitors of the Cheltenham spa outdid themselves in idleness, from the Regency era to the Swinging Sixties.

EDINBURGH, SCOTLAND

Inhouse

28 Howe Street, EH3 6TG. Purveyor of classic furnishings. Features special design exhibitions during the Edinburgh Festival.

The Scottish Gallery

16 Dundas Street, EH3 6HZ. This private gallery has mounted over one hundred exhibitions of European craftsmanship.

GLASGOW, STRATHCLYDE

Glasgow School of Art

167 Renfrew Street, G3 6RQ. An Art Nouveau edifice which still houses the art school. Stands as the main achievement of Rennie Mackintosh, who created this opulent artistic totality at age 28. Of particular note are the highly original library and a furniture gallery.

Queen's Cross Church

870 Garscube Road, G20 7EL. Seat of the Mackintosh Society which organizes weekends and tours; publishes a quarterly journal.

The Lighthouse

11 Mitchell Lane, G1 3NU. As a "City of Architecture and Design," Scotland's cultural and industrial metropolis received Great Britain's second design museum—which is not to be ranked second in any other respect. The former Glasgow Herald Building—Rennie Mackintosh's second public building and itself a product of high design—is today one of the largest museums for architecture and design in Europe. Four galleries continually show interesting exhibitions. In the Mackintosh Interpretation Centre visitors receive a comprehensive introduction to the master's work. From the tower, one can see the Glasgow School of Arts and other buildings by Mackintosh.

LONDON

Aero

96 Westbourne Grove, W2 5RT. A furniture store in hip Notting Hill, which is increasingly becoming the city's design district.

Camden Market

Camden Lock, Buck Street, Chalk Farm Road and Commercial Place. A daily flea market for street-style gear, be it fashion, music or design.

Connolly Luxury Goods Ltd.

32 Grosvenor Crescent Mews, SW1X 7EX. For everyone who values fine leather.

Conran Shop

Michelin House, 81 Fulham Road, SW3 6RD. A design department store in a former garage. Tenrence (sic) Terrance, trans. Conran opened one of his numerous restaurants in the same building. Bibendum is at the top of the list for dining in London.

Covent Garden

This former flower market has the ambience of a Mediterranean piazza with markets for dresses and crafts. It numbers among London's prettiest public places. Furnished by Ron Arad, whose studio is right around the corner, the restaurant Belgo Centraal is worth seeing—and worth trying as well.

Danny Lane

19 Hythe Road, NW10 6RT. Exhibition space, workshop and studio of glass artist and design eccentric Danny Lane.

David Mellor

4 Sloane Square, SW1W 8EE. Main store of England's most famous silversmith. Sells not only Mellor's cutlery but also dishes and housewares.

Design Decoration Building

107a Pimlico Road, SW1 8PH. Showrooms of English designers, furnishing and decorating tips, café.

Design Museum

Butler's Wharf, 28 Shad Thames, SE1 2YD. Opened in 1989 as the first museum in the world devoted exclusively to industrial design. The white Bauhaus-style building with a view of Tower Bridge houses exhibitions of innovative design and several interesting articles of daily use; shows change regularly.

Designers Guild

267–271 Kings Road, SW3 5EN. Parent company of Tricia Guild, the Laura Ashley of the 1990's.

Geffrye Museum

Kingsland Road, E2 8EA. Specializes in one of the great periods in English design, namely furniture and furnishings of the 17th–19th Centuries. Furniture from subsequent periods is shown in the new tract, designed by Branson Coates. Also houses a gallery and a center for furniture from East London.

Habitat

196 Tottenham Court Road, W1P 9LD. Since the late 1990's England's first design chain store is being kept up to the minute by Tom Dixon.

Harrods

Brompton Road, Knightsbridge, SW1X 7XL. A classic department store with a designed interior life. Harrods has its floors styled by designated studios; for example, the shoe department was created by DIN. But even the original interior design, as in the famous food hall, is well worth seeing.

Heal´s

196 Tottenham Court Road, W1T 7LQ. Headquarters of the renowned furniture and decorating company. Several years ago a branch store specializing in kitchens was opened at King's Road 234.

Imagination Gallery

25 Store Street, South Crescent, WC1E 7BL. A studio presenting its own products on the top floor.

Laura Ashley

256–258 Regent Street, WI. Petite floral designs are preferred. The Ashley style is a typically English phenomenon, with a store in every town.

Liberty

210–220 Regent St, W1R 6AH. A classical design department store near Oxford Circus, which made its reputation with Arts and Crafts. Liberty is a big name in cloth and textiles but also offers furniture, antiques, tableware and lamps. Numbers among tourist sights for its Tudor-inspired façade alone.

Lloyd´s

Lime Street, EC3N 7HA. Stemming from the late 1980's, the insurance giant's headquarters serves a PR purpose. The extroverted style of the technoid structure (Richard Rogers, architect) has been the subject of controversy ever since its completion.

Marks & Spencer

458 Oxford Street, W1D 2JR. This department store chain is an English institution. It is famous for its good garments; also its many prepared meals. But M&S is also exemplary when it comes to retail design. For many years the store has resorted to well-known design studios to create a pleasant and no less well-known sales environment.

Moshi Moshi

Carob Place, Canada Square, EC14. A sushi bar near the Design Museum. The interior was designed by Branson Coates.

Next

201–203 Oxford Street, W1D 2LD. This busiest store of the strictly design-oriented fashion chain was styled by in-house personnel.

Pharmacy

150 Notting Hill Gate, W11. An eatery in a pharmacy setting. The outward appearance of this restaurant by artist Damian Hirst caused a stir.

Portobello Road Market

Portobello Road (closed Thursdays and Sundays). England's largest antiques market with over 1,000 dealers.

Sainsburys

55 Bugsbys Way, SE10 0QJ. England's supermarkets are also betting on design. As a typical example representing many others, the new Sainsbury supermarket near the Millennium Dome was designed by Roy Fleetwood.

SCP Limited

135–139 Curtain Road, EC2A 3BX. New furniture designs with old-fashioned virtues.

Soup Opera

Concourse, Cabot Place, Canary Wharf, E14 4QS. DIN Associates won the Week Retail Environment Award with this restaurant which specializes, unconventionally, in soups as fast food.

Westbourne House

Corner of Westbourne Grove and Kensington Park. A nice idea by fashion designer Paul Smith: the ladies' department is furnished as a lady's dressing room, the gentlemen's shop as a club room, and clothing for little ones is sold in a children's room.

Sir John Soane´s Museum

13 Lincoln´s Inn Fields, WC2A 3BP. The typically English private quarters of eccentric genius and architect John Soane who was active around 1800.

Page 369

upper left: the furniture department in Heal's, London

upper right: collapsible traveling cup by Connolly, London

bottom: National Centre For Popular Music, Sheffield, by Branson Coates, 1999

Victoria & Albert Museum

Cromwell Road, South Kensington, SW7 2RL. Financed with profits from the 1851 World's Fair, it was the world's first museum for design or "applied art." The gigantic and venerable building houses all of the beautiful (some more, some less) articles that surround us: jewelry, furniture, carpets, photographs. Fashion is one of its specialties, and the department of product design has now been completely renovated. In William Morris's Green Dining Room one can actually get something to eat. Equally noteworthy is the reconstruction of an office designed by Frank Lloyd Wright.

Vivienne Westwood

44 Conduit Street, W1R 9FB. Showcase of a designer specializing in shocking fashions.

William Morris Gallery

Water House, Lloyd Park, Forest Road, E17 4PP. The home of William Morris's parents is now a museum.

Zwemmers Design

72 Charing Cross Road, WC2 0BB. London's only book store dealing exclusively with design. It is a branch of the renowned photography book store on the next street corner.

LYNDHURST, DORSET

National Motor Museum

Beaulieu, 10 km from Lyndhurst on route B 3056. Approximately 250 cult objects with four or more wheels to be admired.

OXFORD

Oxford Union Library

Frewin Court, St. Michaels Street, OXI 3JD. Frescoes on ceilings and walls dating from 1857, by W. Morris and artist friends. Stained glass windows by W. Morris and E. Burne-Jones, likewise in Christ Church Cathedral.

SHEFFIELD

National Centre of Popular Music

Paternoster Row, S1 2QQ. Four drum-like tracts—design by Branson Coates—where one can learn almost everything about Pop and the contributions made by British musicians.

ST. IVES, CORNWALL

New Craftsmen

24 Fore St, TR26 1HE. England's famous artist's colony also remains a center of craftsmanship, in this case, primarily pottery.

Page 371
Instamatic Kamera by Kenneth Grange for Kodak, 1966

Index

Designers, Companies, Terms

ADDISON: A London-based design consultancy, working with large corporate clients on identity schemes, active in the 1980s. 82

AERO: 84

AESTHETIC MOVEMENT: 19th century movement in architecture and the decorative arts. Key participants E. W. Godwin(1933–86) and J. McNeil Whistler (1843–1903). Promoted the Japanese style.

ALLIED INTERNATIONAL DESIGNERS: Product design studio, founded in 1959 in London by James Pilditch (originally as Package Design Association). Transferred the American "consultant for industrial design" concept to Great Britain. Occasionally collaborates with Sigvard Bernadotte in Stockholm.

ANGLEPOISE: Classic lamp, designed in 1932 by George Carwardine (1887–1948) for Herbert Terry and Sons, England.

ANLEY, James: b. 1972. Jamaica. Interior designer. Cofounder of Jam. 220

ARAD, Ron: 11, **96**, 108, 164, 223, 333

ARCHIGRAM: A Group of visionary architects, including Peter Cook (1936), Warren Chalk (1927) and Dennis Crompton (1935), active in the 1960s, who allied them themselves to Pop culture.

ARCHITECTURAL REVIEW: Founded in 1896; leading British journal for architectural criticism; was a mouthpiece for modernism in the 1930's when Nikolaus Pevsner was one of the managing editors. Contributions by Reyner Benham, among others, in the 1950's. 114

ART DECO: A modernist style which was a decorative alternative to the austerity of the Bauhaus; began to influence not only interior design, but also ceramic and glass design in Great Britain following the 1925 exhibition of decorative and industrial arts in Paris. An example is the staircase from the early 1930's in the Strand Palace Hotel in London. 74, 229

ART NOUVEAU: An inclusive style of design and architecture around 1900 which encompassed all of Europe. In Great Britain, however—perhaps because of the dominance of Arts and Crafts—it was only adopted by individual artistic personalities such as Charles Rennie Mackintosh in architecture and Aubrey Beardsley in graphic art and illustration.

ARTS AND CRAFTS: 10, 52, 61, 74, **102**, 110, 194, 226, 238, 240, 242, 292, 316

ART WORKERS' GUILD: Founded in 1884, this club declared architecture a form of art and was later responsible for the Arts and Crafts Exhibition Society.

ASHBEE, C.R.: 1863–1942. Member of the 19th century Arts and Crafts movement. Designed metalwork and furniture and established the Guild and School of Handicraft. 56, 102, 292

ASHLEY, Laura: 51, **104**, 152

ASTON MARTIN: Car manufacturer. British. Set up in 1914 producing racing cars. Known for its elegant, up-market cars, especially the 'DB-2'. **106**, 256, 260

ATFIELD, Jane: b. 1964 Furniture designer and architect; consistently worked with recycled materials in the 1990's; her company . Made of Waste, specialized in reclaiming synthetic materials; also works with materials such as plywood, canvass and bamboo. Her usually colorful and richly structured designs have a pronounced sensuous and evocative effect. The multicolored chair she designed in the early 1990's while still a student at the Royal College of Art was highly acclaimed.

AZUMI: 108

BACHE, David: b.1926. Automobile designer; began his career at Austin and later switched to Rover, where he redesigned the Land-Rover and the classic R5 und R6. 314

BAIER, Fred: **110**

BALL, Ralph: **112**

BANNENBURG, Jon: b.1929. Interior designer active in the 1960s and 1970s. Moved into yacht design.

BARBOUR MANUFACTURER: Established in the 19th century, of utility, all-weather clothing. The ' Barbour jacket' became a status symbol among 'Sloane Rangers' in the 1980s. 151

BARMAN, Christian: **114**

BARNBROOK, Jonathan: **115**

BAYLEY, Stephen: b. 1951. Design historian, responsible, in collaboration with Terence Conran, for the formation of the Boilerhouse Project in London in the early 1980s and the establishment of the Design Museum in the Docklands at the end of the decade.

DESIGN WEEK: Weekly design magazine, established in the early 1980s. 294

DESIGNERS GUILD: 158

DIA, (Design and Industries Associates): 58

DILLON, Jane: 160

DIN, Rasshied: 1979 graduates from Birmingham Polytechnic; DIN Associates. **162**

DIXON, Tom: 11, **164**, 192, 223, 364

DORN, Marian: American. 1899–1964. Textile designer married to British graphic designer, E. McKnight Kauffer. Created carpets and fabrics with strikingly modern designs on them.

DRESSER, Christopher: 1834–1904. Botanist and designer. Important proto-industrial designer who created modern-looking designs in metal, ceramics and glass. 54, **168**, 226

DRYAD: Manufacturer, active in the 1920s and 1930s, of cane furniture, based in Leicester. The Dryad family played a key role in the activities of the Deign and Industries Association.

DUBREUIL, André: French. b. 1951. Interior and furniture designer, active, until recently, in London. Collaborated with Tom Dixon on the interior of the Rococo Chocolats boutique in London's Kings Road. 166, 223

DUNHILL: Established British manufacturer of small luxury goods—cigarette lighters, fountain pens etc.—associated with the ideas of tradition, status and quality. Recently entered into men's perfume.

DUNNE, Tony: Young designer with a special interest in computer interfaces. Teaches in the Royal College of Art's Computer-related Design department. Works in partnership with wife, Fiona Raby.

DYSON, James: 84, **170**, 276

ECKO (E.K. Cole Ltd.): British manufacturer of radios and plastic products in the 1930s and immediate post-war years. Known for its collaborations with leading designers, among them Serge Chermayeff and Wells Coates. 58

EL ULTIMO GRITO: 108, **174**

ELLE DECORATION: Monthly magazine (British equivalent of its French counterpart), formed in the 1980s, which focuses on the decoration of the domestic interior with a reputation for a high level of stylishness and chic.

ERCOL: British furniture manufacturer, based in Hugh Wycombe, formed in the early post-war years and known for its re-working of the traditional Windsor chair. Played an important part in the Contemporary movement in the 1950s.

ETTETGUI, Joseph: Morrocan-born retailer who developed a number of stylish clothing outlets and restaurants in London from the early 1980s. Employed leading designers to create his store interiors notable among them Eva Jiricna and Norman Foster. 142, 311

FAT: 175

FESTIVAL OF BRITAIN: An important landmark event of the early post-war years, held on the South Bank of the River Thames, which gave many designers their first opportunity to show their new designs, among them Robin Day, Hugh Casson and Jack Howe. 66, 149, 156, 306

FILOFAX: A long-established British manufacturer of leather-bound personal organisers which became an obligatory accessory for the style-conscious 'yuppies' of the 1980s. Paul Smith was among the first to sell them. 296, 324

FINMAR: The British agent for Alvar Aalto's furniture in the 1930s Finmar helped bring European modernism to Britain in the inter-war years.

FITCH, Rodney: Designer. Fitch started out in the employment of Terence Conran but broke away to create his own design consultancy, focusing on shop fitting and corporate identity, in the 1980s, rising to become one of the largest and most powerful design group of that era. His firm went into liquidation at the end of the decade, however. 77, 139, 310

FLEETWOOD, Roy: 11, 174, **176**

FOSTER, Norman: 11, 82, 112, 176, **178**, 199, 286, 311

FRAZER, Stephen: **180**, 294, 296

GALLIANO, John: **182**, 248, 318

GARDNER, James: 1907–1990. Exhibition designer responsible for the Britain Can Make It Exhibition of 1946 and Battersea Pleasure Gardens at the Festival Of Britain. 1947 became a Royal Designer for Industry.

GARRET, Malcolm: b. 1956. Graphic artist;the anarchistic-eclectic bent he initially put to use for independent labels on the punk scene resulted in the late 1970's and early 1980's in a series of radically different cover designs; the sleeve for the

Buzzcocks' single *Orgasm Addict,* which features a surrealistically alienated female body is typical for the manner in which he draws on historical material. He also worked for magazines, mixed type faces and design layouts for novels. In the late 1980's he produced a poster for Boy George, which achieved mainstream acceptance for the irregular and jumbled typography of punk. 350

GILL, Eric: 77, **186**, 228

GIMSON, Ernest: 1864–1919. Architect and designer, born in Leicester. A member of the arts and crafts movement Gimson set up a furniture workshop in the Cotswolds with the Barnsleys. His designs had a strong traditional, rustic feel to them.

GODWIN, E.W.: b. 1833–86. Architect, furniture snd stage designer. Strongly influenced by the Japanese style and a proponent of Aestheticism. Collaborated with Whistler. 54

GODDEN, Robert: b. 1909. Architect and designer. Worked across a range of media. 1948–71 was Professor of jewellery, silversmithing and industrial glass at the Royal College of Art. 1947 elected a Royal Designer for Industry.

GRANGE, Kenneth: 77, **186**, 284

GRAY, Milner: 1899–1990. Industrial and graphic designer. From 1945 was a founding partner, with Misha Black, of the Design Research Unit. Had worked with the Ministry of Information during the war. Designed corporate identity programmes for British Rail and Austin Reed.

GROPIUS, Walter: 56, 212

GREY MATTER: British design consultancy, based in London, worlion in the areas of interiors and corporate identity programmes, active in the 1980s.

GRIMSHAW, Nicholas: Architect in the High Tech idiom. Responsible for the design of Eden, an environmental centre in Cornwall, England.

GRCIC, Konstantin: German. Young furniture designer, trained in England, who designs pieces for SCP in London. His Mono tables are among his most recent project. 320

GUILD, Tricia: b. 1948. Textile designer, Founder of Designers Guild in 1970, author of a number of interior design books. 104, 158

HABITAT: 11, 73, 89, 92, 144, 152, 163, 166, **192**, 282, 289, 310

HAMNETT, Katherine: b. 1947. Fashion designer. Set up her own company in 1979. Known for her political slogan T-shirts produced in the mid 1980s.

HARMAN-POWELL, David: Product designer. Has worked with the plastics industry since the 1950s. Well-known for a number of pieces among them his 'Nova' tableware for Ekco Plastics Ltd. of 1967.

HEAL, Ambrose: b. 1872 Contractor and furniture designer ConranDD149. 58, 194

HEAL'S: 146, **194**

HENRION, FHK: French. 1914–1991. Exhibition and graphic designer. Active in England from the 1930s. Designed posters for BOAC and London transport and a corporate identity scheme for KLM. 1959 elected Royal Designer for Industry.

HERITAGE INDUSTRY: **196**

HERITAGE, Robert: b. 1927. Furniture designer. Set up his own studio in 1953. Professor of Furniture Design at the Royal College of Art 1974–85. Best known for his lighting for Concord.

HIGH TECH: An architectural and design style of the 1980s which brought an industrial aesthetic to the consumer market. While Norman Foster, Michael Hopkins and Nicholas Grimshaw were among its best known architectural protagonists Era Jiricna and Ron Arad brought it into the areas of interior and product design. 98, 112, 178, 180, 221, 311, 338

HILLE: British furniture manufacturing company, established in the early century but best known in the post-war years through it collaborations with the designers Robin Day and Fred Scott. 68, 148, 156

HILTON, Matthew: **200**, 320

HIPGNOSIS: Graphic design studio

HOLLINGTON, Geoff: **202**, 320

HOWE, Jack: Industrial designer, active in the 1950s. Designed the litter bins for the festival of Britain.

HMV: British manufacturer of audio equipment and electrical appliances from the 1930s. Best known for its collaboration with the designer, Christian Barman. 114

i-D MAGAZINE: British style magazine, established in 1981, by its founder and editor, Terry Jones.

IDEO: San Francisco- and London-based design consultancy, working with the new computer industries in both countries.

JONES, Allen: b. 1937 Painter, pop artist with a predilection for latex; chair, table and hat rack made of life size female figures, 1969; costumes and stage design for the musical *Oh! Calcutta!,* 1970. 290

JOURNAL OF DESIGN: See Henry Cole

JONES, Owen: Mid 19th century design reformer. 1809–1874 associated with the circle of critics around Henry Cole. Designed textiles and wrote influential 'Grammar of Ornament'. 54

KAMALI, Nazanin: 94

KAPLICKY, Jan: Czech 'High-tech' designer. Worked in the office of Norman Foster in the 1970s before establishing his own architectural firm, Future Systems, which is based in London.

KENWOOD: British manufacturer of domestic appliances. Its founder, Kenneth Wood, had a progressive approach towards design leading him to employ the product designer, Kenneth Grange. His Kitchenmachine food mixer of 1964 is among the notable of his designs for the firm. 77, 180, 188

KING, **Perry**: 1938; a product designer who went to Italy in the 1960's; worked first for Ettore Sottsass and later founded the King Miranda Studio.

KINSMAN, **Rodney**:1943 born in London. 1965 Kinsman graduates from Central School of Art and Design. 1966 OMK gegründet von 282

KORN, **Arthur**: A Different World 176.

LANCASTER, Nancy: American. 1897–1994. Interior decorator and co-owner of Colefax and Fowler—the firm which created the English Country Look—between 1950 and 1977.

LATIMER, Clive: Furniture designer. Latimer collaborated with Robin Day in the late 1940s, winning a prize with him from the Museum of Modern Art, New York. He designed a series of furniture pieces in aluminium for Heal's. 148, 154

LEACH, Bernard: 1887–1979; a potter; pioneer and champion of the *Crafts Revival.*

LINLEY, David: British. Son of Princess Margaret and Lord Snowdon, trained as a furniture-maker at the Parnham School. Set up a shop in London selling his own creations in the 1980s.

LITTLE, Mary: b. 1958. Furniture designer, active from the 1980s, creating craft-based pieces in an eclectic style. Spent time in Milan in the '80s and collaborated with Memphis in 1988.

LLOYD NORTHOVER: British design consultancy, specialising in corporate identity schemes, active in the 1980s. 139

MARX, Enid: 1902–96. Textile and graphic designer. Best known for her fabric designs for London Transport of the 1930s. She was a member of the Utility Advisory Board during the war. Elected a Royal Designer for Industry in 1944.

MAUGHAM, Syrie: 1879–1955. Interior decorator active in England in the 1930s. Wife, for a time, of Somerset Maugham. Best known for the luxurious bathroom she designed for Margaret Argyll and for the white drawing room she created for her own house.

MCDOWELL, Alex: Graphic artist; worked in the field of pop music, including both cover design (among others for Iggy Pop) as well as music videos; his stunningly original work was trend-setting for later designers like Neville Brody. Founded companies such as the design agency Rocking Russians, the State Arts T-Shirt Company, 3 Kliks Video and Direct Hit Records. His clip *When All's Well* for the group *Everything but the Girl* is considered a classic. 128, 140

MCGRATH, Raymond: Australian. 1903–77. Modernist architect and designer active in London in the 1930s. In the early decade he was the consultant for the interiors of the BBC Broadcasting House.

MCLAREN, Malcolm: b.1947. Singer and pop impresario; founded Sex Pistols with Vivienne Westwood; later devoted himself to debunking cultural myths like Hiphop or the Viennese Waltz.

MCQUEEN, Alexander: 248

MELLOR, David: 68, **250**

MG: 51, 216, **252**, 260

MILLENNIUM DOME: A huge dome, designed by the architect Richard Rogers, erected in greenwich to celebrate the MILLENNIUM. Many of Britain's leading architects and designers—Nigel Coates, Eva Jiricna and others—were involved with designing elements of the interior. 9

MINALE, Marcello: 254

MINALE TATTERSFIELD: 254

MINTONS: 149

MOGGRIDGE, Bill: 258

MOORE, Simon: Glass designer. Leading figure in the British art-glass movement of the 1980s. Was involved with the group of designers based at the Glasshouse in London's Covent Garden.

MORGAN: Motor company established in 1909 known for its high quality, hand-built, open top cars with characteristically rounded forms. 216, 256, **260**

MORRIS MOTORS: Motor company established in 1912, the first to mass produce cars along Fordist lines. Best known in the post-war years for the Morris Minor of the late 1940s and the 'Mini' of a decade later, both designed by Alec Issigonis.

MORRIS, William: 10, 52, 76, 102, 150, 192, **262**

MORRISON, Jasper: 11, 84, 108, 164, 200, 210, 240, **266**, 320

MOULTON, Alex: 72, **272**

MR. FREEDOM: Better known as Tommy Roberts who played a key role in the retail side of the London-based Pop design movement of the 1960s. Opened a show shop in Kensington which was designed by Jon Wealleans.

MURDOCH, Peter: 72, **274**, 289

MURPHY RADIO: Radio manufacturing company active in the middle years of the century. Employed the designer R.D. Russell to design some progressive models.

MURRAY, Keith: 275, 276, 346

NASH, Paul: 1889–1946. Painter and designer. Designed textiles for London Transport in the 1930s and is best know for an all-glass and black bathroom he created for the dancer, Tilly Losch, in the same decade. He also worked on ceramics and glass.

NEWEL, Steve: American. Glass designer, active in London in the 1980s and key member of the British art-glass movement. Member of the Glasshouse in Covent Garden. 276

NEWSON, Marc: Australian. b 1962. Furniture and industrial designer. Worked with Ron Arad in London in the 1980s. Best known for his 1985 'Lockheed Lounge' steel chair installed in the lobby of the Paramount Hotel, New York. 11, 279

OGLE DESIGN: British design company, set up by David Ogle but after his death in 1962 was run by the Czech designer, Tom Karen. Known for its design of the TR130 Bush radio.

OLIVER, Vaughan: 280

OLLINS, Wally: b. 1930. Founded the company Wolff Olins, with partner Michael Wolff in 1965. 358

OMEGA: 1913–19. Studio for interior design founded by art critic Roger Fry and modeled after the Wiener Werkstätter and Paul Poiret's Studio Martine.

PEL: Practical Equipment Limited, British manufacturer of tubular steel furniture, active in the 1930s.

PENTAGRAM: 73, 188, 254, **284**, 311, 318, 348

PETERS, Michael: b. 1941. Established influential design consultancy, specialising in packaging, in the 1980s. The group went into liquidation in 1990.

PESNVER, Nikolaus: German. 1902–1983. Art Historian. Wrote seminal book "Pioneers of Modern Design" when based in London in the 1930s.

PICK, Frank: Underground.Headed the construction of the Ministry of Information in 1939.

POOLE POTTERY: Dorset-based family pottery manufacturing company which developed modern designs for its wares in the 1930s. Highly collectable today.

POP DESIGN: 175, **288**, 299

POULTON, Neil: British designer, trained at the Domus Academy in the 1980s. Best known for a plastic pen, designed in the '80s, which changed colors as layers were worn away.

POWELL-TUCK, Julian: 292

PRIESTMAN-GOODE: , **294**

PRINGLE: Company, of Scottish origin, established in the early century, known for making 'classic' knitwear from lamb's wool. Popular with tourists. 151

PRITCHARD, Jack: 212

PSION: 84, 190, **296**

PUNK: 9, 61, 78, 81, 122, 175, **298**, 308, 330, 354

QUAD ELECTRONICS: British manufacturer of high performance audio equipment known for the high quality of its design input.

QUANT, Mary: 71, 288, **300**, 310

QUEENSBURY HUNT LEVIEN: **304**

RABY, Fiona: British architect, active in the 1990s, who works with her husband, Tony Dunne, in the area of interaction design.

RACE, Ernest: 63, 148, **306**

RAVILLIOUS, Eric: 1903–1942. Wood engraver and ceramics decorator. Known for his designs for Wedgwood from the 1930s, prominent among them 'Boat Race' design. He also worked on glassware for Stuart Crystal. 346

READ, Herbert: 1893–1968. Author; his book *Art and Industry* (1936) declared the beauty of the machine for the first time in England; he was a proponent of the ideas of Walter Gropius and in 1944 became the first director of the Design Research Unit.

REID, Jamie: 299, **308**, 332

REILLY, Paul: b.1912 Businessman and journalist. Director of the Design Council in the 1960s. Reilly played an important role in the paradigm shift from Arts and Crafts to Modernism.

RETAIL DESIGN: 162, 221, 229, **310**, 348

RISS, Egon: Architect

ROBERTS, Weaver: British design consultancy, specialising in corporate identity and product design, active in the 1980s.

ROVER: 98, **312**

ROWLANDS, Martyn: b. 1920. Industrial designer responsible for designs for Ecko Plastics in the 1950s.

ROYAL COLLEGE OF ART: Leading School of Art and Design, based in Kensington Gore, London, established in 1937, and specialising in postgraduate work across a wide range of disciplines. Many of Britain's leading designers have graduated from there. 11, 112, 118, 160, 164, 170, 210, 230, 232, 266, 292, 294, 348, 356

ROYAL DESIGNER FOR INDUSTRY: Furniture designers.

ROYAL DALTON: British ceramics manufacturer set up in 1846 to make stoneware pipes but subsequently moved into the production of fine pieces of pottery designed in the fashionable styles of the day. Their pieces represent one face of British traditional design.

RUSSELL, Gordon: 61, **316**

R.D. RUSSEL: 1903–1981. Architect and designer. Brother of Gordon Russell and wife of textile designer Marian Pepler. Best known for his modern-style radio cabinets for Murphy designed in the 1930s. Was Professor of Furniture at the Royal College of Art from 1949–1964.

SAVILLE, Peter: b. 1955. Graphic designer. Emerged from Punk culture, established his own company in 1983 and joined the Pentagram group in 1990. He has worked across a range of projects from advertising, to publishing to music and video. 286, 299, **318**, 331, 350

SCHREIBER, Gaby: Austrian. 1912–1990. Interior and industrial designer. Worked in London in the 1930s but is best known for her designs for plastic products for Runcolite from the 1940s. Worked on a range of public interiors in the '50s and '60s. 67

Acknowledgements

Special thanks to Mr. Andrew Summers of the Design Council in London, John Davis of the Design Council Slide Collection in Manchester, Catherine Moriarty of the Design Council Archive in Brighton as well as Lucy Swift of the Design Department of the British Council in London.

The assistance of Dr. Elke Ritt, Ms. Barbara Jahn und Ms. Sabine Soelken of the British Council in Cologne was particularly helpful.

In addition, we would like to express our gratitude to Mr. Gerard Forde of the Design Museum in London and Mr. Gareth Williams of the Victoria and Albert Museum in London.

A heart-felt "Thank-you" also to all designers, companies and institutions who have supported this project and to Mr. Colin Webb of Pavilion for his forbearance.

Collaborators on this book: Donatella Cacciola, Janina Kossmann, Anita Mayer, Jutta Nerkewitz, and Astrid van der Auwera.

Other titles in the Design Directory series are:

Bernd Polster:
DESIGN DIRECTORY SCANDINAVIA
ISBN: 1 86205 307 3

Claudia Neumann:
DESIGN DIRECTORY ITALY
ISBN: 1 86205 312 X

Marion Godau, Bernd Polster:
DESIGN DIRECTORY GERMANY
ISBN: 1 86205 333 2

This edition published in
Great Britain in 2001
by PAVILION BOOKS LIMITED
London House, Great Eastern Wharf,
Parkgate Road, London SW11 4NQ
www.pavilionbooks.co.uk

©2001 Howard Buch Produktion
Bonn, Germany

Concept and realization:
Howard Buch Producktion
editor: Bernd Polster
art director: Olaf Meyer

Text by Penny Sparke
© 2001 Universe Publishing

ISBN 1 86205 330 8

Printed in Germany
10 9 8 7 6 5 4 3 2 1

This book can be ordered direct
from the publisher. Please contact
the Marketing Department.
But try your bookshop first.

Cover picture credits:

front: *Dual Cyclone V4* vacuum
cleaner by James Dyson, 1996

back: badge showing design by
Jamie Reid, 1977

bottom: Mackintosh's *Rose and
Teardrop* textile

Photographs and illustrations that are not listed separately are reprinted by courtesy of the designers and companies.

Unless otherwise indicated, the copyrights are with the respective designers and companies. In a few cases it was not possible to identify the copyright holders. Legitimate claims will be settled according to customary agreements.

The text on the following pages is written by Bernd Polster: 94, 106, 108, 116, 142, 168, 186, 210, 216, 242, 252, 260, 277, 296, 312, 328, 320 and 356

Design Council Archive at the Design History Research Centre Brighton, 26, 50, 65 (b.l.), 69 (b.r.), 70, 75 (t.l.), (b.r.), 79 (t.l.), 137 (b.), 145 (t.l.), (t.r.), 149, 150 (l.), 151 (l.), 213 (t.), 289 (r.), 306, 307, 346

Design Council Slide Collection, Department of History of Art and Design, Manchester Metropolitain University, 19, 22, 34, 41, 46, 47, 55 (b.l.), (t.r.), 57 (t.r.), (b.l.), 65 (t.), 69 (t.l.), 79 (b.l.), (b.r.), 102, 103, 105, 117, 121 (t.), 150 (r.), 151 (r.), 155 (b.l.), 169 (t.), 193 (t.l.), 195, 196, 197, 213 (b.), 227 (t.), 239 (t.r.), 265 (b.l.), 273 (t.), 275, 274, 288, 310, 317, 334

Jean Luc Bernard 223, **Ugo Camera** 351 (l.), 355 (b.r.) (l.) (t.r.), **Clareville Studios Limited** 251 (t.l.), **Mario Carrieri** 13, 235, 237, **Corning Museum** 225 (l.), **Reginald Davis** 301 (b.r.), 303 (t.r.), **Design Council/DHRC, University of Brighton** 2, **Design Council Studio London** 251 (b.l.), **Terence Donovan** 301 (l), **Chris Frazer Smith London** 87, 133, 134, **J. Garcia** 174, **Thomas Goode** 327 (b.r.), **Hans Hansen** 181 (b.l.), **Julian Hawkins** 108, 109, **Dennis Hooker** 156, **Gary Hunter London** 39, **Christoph Kicherer** 97, (b.), **London Transport Museum** 229, 115 (b.), **Mauro Masera** 83 (b.), **Niall McInerney** 351 (r.), **Chris Moore** 325, 327 (l.), **Mike Murless** 48, **National Motor Museum** 215 (b.), **Keith Parry** 195 (t.l.), **Bruno Pellerin** 249, **Arthur Sanderson & Sons Ltd. Archive, Uxbridge** 265, **David Simmonds** 363 (b.), **Schoeller & Rehingen PR** 355 (t.r.), **Patrice Stable** 183 (l.), 185 (l.), **V&A Enterprises, Victoria and Albert Museum, London** 263, 265 (t.r.), **Vogue Magazine** 289 (l.), 301 (t.r.), **Peter Wood** 43, 225 (l.), **Nigel Young** 181 (t.), (b.r.), **Andrea Zani** 54 (t.r.), 239 (b.)